ADDICTED TO

THE MONKEY MIND

CHANGE THE PROGRAMMING

THAT SABOTAGES YOUR LIFE

JF BENOIST

Published by Pakalana Publishing Sep, 2018
ISBN: 9780692978597

Editor: Danielle Anderson
Typeset: Greg Salisbury
Book Cover Design: Judith Mazari
Portrait Photographer: Brady Simmons

Disclaimer: Jean-Francois (J.F.) Benoist is an Option Process® Certified Mentor-Counselor who teaches methods of self-reflection but does not prescribe or diagnose in any way. The materials and services offered by Benoist are intended to encourage and to teach skills that support positive attitudinal and relational change.

This book is not intended to replace or simulate medical advice of any kind. The contents of this book are intended to be used as an adjunct to a rational and responsible healthcare program prescribed by a healthcare practitioner. The author and publisher are in no way liable for any use or misuse of this material.

A Note on Privacy
Confidentiality and discretion are the highest priorities in J.F. Benoist's work. Because of this, Benoist has taken real life types of events to create simulated stories and characters in this book. Any resemblance to any specific person or persons is purely coincidental.

To my beloved wife, Joyce

CONTENTS

MEET KEVIN

Kevin arrives home one evening after working a twelve-hour shift at the hospital. He goes straight to the fridge, pulling out a bottle of beer. He grabs a bag of chips off the counter and shuffles tiredly into the living room, where he sinks into the couch and turns on the TV.

He soon hears his wife stomping down the stairs.

"Kevin! I can't believe you!" Jamie screams, still out of view of her husband.

He sighs and responds, "What did I do?"

Jamie enters the room and throws an envelope at Kevin.

"You didn't drop off the contract at the realtor's! That was the *one* thing I asked you to do with the offer on this house! I just called Judy to apologize, and she said we're too late—they accepted someone else's offer," Jamie hisses, looking at her husband in disgust.

Kevin takes a long gulp of his beer, his attention still focused on the TV. He finally responds, "I'm sorry. Work has been so crazy lately that I…"

Jamie cuts in, "Oh, work is the problem, is it? Let's talk about your *work* for a second. I got a call from your nurse friend Patti today. She was calling to ask if you were sick since you hadn't gotten to work yet … at *ten o'clock*. You left at seven this morning, Kevin. What did you do for those three hours before you decided to show up to work?" Jamie interrogates, moving to block his view of the screen.

Exaggerating his sigh, Kevin takes a moment to think before responding. "I wasn't feeling well this morning and had to take some time before I could go work my shift," he answers matter-of-factly, now looking his wife in the eyes.

"Oh, that is such bull!" Jamie shouts, throwing her hands in the air. "You were parked at some liquor store, downing vodka or who knows what." She pauses and takes a deep breath before quickly running her fingers through her hair. "I can't look at you right now," she says quietly, focusing on the rug. She walks away, leaving Kevin alone with his racing thoughts.

Can't you do anything right? You're irresponsible. You're stupid. Jamie deserves better than you.

Kevin jumps up, desperately wanting to silence this critical voice in his head. He quickly walks out the front door, and soon he's putting the keys into his truck's ignition and speeding into the parking lot of the bar two blocks away. As he parks, his mind will not let up on him.

Now what? You're going to drink away all your problems? Own up to something for once. Stop running away from your troubles, Kevin.

Slamming his truck's door, he jogs into the bar and demands a double whiskey from the bartender. As soon as the glass is in front of him, he drains it.

"Another," Kevin instructs.

"Rough day?" the bartender asks.

Kevin cracks his neck and lets out a cynical laugh. "You could say that. Whatever I do is just never good enough for my wife."

"Oh, yeah?" the bartender comments with raised eyebrows.

Kevin shakes his head bitterly and takes another swig. "Never. She comes from this family where all of them are CEOs or lawyers. So when I got kicked out of med school, they basically shunned me. I mean, they had to know how hard that was for me, you know? I was the one who wanted to be a doctor in the first place! But they didn't seem to care at all. Not even my wife. That's really messed up to do to someone, if you ask me," Kevin says sharply.

"Why'd you get kicked out of med school?" the bartender curiously inquires.

Unconsciously, Kevin responds by motioning to his glass. Catching himself, he uncomfortably shrugs it off and replies, "Um, I don't really want to talk about it. Get me another, will ya?"

This goes on for several hours. By the time the bar is closing, Kevin can barely see straight. Not wanting to leave his truck behind, he decides to drive home anyway. After all, it's only a few blocks.

The streetlights illuminate blurry images on Kevin's ride home, and he struggles to decipher them. He jerks his head to the right when he thinks he sees a person walking on the sidewalk. "Just a tree," Kevin slurs with a laugh.

As he's about to pull into his driveway, he sighs a breath of relief at making it home safely. Suddenly, he sees a blob dart in front of his truck. Or did he? Kevin blinks his eyes and keeps his foot on the gas. "It's nothing," he reassures himself.

Then he feels the bump.

Slamming on the brakes, Kevin jumps out to see the damage. His breath escapes him when he sees the source of the bump.

His neighbor's chocolate lab.

Kevin's stomach drops. His mind is spinning. He can't see straight. He leans against the car for support until he can't hold it back anymore; he turns into the lawn and vomits. As he wipes his mouth, he wonders if it's from the alcohol or the disgust at what he's just done.

He checks the dog's mouth, desperately hoping to feel a breath.

Nothing.

Panic sets in. It's 2:00 a.m.—what is he supposed to do with this dog? He can't tell his wife. He can't wake up the Browns. Kevin rubs his suddenly pounding head. He can't deal with this right now. So he does what he thinks is his next best option: dragging the dog's body into the bushes.

After clumsily hiding the body and rearranging the shrubs, he leaves the truck parked where it is, its bumper sticking out into the road. Fumbling with his keys, he finally finds the match to the front door and stumbles in, simultaneously collapsing on the sofa and falling into a deep sleep.

The next morning, Kevin awakes to Jamie shaking his shoulder.

"Kevin! Hey, have you seen Max? The Browns just stopped by and said they can't find him," Jamie says, her nose scrunched in concern.

As Kevin opens his eyes, he grabs the cushion for support. By the time he's able to focus Jamie into one image, last night's details have flashed through his mind. He swallows hard and closes his eyes.

"Nope," he mumbles, shaking his head.

He can hear Jamie sigh and walk out the back door, yelling for the dog that will never come. As Kevin sits up, he places his head in his palms. "What did you do?" he asks himself.

He collapses in defeat, mourning the creature he killed and the person he has become.

INTRODUCING THE MONKEY MIND

Kevin's life is not what he pictured. What he truly wants is to be happily married, start a family, have a successful career as a doctor, and connect with those around him. Instead, he's experiencing marital issues and career struggles, and he has a serious drinking problem.

What Kevin doesn't realize is he's stuck in a mindset that is dragging him down in life. Imagine this mindset as if it were a computer: someone had to come along and program the computer to operate as it does.

So how does this kind of programming get created in the first place? It comes from the thousands of messages we heard repeated over and over to us as we grew up, many of which had an underlying tone of pressure.

"You only got a B on that test?"

"You never clean up after yourself! Why are you so lazy?"

"Why can't you ever do as you're told?"

"If you keep this up, you'll never amount to anything."

These messages, and many more, are what shaped our programming. Our parents and teachers told us these things in an attempt to help us be accepted and successful; they thought they were pushing us to do better by using punishments and reprimands as motivation. However, what this constant influx of negative messages really did was teach us that the best way to motivate ourselves is through *shame*.

These indirect, shame-inducing messages led many of us to develop a sense of inadequacy, making us feel like we're not "good enough" in some areas of our lives. With this self-deprecating mindset, we've learned to put an immense amount of pressure on ourselves to act a certain way.

As a result, we find ourselves altering our behavior and subtly performing for those around us. We say we're fine when inside, we're falling apart. We fib and claim our email wasn't working instead of admitting we forgot to send it. We walk our best walk and talk our best talk, all in the hopes that others will like, love, or—at the very least—tolerate us.

After years of focusing externally, we've learned to look outside ourselves for the cause of our problems. When we get upset, we blame others or outside circumstances. We get caught up in believing that what others think of us, and what happens to us, are what dictate our experience.

In actuality, our beliefs about ourselves and the world—which were formed through our programming—are what determine our everyday experiences. While our programming was primarily developed through those shame-inducing messages from the adults who raised us, it also incorporated other impactful experiences we went through in life: bullying, trauma, heartbreak, or failure.

Over time, our beliefs slowly transformed into the negative mindset that directs how we view our world today: the Monkey Mind.

We call this mindset the Monkey Mind because it is less mature and evolved than the other aspects of our mind and thought processes. It's quick to react to something it doesn't agree with, as well as blame something or someone else for our problems. It wants to keep us focused on how everything outside ourselves is why our lives aren't the way we want them to be:

If your job wasn't so demanding, you wouldn't be so stressed.

If that road hadn't been closed, you wouldn't have been late, and that date would have gone better.

If your mother didn't have such high expectations of you, you'd have a closer relationship.

The Monkey Mind also keeps a memory bank of all the criticisms and judgments we've adopted from our programming. If we ever get to the point where we stop blaming others and want to take responsibility for our circumstances, the Monkey Mind loves to remind us about the shame-inducing beliefs we've developed about ourselves:

You haven't gotten that raise yet because you're not smart enough. Everyone knows it.

That date went terribly because you look fat in this shirt, and no one is attracted to you.

Your family is embarrassed by your failure. That's why they never come visit.

This inner critic makes it extremely challenging to create the life we want for ourselves, as it produces an immense amount of anxiety that whittles away at our confidence, driving us to do a number of things: drink, use drugs, isolate ourselves from others, yell at our kids, get divorced, give up on our dreams—the list is endless.

We've gotten to the point where we aren't aware of how much our anxiety rules our lives. When we're in line at the bank, we're anxious because it's taking too long. When we forget to call a client, we're anxious because we might have lost the deal. When we don't wear makeup to the grocery store, we're anxious about how others are perceiving us. The anxiety is so constant that we don't even question it.

Throughout the generations, we've *normalized* the Monkey Mind's critical voice and the vast amounts of anxiety it creates. For example, think about how many of us grab a drink at an event to "take the edge off." Where does this "edge" come from? It's the Monkey Mind, creating stories and judgments about the way we need to act. Because we're not conscious of this inner critic or equipped to deal with it, this ritual of drinking to minimize anxiety has become completely socially acceptable.

To move past the anxiety our Monkey Mind has created, we must listen to a different perspective: the Observing Mind.

The Observing Mind does not look to other people or situations as the source of our troubles. Instead, it offers an objective perspective, uninhibited by our judgmental programming. This point of view understands that the source of our upset or delight is within ourselves. The Observing Mind is able to offer this wisdom by witnessing and learning from the Monkey Mind. Oftentimes, being aware of our shadows allows us to see the light we can offer to the world.

Shifting into the Observing Mind's perspective is so powerful because our mindset affects everything we do. When we move away from the Monkey Mind's judgmental perspective, we open ourselves up to an abundance of opportunities and experiences. Relationships that once seemed doomed can begin to flourish. Endless cycles of addictive behavior can be resolved. An unattainable joy now becomes accessible. A life driven by passion and purpose is now within reach. When you address the root cause of your problems—your programming—everything else will start to fall into place.

WHAT YOU'LL FIND IN THIS BOOK

Learning about the Monkey Mind can come as a shock for some people, because many of us do not have an accurate assessment of our own programming. Some of us might even say that we don't have any negative programming because we had "great" childhoods.

While it could be true that we grew up in warm, loving households, the fact still remains that we grew up in a shame-based society that fueled the Monkey Mind. The skill of not blaming or judging others or ourselves is rarely taught in any school or university. Even those who love us the most don't usually have the tools to teach us reliable, repeatable ways to create a healthy state of mind.

In this book, we will explore why your thoughts are so erratic; why your emotions sometimes spiral out of control; why some days you feel great, but other days you're so anxious that you drink, use drugs, snap at your partner, sabotage your career, or feel so depressed that you can't get out of bed. We'll explain why—and how—we became addicted to our Monkey Minds.

With the Observing Mind's guidance, we will finally shed the programming we received growing up. We will feel more connected with others and experience far less anxiety in our day-to-day lives.

After teaching the skills of the Observing Mind for over twenty years, I've compiled many proven techniques for gaining mastery over our feelings and thoughts. What I offer to you in this book are the tools to put yourself back in the driver's seat of your life. By following the journeys of the characters in this book, you will develop skills of observation, awareness, and emotional fluidity to help you change the course of your life.

Since we learn best experientially, there are opportunities throughout this book for you to practice the skills of the Observing Mind firsthand. When you apply these skills to your own life, try to remain curious and keep an open mind and heart. You may be surprised to find what new awareness pops up when you fully open yourself up to this work.

My goal is to teach you specific, useful skills you can actually put into practice, so you can finally shed your sabotaging programming and create the life you deserve.

Part 1

GETTING TO KNOW
THE MONKEY MIND

Chapter 1

IT'S YOUR MOVIE

To visualize the roles of the Monkey Mind and the Observing Mind, imagine that your life is like a movie. You're in every frame, since you're the star of your movie, and a voice comments on the action as it happens.

Let's imagine one scene of your movie right now. You're on a first date with someone you find very attractive. You're both dressed elegantly. After a wonderful, romantic time at your favorite restaurant, you decide to go for a stroll through a beautiful park. You walk hand in hand down a flower-lined path, which leads to a tall fountain. You and your date lean over, wanting to get a peek of the moon's reflection in the water. Just then, the fountain comes on, completely drenching you both.

Now, notice your reaction. Is this movie a comedy or a tragedy? It all depends on what director you're getting your cues from and how they interpret the events.

When the Monkey Mind is in charge, it uses your self-judgments to create dramatic storylines. Anxiety fuels this critical story, throwing plot twists and dramatic turns into the movie of your life. Its non-stop chatter is full of opinions and distractions.

After you get soaked by the fountain, the Monkey Mind would go into a tizzy. *This is horrible! Just imagine what your hair looks like right now! You're going to have to go home early to change before you even got a chance to know each other. This date is completely ruined. Why do you even try to meet anyone?*

When you listen to the Monkey Mind, you may feel a variety of emotions such as anger, disappointment, sadness, shame, fear, and depression.

In contrast, the Observing Mind prefers a good documentary to a drama. It calmly and simply describes the events as they happen without overlaying any dramatic stories or personal opinions. After you get splashed by the fountain, it would simply say, *Wow! You're all wet! What do you do now?*

The Observing Mind is much like the camera that simply records what is happening. It's curious, but it doesn't judge the situation. When you look at life through its eyes, you can learn how to question everything and decide exactly how to create the changes you desire.

While the Monkey Mind frets about problems, the Observing Mind shifts your focus toward solutions. It is looking, listening, and feeling for the path away from anxiety.

Who do you want directing your movie?

Let's watch a scene from Elizabeth's movie to see who she chooses.

MEET ELIZABETH

It's a sunny morning, and Elizabeth is enjoying her breakfast out on the terrace. She's already dressed and ready for the day. Her husband, who has slept in, yawns as he pulls up a chair next to her.

"Glad you could join me," Elizabeth comments with a chuckle.

"Good morning," Ted responds sleepily.

"You don't look so good, honey. Did you have another crazy dream last night? You know, Aunt Margie always said that's a sign of unmanaged stress," Elizabeth sweetly suggests.

Her husband reaches for the newspaper without responding.

Elizabeth doesn't give up. "Did you take those supplements I got you? They're supposed to help with anxiety."

He grunts.

"You should take better care of yourself. You're working too much," she advises, her voice growing louder.

Still no response.

"I think we should invite Jen and Bill over for dinner tomorrow. The kids could all go upstairs and watch a movie or something. What do you think?" Elizabeth asks, an edge forming in her voice.

Ted pours cream into his coffee and keeps reading.

Sharply, Elizabeth demands, "Ted, are you even listening to me?"

"What? Yeah, of course. I have a work call tomorrow night. Can't we do dinner another time?" he says, still looking at his newspaper.

"Again? Ted, we haven't seen our friends in weeks. Can't you do it another day?" Elizabeth asks, a small plea in her voice.

"No, I can't. I've been trying to get this call scheduled for weeks. We can just have them over next weekend," Ted replies, his voice tinged with annoyance.

"That's what you said last weekend, when we canceled with Barry because you had to work late. I'm sick of always coming second to work. We don't do anything anymore. Ted!" Elizabeth erupts, snatching the newspaper out of Ted's hands. "Look at me when I'm talking to you!"

Ted's jaw clenches as he grabs the paper away from his wife.

"Sorry I have to make a living, Elizabeth. My clients aren't going to take 'my wife wanted to have company over' as an excuse for not winning their case. Now, please, let me read the paper." Ted loudly snaps his newspaper back into position, hiding his irritated face from his fuming wife.

"Fine," Elizabeth mutters. "I'm leaving for my haircut, so you won't be distracted from your precious paper anymore." She leaves the breakfast table feeling discontented and drives off to her hair appointment.

Elizabeth doesn't know that she's in charge of her own life. She wandered onto the set this morning and started playing a bit part in a film that someone else seems to be writing. She believes that life is happening *to* her. Will her scene move toward comedy or tragedy?

LISTENING TO THE MONKEY MIND

Elizabeth coincidentally arrives at the salon just behind Paula, her high-energy friend from college who is rarely seen in anything but yoga gear and designer sunglasses.

Paula is the personification of the Monkey Mind. She loves to stir the pot and lives for drama, and if something is awry she wants to hear every detail. Whenever Elizabeth bumps into her collegiate friend, she always ends up getting worked up about something.

In no time at all, Paula is digging for a story. "So what did Ted do this time?"

Elizabeth begins, "He doesn't want me having anyone over *again*, even after…"

Paula interrupts, as the Monkey Mind loves to do, with an opinion. "Men are so selfish! My husband is the exact same way. And he does this to you all the time. Remember last month when you set up that tango lesson? What did he say again? That he was working late and couldn't go? Probably 'working' with that sleazy secretary of his, if you ask me," Paula mumbles out the side of her mouth.

Elizabeth swallows deeply and admits, "He *has* been working even later than normal…"

"Mmm hmm," Paula utters knowingly as the stylist brushes bright, blonde highlights onto her hair. "You don't have to tolerate this kind of behavior. There are a million men who would be thrilled to have you!"

Elizabeth scoffs. "Yeah, right," she responds sarcastically, her cheeks growing red.

Paula turns her head toward the stylist and tells her, "Elizabeth here is the *worst* at accepting compliments. She always has been," Paula says sharply.

Clearing her throat, Elizabeth quickly changes the subject back to her husband. "Do you really think he could be cheating?" she asks nervously, leaning over to Paula.

"How many times has Ted disregarded you like this? He's so focused in his own little world. It really wouldn't surprise me," Paula insists.

Now, Elizabeth is fully jumping onto the negative bandwagon. "God, you're right. How have I been so stupid? He never makes time for me or anything *I* want to do!"

"You should come and stay with me for a few days and teach him a lesson," Paula offers smugly. She seems to enjoy the drama she's created.

"That would show him!" Elizabeth snaps triumphantly.

"It sure would!" Paula yells as she's ushered to another chair.

With Paula's disapproving voice gone, Elizabeth is once again alone with her thoughts. She whispers under her breath, "I doubt he would even miss me…"

When Elizabeth leaves the salon, she's in more distress than when she arrived. With Paula's help, she has convinced herself that her marriage is on the verge of ending.

With the Monkey Mind directing her movie, Elizabeth finds

herself in a war film full of drama and conflict. Her husband is cast as the enemy and their home is the battleground.

In the past, this exchange would have driven Elizabeth into a drunken stupor. Whenever she felt pain, emotional or otherwise, she drowned it out with her friend, Chardonnay. Recently though, she has been diligently working to overcome her addiction. Will this be the trigger that pushes her back to her old ways?

LISTENING TO THE OBSERVING MIND

On her way home from the salon, Elizabeth finds herself en route to her favorite liquor store, certain her marriage is over. As she's about to pull into the parking lot, her Observing Mind pushes through the Monkey Mind's babble.

What is triggering you to want to drink right now?

This single awareness helps Elizabeth swerve out of the store's parking lot. Instead, she pulls into the lot of the park across the street. She steps out of her car, taking a moment to bask in the warm sun.

As she's stretching, Elizabeth's eye catches the neon "Open" sign of the liquor store. Her mouth starts to water for a bottle of Chardonnay, but her Observing Mind's comment rings in her thoughts. She turns away from the temptation and starts power walking toward the stream in the park. She whips out her cell phone and gives her friend Sarah a call.

Sarah has a very different approach to living than Paula. Sarah's goal isn't drama; it's clarity, empowerment, and peace. She represents what our Observing Mind can offer us when deciding how to act in a stressful situation.

"Elizabeth!" Sarah exclaims, "I've got one more day here on assignment, and then I'm coming home. I can't wait to have lunch with you and catch up!" Sarah is a reporter for the local newspaper. The two have been inseparable since they were young and even worked together in the press room before Elizabeth became a stay-at-home mom.

Sarah has been a strong supporter of Elizabeth during her struggle with alcohol. Whenever Elizabeth is close to bingeing, she gives Sarah a call instead.

"I wish I was there with you right now," Elizabeth bemoans.

"What's up?" Sarah asks. "How are you?"

"Oh, you know. Having to put up with Ted's crap as usual. I think this might be it," Elizabeth declares, her voice catching.

"What happened this time?" Sarah says with a sigh. This is not the first time Elizabeth has predicted her marriage to be doomed.

"He's so selfish… he doesn't care about me at all." Elizabeth's voice breaks. "I think he's having an affair!"

"You're not drinking, are you?" Sarah interjects.

Elizabeth bites her lip. "No, I almost went to the liquor store, but I came to the park instead. I'm walking by that duck pond you like right now," Elizabeth relays, kicking a stone into the water despondently.

"Oh, good. Good for you," Sarah celebrates.

Elizabeth shrugs it off and doesn't respond.

"OK, so you know the drill: who, what, why, where, when?" Sarah instructs.

"Well, this morning I was *happily* talking with Ted at breakfast, and he just kept on reading the newspaper and ignoring me. And then, when I asked to have some friends over for dinner tomorrow night, he said that he has to go into work, and that his clients don't care about what 'his wife' wants! He's probably going in to meet up with that awful secretary of his," Elizabeth angrily explains.

"Elizabeth, it's quite a leap from 'he has to work tonight' to 'he's having an affair'! Forget about the story for a minute, honey. What are you feeling right now?" Sarah inquires.

Elizabeth takes a second to dissect her feelings. After taking a breath, she says, "I thought I was angry, but the truth is, I feel sad."

"Yeah, I get it. If I thought my husband was having an affair, I'd feel sad too," Sarah kindly responds.

Elizabeth begins to softly cry and reaches for some tissues out of her purse. "Oh, Sarah, I feel so lonely."

"I'm right here for you, Elizabeth."

"I mean, if Ted really cared about me, he would want to spend time with me, or at least *talk* to me," Elizabeth insists.

"Maybe this has nothing to do with you," Sarah states. "Maybe he just needs some space. He did come and have breakfast with you this morning, didn't he?"

Elizabeth pauses, considering this possibility. "I suppose he did… I mean, that hardly makes up for how he's been treating me lately though," Elizabeth persists stubbornly.

"Maybe that's all he's capable of doing for you right now," Sarah calmly suggests.

"Well, geez, sitting silently with your wife at the breakfast table doesn't really qualify him for 'Husband of the Year,'" Elizabeth quips sarcastically.

"Have you asked Ted if anything is going on with him?"

"Oh, he'd never admit to anything being wrong. He's a *man*, Sarah."

"Maybe you should try asking him anyway," Sarah proposes.

"Say I do try, and he responds with his favorite phrase: 'I'm fine.' Then what do I do?" Elizabeth asks sincerely, her anger starting to fade.

Sarah considers this for a moment. "Well, what if you spent time with your friends this weekend and give him some space? Maybe what he needs right now is not to talk about it, but to see that you're there for him," she recommends.

"I'm just tired of having to do everything. I feel like I'm alone in this marriage," Elizabeth laments.

"If you want something to change, change it. Don't sit around waiting for Ted to be someone he's not," Sarah kindly but firmly states.

"I know. I know. I need to not build up the story in my head and just go talk to Ted. But it's easier to complain to you than actually do something about it!" Elizabeth says with a small laugh, dabbing at her eyes. "Thanks for being there when I need you, Sarah. I'll let you know how it goes."

As Elizabeth finishes her lap around the park, she feels grateful to have someone like Sarah who isn't afraid to ask the hard questions. Sarah is using the same no-nonsense attitude to help Elizabeth through this relationship issue that she used to help Elizabeth stop drinking so many months ago.

When Elizabeth gets home that evening, Ted is working away behind his office door. Elizabeth is tired and wants to go to sleep—she'll talk to Ted tomorrow. For now, she sends off a text to Bill and then calls it a night.

The next morning, Elizabeth awakes to an empty bed. She can already hear keyboard clicks from down the hall. She slowly stretches, then slips out of bed and walks to Ted's office door. After taking a deep breath, she knocks on the door.

"Come in," Ted shouts through the wall.

Elizabeth walks in and stands in front of her husband's desk, placing herself directly in his line of sight. However, his eyes are still glued to his computer screen. She simply looks at him for a few moments, then firmly says, "Yesterday at the hair salon, I told Paula about our argument over breakfast. She said that you don't appreciate me, and there are a hundred other men who would."

Ted rolls his eyes and cuts in, "Oh, come on! Paula is such a…"

"Please let me finish," Elizabeth calmly replies, standing her ground. "I was so worked up I wanted to get a drink."

Ted inhales sharply at this possibility and looks up at his wife.

"But… I didn't."

Exhaling loudly, Ted smiles slightly. "That's great you didn't, hon."

His computer dings and his eyes flash back to the screen.

Elizabeth continues, "Yeah, well, instead I called Sarah. And she told me that she thinks you have some issue going on that's not about me. Maybe work or something. So I want to know what the real answer is," Elizabeth declares confidently.

Ted, still looking at his computer, replies, "I've just been swamped with work, Elizabeth. Don't make a big thing out of it."

Elizabeth huffs, "Fine." She clears her throat. "Well, I'm off to have lunch with Bill and Jen today, since we aren't having them over for dinner. I figured that just because you can't see them, doesn't mean I can't."

Ted nods in agreement. "Great idea," he responds mindlessly.

"I'm going to drop Josh off at soccer practice on the way, if you can pick him up after," Elizabeth relays.

"Yeah, yeah. Fine," Ted replies.

"Well, good luck with your work," Elizabeth says coldly as she walks out the door. She turns to say something, but his attention is completely gone. She sighs and pulls the door closed behind her.

Chapter 2

RAISED BY THE MONKEY MIND

We've introduced the Monkey Mind and the Observing Mind as two different people in Elizabeth's life because sometimes it's easier to recognize their voices when we place them outside ourselves. But, don't be confused; both of these voices are present in our own minds. Even when no one else is around, our thoughts give a running commentary on our lives, and we are listening to one voice or the other.

Each person's Monkey Mind is unique, shaped by the experiences they went through growing up. Understanding someone's Monkey Mind starts with looking into the past—a flashback, if you will.

Let's take a look at how Kevin developed his Monkey Mind. Then we'll look at how Elizabeth's Monkey Mind continues to influence her as an adult.

PARENTAL "LOVE"

One day, six-year-old Kevin is outside playing soccer with his brother when he trips and falls, scraping his knee. His eyes start welling up, and he limps over to his dad to show him the bloody gash. As Kevin starts to describe what happened between sobs, his dad cuts him off and leans down next to him.

"You're fine, Kevin. Stop that. It's just a cut. Do you ever see your brother cry when he falls down? Of course not. Do you want everyone to think you're a sissy? Kevin, I said that's enough! Stop that or I'll really give you something to cry about. Go rub some dirt on it and play with your brother." He then turns away and goes back to trimming the hedges.

To Kevin's dad, this was a forgettable incident. Although his approach appears harsh, his father is well-intended: he wants his son to fit in with his peers. He believes that the way to stop Kevin from being teased is by scolding him when he does something that others may judge.

For Kevin, however, this kind of shame-inducing encounter happened hundreds of times throughout his childhood. He received similar messages from his family and friends, which all played a role in shaping his programming. This created a lot of anxiety for Kevin—which the Monkey Mind only adds to with its stories. As a result, these "small" encounters snowballed over time, resulting in Kevin developing a belief that many men share: showing emotion is weak.

Fast forward twenty years, to the present day.

~

Since Jamie found out that Kevin ran over the Browns' dog, she has barely been speaking to her husband. When they do speak, the conversation usually consists of words of hurt and disappointment.

One night, as Kevin is sitting alone on the couch, his phone rings. It's his mother. She tells Kevin that his favorite uncle, Roger, has passed away suddenly. After saying good-bye to his grief-stricken mother, Kevin sits in a daze on the sofa. Jamie happens to walk by him on her way to the kitchen and notices his unusual demeanor.

"What's wrong?" Jamie suspiciously asks.

"Um… Uncle Roger died," Kevin quietly states, still in shock.

Jamie quickly sits down next to her husband. "Oh my gosh, I'm so sorry. Is there anything I can do?" she asks kindly, all animosity gone from her voice.

Kevin looks away, gritting his teeth as he tries to keep his emotions in check. "No. I'm fine," he responds flatly.

She leans in closer to him, gently hugging his arm. "I know how much your uncle meant to you. Really, just let me know how I can help," she says.

Kevin's vision starts to get misty. He jumps up, accidentally throwing Jamie off him in the process.

"I'm fine. Please, just let me be," Kevin mutters, still unable to look her in the eyes.

Jamie lets out a big sigh and stands up. She turns around before reaching the kitchen door and says, "You know, time and time again I tell myself that you'll get over this shutdown thing you do. But every time, you prove me wrong. What's the point of being in a relationship if you won't let me in? I honestly don't know if I can do this anymore," she whispers.

As the door clicks behind her, Kevin stumbles over to his cabinet and pulls out his whiskey, desperate to get away from the sea of grief, shame, and anger that threatens to overwhelm him.

Situations change, and we evolve and grow, but our mindset isn't as flexible as we think it is. The Monkey Mind latches on to what occurred in our childhood, and it uses those events to color all of our interactions—oftentimes without us even knowing it. Look at Kevin. He learned over and over throughout his childhood that being vulnerable is bad. As a result, when he is in a mature relationship as an adult, he cannot open his heart to his partner, despite her repeated requests.

If Kevin wants to maintain a healthy relationship, he needs to first become aware of his Monkey Mind. Once he understands how his belief that showing emotion is a form of weakness is not true, he can start to learn how to be authentically open with his wife and finally release the programming that is holding him back.

FROM CHILDHOOD TO ADULTHOOD

The strongest or most repeated messages we received in our childhood become the core issues that impact us as adults. Any situations that touch on these particular issues can trigger the Monkey Mind to chatter incessantly, increasing in volume as our anxiety rises, to the point where we'll do just about anything to shut it up.

Elizabeth wipes her sweaty palms on her black skirt, smoothing the crease in it. She climbs into the passenger seat of her father's car, pulling the door shut a little too hard behind her. Her father sits down with a "humph" and turns the key in the ignition.

"Mom's not riding with us?" Elizabeth asks with an edge to her voice.

Her father doesn't reply for several moments, adjusting each mirror ever so slightly. Finally, he mumbles, "No. She's riding with Ted and the kids."

The two sit in silence for several miles, without even the radio on to cut the uncomfortable tension in the air. Elizabeth closes her eyes and gathers her courage before finally turning to her father. "How are you doing with all this, Dad? You haven't said a word about Grandma since she passed... do you want to talk about it?"

Elizabeth's father's jaw clenches as his hands tighten on the steering wheel. "No, I do not," he replies flatly.

Releasing her held breath, Elizabeth nods understandably. However, she can't shake the feeling that he's holding something back. "Are you sure? Because it just seems..."

Slapping the top of the steering wheel, Elizabeth's father shouts, "Goddamn it, Elizabeth! I said I don't want to talk about it, so stop bringing it up!"

Elizabeth can feel her own anger starting to rise. "I know you, Dad. Your mom just died. That's not something you can just shrug off! You're just going to bottle this all up and never process it, and you're going to..." Elizabeth stops herself, her face growing red.

Her father locks his eyes on the road ahead and icily shoots back, "I'm going to what? Drink myself into a stupor? No, I think you need to look into a mirror to find that person. I'll be just fine."

"No, you'll just go start another affair," Elizabeth spits as her anger gets the better of her.

A scowl forms on her father's face as he sits quietly for a moment. "One thing I inherited from my mother was a sense of respect, something that your mother and I seemingly failed to pass on to you," he hisses. "I am done having this conversation with you."

Abruptly, he turns into a gas station parking lot. "I need some air," he mumbles. He slams the door as he walks over to the grass and lights up a smoke.

Elizabeth takes a shaky breath, watching her father take deep, angry drags of his cigarette. She hops out of the car and quickly shuffles into the store, the critical voice in her mind hurling judgments toward her. Before her father even notices she's left, Elizabeth is back in the car, a fifth of vodka pinned against her body under her coat.

Reluctantly, her father trudges toward the car. As he's starting the engine, he clears his throat, releasing a smoky smell into the cabin. "I don't want you staying at my house tonight," he growls. "After the service, you can go and collect your things. I expect you to be gone by the time I return."

Elizabeth throws her hands in the air with a cold cackle. "You're not serious! I made one little comment and now you're kicking us out? Where are we supposed to stay tonight, Dad? A hotel?"

Her father keeps a straight face, staring ahead. "The kids and Ted are welcome to stay. It's just you who isn't."

Elizabeth turns to face the window and sinks back into the leather, tears slowly sliding down her face. She musters every bit of strength to cry as silently as possible, so her father won't get the satisfaction of knowing that his words hurt her.

As they pull into the funeral home's parking lot, Elizabeth throws the car door open before her father even has it in park. Wiping away the trail of her tears, Elizabeth hurries in the door with the bottle still hidden under her coat. She quickly locates the restroom and locks herself into a stall. Throwing the toilet lid down with a bang, Elizabeth plops down and starts digging through her purse vigorously.

Finding her phone, she frantically calls Sarah. No reply.

Elizabeth stomps her heel loudly, the tears resuming their pace. She forgot Sarah is on assignment and unreachable for the next month.

Her Monkey Mind's voice is now deafening. *Your dad's right. No one wants you. You're not good for anything.*

Hands shaking, Elizabeth uncaps the bottle of vodka.

As soon as the alcohol touches her lips, Elizabeth cries even more. But she can't stop. She drinks and drinks until she nearly empties the entire container. All she wants is for the pain to go away, and soon she feels the familiar numbness start to spread.

Plopping the bottle in the trash can, Elizabeth glances at herself in the mirror—her makeup is running, and her hair is starting to look disheveled. The longer she looks, the blurrier her reflection becomes.

When she steps out of the bathroom, her husband is waiting for her.

"Everything all right, Elizabeth? You've been gone for almost half an hour. The service is about to start," Ted begins.

"I'm fine," Elizabeth replies, slightly slurring her words.

Ted can smell the alcohol on her breath, and his jaw clenches. "Elizabeth, you didn't…"

"We can talk about it later. Right now, I'm going to go say good-bye to my dead grandmother," Elizabeth remarks unemotionally.

She walks toward the service, leaving her distressed husband behind, and takes her seat in the front row between her two children. Elizabeth's mother is next to her son, daintily dabbing away at her tears with a handkerchief. Next to Elizabeth's mother sits her father, stone-faced.

Suddenly, Elizabeth's son is poking her. "Mom—that's you," he whispers, motioning to the podium. Elizabeth feels everyone's eyes on her, and she realizes it is her moment to speak.

She makes her way up to the front. As she passes by her grandmother's body, a shiver runs up her spine. She looks out at the crowd, all waiting to hear her compassionate words.

The vodka has made her head fuzzy, and she can't remember how she wanted to begin. Actually, she can't think of anything to say at all. Then, looking down at her grandmother's face, Elizabeth thinks of the perfect thing to share.

"My grandmother was a woman of high morals. She coveted honesty, responsibility, and," Elizabeth pauses, looking her father directly in the eyes, "respect."

Her father returns her gaze with such contempt that, for a moment, she thinks he's going to pull her away from the microphone.

She continues, "Grandma Elsie was very passionate about instilling those ideals into each of her children, then grandchildren, then great-grandchildren," Elizabeth says, looking over to her own kids. When she sees their mournful faces, she can no longer put on a front. Her eyes tear up as her true emotions start washing over her.

"I remember one day, when I was very little, we were walking by a homeless man asking for change. He was in a wheelchair, and he was missing a leg. I asked Grandma very loudly, 'Gram Gram, why does that man only have one leg?'" A few chuckles emerge from the crowd.

Elizabeth chuckles as well, hiccupping slightly. Soon, a warm, reminiscent smile settles on her face. "Grandma had noticed the man was wearing a military cap, so she said, 'Let's go ask him.' So I went and asked him how he lost his leg, and he explained how he was a veteran and had lost it in the war. My grandmother went on to explain to me that every single time I ever see a veteran, I should thank them for their service. And from that day on, I always did," Elizabeth recalls fondly. "My grandmother lived a love-filled, joyful life, and I know how much she touched each heart here today. So let's make a toast to Grandma," she says, reaching her hand out for her glass.

However, Elizabeth's hand only cups air. There is no glass in front of her. A smattering of whispers seeps up from the seats, and Elizabeth can feel her cheeks grow hot.

"Ceremoniously, I mean, of course," she quickly corrects, pretending to lift a wine glass into the air. A few people follow her cue, but the majority of people look back at her, perplexed. Elizabeth swallows hard and bows slightly, then quickly walks back to her seat. As she does, she looks over at the five most important people in her life.

Her husband won't look at her. Her daughter stares at her with tear-filled eyes, seemingly beside herself about her mother drinking again. Her son's face is white, and he's staring at the floor with embarrassment. Her mom still has her eyes closed, completely focused on her own grief—she didn't seem to notice what her daughter just said. Her father looks at her with a cold, furious glare.

Elizabeth looks back at these people, the people she loves most in this world, and her Monkey Mind has only one thing to say:

You're worthless.

And Elizabeth wholeheartedly believes it.

Chapter 3

WHERE OUR PROGRAMMING COMES FROM

We've just seen how influential Kevin's and Elizabeth's parents were in creating the basis for their programming. To understand how our own patterns of anxiety started, we need to look back at our childhoods and the messages we received from the world around us.

Think about how you viewed the world when you were four or five. Doesn't the world seem to revolve around you? Mom and Dad feed you, bathe you, and give you their attention—this is all you see. You think that any emotion Mom or Dad has, positive or negative, is directly related to you. This is because, as children, we don't have the maturity to discern otherwise. We absorb everything that we witness our parents say or do like a sponge. Unfortunately, this means when we witness an argument or tension, we absorb that uncomfortable feeling too.

These anxious feelings formed the basis of our programming, which was then slowly built upon as we developed the ability to form beliefs. Years of stress-filled situations added to this programming, coming from a wide range of experiences and responses. Our parents did not have to yell at us or scold us to create this programming; even people who think they had a perfect childhood may have developed anxiety through other kinds of interactions. This could include experiencing a lack of control, not having enough of a supportive structure, or living through a trauma at any age.

So what exactly did the beginnings of our programming look like when we were children? Let's look at the programming-forming messages received in two very different households to understand this concept more fully.

The Smith Family

Five-year-old Patrick is playing with his toy trucks in his family's living room, where his parents just put in new, luscious carpet. He's carried away in his make-believe world, wildly spinning a plastic bulldozer around. Before he knows it, he has knocked over his cup of grape juice. A purple puddle starts growing on the carpet. By the time Patrick notices, the puddle is the size of a melon.

Immediately, Patrick's heart starts to race.

Patrick's mother comes into the room to check on him and instantly sees the stain. She's furious.

"Patrick Michael! How many times did I tell you not to bring any drinks in here? Do you have any idea how much that carpet cost? There's no way that's ever going to come out! Just wait until I tell your father about this," Mrs. Smith rants.

"Mommy, I'm sorry. I, I didn't mean to…" Patrick whispers as the tears run down his cheeks.

"I can't believe you did this! Go to your room. NOW!"

Patrick jumps up and runs to his room, burying his face in his pillow.

How many of us can relate to growing up in a household similar to this? If we made a mistake, we were scolded and disciplined for it. However, we were still at the age where we didn't know what to do with these anxious feelings—so we just held on to them.

Imagine, though, being raised in a home where they didn't use these harsh words and punishment.

The Walton Family

Charlie is playing around with his friend in his dining room. They find a ball that had fallen behind the china cabinet, and they start playing catch. Charlie throws the ball a little too hard, and his friend misses it. The ball crashes into one of his parent's china plates from their wedding, which explodes into a puzzle of small shards. Hearing the commotion, Charlie's dad hurries into the room.

Five-year-old Charlie is sharing the same reaction Patrick had—his heart is racing and he can't catch his breath. However, instead of chastising his son, Mr. Walton takes a deep breath and calls Charlie over to him. Charlie can't bring himself to look his dad in the eye, so he focuses his gaze on the floor.

Mr. Walton bends down and warmly wraps his arms around his son. He simply holds Charlie, not saying anything, while breathing calmly. Soon, Charlie feels his nervous shakes fade away and his heart rate start to return to normal. Finally, he unconsciously synchronizes his breath to his father's.

After several minutes of silence, Mr. Walton releases Charlie. "How ya feeling, buddy?" he asks.

"Better," Charlie quietly responds, his green eyes reflecting off his father's. "Sorry about your plate, Dad."

"These things happen sometimes," Mr. Walton replies. "But let's not play catch in the house anymore so it doesn't happen again, OK?"

"OK. I won't do it again."

"Sounds good. I'll let you tell Mom about this when she gets home."

"OK. I will," Charlie agrees, without an ounce of uneasiness in his voice.

"Good. Let's clean this up, and then you can go outside and play with Billy."

Charlie helps his dad clean up the mess and then goes outside with his friend, continuing their play session under the sun. Charlie seems as happy as ever—you would never be able to tell he just broke a treasured family item. In this scenario, Charlie recognizes that what he did was a mistake. He feels guilty for what he did, but he doesn't take on the belief that he's a bad person for it. He's able to see this event as a learning experience, and he will not play with balls in the house again.

So what is the difference between the Smith Family and the Walton Family? The first family holds the belief that we need to be reprimanded for our mistakes, while the second family believes that acceptance is the way to create change.

The first family sets the foundation for the Monkey Mind; the second nurtures the Observing Mind.

Even though most of us didn't grow up with parents like Mr. Walton, we can still learn how to respond through his mindset.

WE ALL HAVE A MONKEY MIND

Kevin was also raised in the Smith family. Both he and his brother, Patrick, received condemning messages from their mother and father nearly every day for eighteen years. And how has Kevin turned out today? His marriage is in shambles, he's dealing with the ramifications from drunkenly running over a dog, and he's consumed with grief. Kevin is in bad shape.

The day I meet Kevin is a few days after the loss of his uncle. I am browsing through a local farmer's market when I notice a man next to me wearing a Pittsburgh Penguins hat, which instantly grabs my attention. However, before I say anything to him, I simply observe this man for a few moments.

He's holding a potato in each hand, looking at them side by side. The focused look on his face would suggest that this is the most difficult decision he's had to make all week. The heavy bags under his eyes and sweat soaking through his shirt show he's having a rough day.

Given the distress I see this man in, I decide to strike up an honest conversation with him.

"Go Penguins!" I say with an enthusiastic smile, walking up next to him.

My voice seems to shock Kevin out of his potato-trance. He looks at me with bewildered eyes. "What? Oh, yeah. Go Penguins," he replies softly, shifting his gaze back to the spuds.

"I'm J.F. Benoist," I say, extending out my hand.

Kevin looks back over to me, surprised to find I'm still there. "I'm Kevin," he uncertainly responds, accepting my handshake.

"Looks like you had a rough night," I state bluntly.

"Um, yeah. I'm pretty hungover. Seems like I always am nowadays," he mumbles, dropping his eyes as if to escape from the conversation.

"Oh, I remember those days. I sure wish I had someone I could relate to when I was going through that. Are you doing OK? Do you want to talk about it?" I gently ask.

He looks me straight in the eye, a quizzical expression on his face. "Most people don't go up to strangers and ask that," he responds nervously.

"You're right," I agree. "It's probably hard to imagine that a stranger could care, especially when people you *do* know ask 'How are you?' and usually don't genuinely want to know."

"And you *do* want to know?" Kevin asks quietly.

"Yeah, I do," I warmly reassure him. "Do you want to take a walk?"

"Uh…" Kevin responds. Looking down, his eyes dart from side to side as he considers his options.

Finally, he reestablishes eye contact. "Sure. Why not?"

He drops his potatoes back into the vendor's cart, and we start our stroll through the market. Casually sticking my hands in my pockets, I comment, "I used to struggle with some pretty major addiction problems. Alcohol, drugs, depression… I was in a bad place. But then, I started studying with some mentors, and after a few years, I realized something."

"What did you realize?" Kevin asks, looking around us uncomfortably.

"We're all suffering, Kevin. We isolate ourselves and pretend like we're not struggling, but we are. But at the same time—it's not our fault. We're doing the best we know how. Sometimes, it just takes a connection with the right person to really change your life."

Kevin has turned away from me, exhaling deeply. He looks back to me and asks, "How are you so comfortable sharing this with me? We met two minutes ago, but you're talking like we've known each other for years. How are you able to do that?"

I smile softly and continue walking. "I'll show you. Do you see that woman over there, fumbling to get something out of her purse? She's a stranger to both of us, yet I still know that she's going through some sort of hardship in her life. Maybe her son isn't doing well in school. Or maybe she's late on her big report at work. I may not know what it is, but there's something," I explain.

Kevin watches the woman successfully locate her keys and yank them out of the bag. Soon, she fades into the crowd.

"What about that man in the brown jacket, Kevin?" I inquire.

"What's your first impression of him?"

Kevin looks over and sees the man I've pointed out laughing while speaking on the phone. "Well, right now he looks pretty happy," he notes.

"You're right. He does look pretty happy. But maybe he's going through a divorce. Or maybe he was adopted, and he has a hard time feeling wanted by anyone. Regardless of how he looks right now, there's something that he's struggling with in his life," I predict.

Kevin stops walking and asks, "Why are you telling me this?"

I take a deep breath before answering. "Because, Kevin, I can see that you're struggling with something very heavy. I've been working with people for a long time, and I can spot someone who has a lot of pain behind their eyes."

Kevin releases a shaky breath. "You can see that, huh?" he whispers, wringing his hands nervously. The two of us sit down on a bench and continue to talk for the next hour. He tells me about his failing marriage, his disappointment in himself, and his struggles with alcohol.

"Kevin, it sounds like you've been through a lot. I can really identify with that myself. But, despite all these struggles in your life, why is it that you drink?" I bring up.

Immediately, I see Kevin's wall start to go back up, and he leans away from me. "God, I'm so sick of everyone asking me that! I don't know, OK?"

"I don't think you're hearing what I'm asking," I calmly reply.

Kevin's curiosity trumps his anger. "What do you mean?"

"If you're so sick of everyone asking you why you drink, are you really trying to find the answer? Or are you just hearing the question as a criticism?" I ask.

Kevin pauses a moment. "Huh. I guess I am taking it negatively," he admits, surprised at his own response.

"Don't be so hard on yourself, Kevin. There's a deeper reason for your drinking. You just have to be willing to open yourself up to find it." As I stand to leave, I add, "I need to head off to an appointment, but I want to thank you for your honesty today. It's really resonated with me. I hope that you figure this out. I think you deserve it." I extend my hand, and we part ways to go about the rest of our days.

Still trying to process his encounter with me, Kevin heads back to the produce booth to buy the potatoes. He picks up five without giving them a second look and hands the money over to the clerk. Suddenly he has a lot more on his mind than which potato is roundest.

Like Kevin, many of us unconsciously assume that people are judging us when they ask questions or make statements about things we're already ashamed about. We rarely are able to take a step back and really hear the question that's being asked. This is the Monkey Mind guiding our thoughts and feelings. Unfortunately, what we don't see is how this shameful mindset is sabotaging our lives.

If your goal is dismantling your negative programming, the Observing Mind can be your biggest ally. It can show you where to find the clarity and peace in every scene in your life. Cultivate your friendship with the Observing Mind, unplug from the Monkey Mind, and relieve yourself from your anxiety, addiction, and relationship issues.

Of course, taking this step will involve dedication and practice, just like any change in habit. To do so, the next step is understanding how our beliefs about others and about ourselves influence the Monkey Mind.

THE MONKEY MIND

VS.

THE OBSERVING MIND

The Monkey Mind

Pushes dramatically
Focuses responsibility on others
Panics and feeds anxiety
Makes drama and stirs up emotion
Sees everything as an emergency
Wants things to change—NOW
Confuses the story with reality
Assumes it knows the truth
Jumps to judgments and immediate opinions
Is consumed by a nonstop stream of thoughts
Rushes and pushes you to react right away
Keeps creating the same result

The Observing Mind

Exudes calmness and clarity
Focuses responsibility inward
Remains present in anxiety-inducing situations
States simple facts
Sees everything as a situation that is unfolding
Accepts what is and explores possible changes
Understands that the story is just a story
Assumes there's something useful to learn here
Asks questions and considers other points of view
Leaves space in its thinking
Allows you to respond at your own pace
Creates new possibilities

Part 2

THE POWER OF BELIEFS

Chapter 4

BELIEFS COME IN MANY FORMS

A belief is a recurring thought that you always assume is true; it seems so obvious that you never even think to question it. It's important to be aware that we each hold a mind-boggling range of beliefs that are creating our reality. If you want to change some part of your reality, you are going to have to change some of your beliefs.

Let's look at several examples of common beliefs.

COMMON BELIEFS

We may believe something about people in general, or about a particular person: "They're lazy." "My father will never understand me." "Money means everything to her."

We can also take something that may be true sometimes and

believe that it's always true: "His family hates me." "She's a liar." "I have the smartest children."

We can have beliefs about what's good and bad, right and wrong. Some of these beliefs serve us well, but sometimes they lead us to see in black-and-white absolutes, and we miss the many colors that exist in the world: "All politicians are corrupt." "Doctors know all the answers." "Lying is bad."

We each develop basic beliefs about the safety and benevolence of life: "Life is unfair." "God is on our side." "It's every man for himself."

Some beliefs are strategies designed to protect us: "Never talk to strangers." "Don't eat junk food." "Men can't be trusted."

And then there are our core beliefs, the stories we return to over and over in very unrelated situations. These beliefs are at the heart of our life and identity: "I'm bad." "I'm good." "I'm smart." "I'm stupid." "I'm blessed." "I'm not good enough." "There's something wrong with me." "I'm not lovable."

The Monkey Mind dominates our thoughts with stories related to our self-defeating core beliefs. These are the beliefs that developed from our programming, and many of the thoughts we have are in some way related to these core beliefs.

The Observing Mind takes a step back from our self-destructive beliefs and questions the validity of these ideas. Is it true that I'm bad? Is it true that I'm not lovable? Once you can create some space from these thoughts, you can see how false these beliefs oftentimes are.

To begin to identify beliefs, imagine a person is looking at an abstract painting. They think, "What is this painting even about?" Their belief in the moment is, "I should be able to figure out the meaning behind this art more easily."

Now, to experience this yourself, look at a painting and write down your thoughts about the art piece. Then start to identify your beliefs from those statements.

When we start to gain awareness of how present our beliefs are throughout our daily lives, we can start to become one step removed from the Monkey Mind's stories and begin to take back control of our lives.

Chapter 5

THE PURPOSE OF OUR BELIEFS

The majority of beliefs we've stored in our memory banks were developed to take care of ourselves in some way or form. Unfortunately, the beliefs that may have helped us when we were younger are often counterproductive in our lives today.

Let's see how a belief can start out beneficial but end up being detrimental.

GABRIELA'S STORY

When Gabriela was eight years old, her mother took her along to her colleague's house. While the two adults were chatting, Gabriela wandered into the kitchen, where she found the family dog eating out of its dish. Thrilled at the discovery, Gabriela ran over and started petting the dog's back.

This particular pooch was very territorial around food, and in one swift movement, he turned and chomped down on Gabriela's hand—hard.

Blood dripping down her arm, Gabriela ran back to her mother in tears. Upon seeing the damage, Gabriela's mother started hyperventilating and naming off the different infections Gabriela could get. By the time they arrived at the hospital, Gabriela was nearly convinced they were going to need to amputate her hand.

While the wound healed up just fine, Gabriela never shook the emotional distress from that day. She developed the belief that all dogs are dangerous, and she soon found herself avoiding getting near any dog again.

Now, as an adult, Gabriela is (in a way) still taking care of herself by holding the belief that all dogs are dangerous—she won't ever get bitten by a dog if she's never around one. However, holding this belief has several other consequences.

Gabriela feels a lot of unnecessary fear and anguish whenever there's a dog nearby. She goes out of her way to avoid a lot of pups that aren't dangerous at all, and she doesn't get to meet the wonderful dogs she might actually enjoy. Many animal lovers would say that's a big price to pay.

On a more personal level, this old belief could harm Gabriela's relationships.

One night, Gabriela gets a call from her friend Dev. "Gabriela! You're coming to the party tonight, right?" Dev eagerly asks.

"Of course!" Gabriela responds, swiping another coat of lipstick on her lips. "I'm getting ready to leave in about fifteen minutes."

"Great! Shannon and Anthony are going to be here too... Down! Bad boy!" Dev suddenly yells, a bark echoing in the background.

"Oh, is there a dog there?" Gabriela anxiously asks, feeling her palms start to sweat.

"Yeah! Moose is here. You've met Moose, haven't you? He's a big sweetheart!" Dev gushes, clearly petting Moose on the other end of the phone.

"No... no, I haven't. OK, well, I'll text you when I leave," Gabriela says, trying to hide her discomfort.

"Sounds good. See you soon!" Dev replies, not picking up on the change in Gabriela's voice.

Gabriela paces her apartment, trying to make the knot in her stomach go away. Her Monkey Mind seizes its opportunity.

His name is Moose? He's going to be massive! What if he wants to play or gets mad? You could lose a finger! There's no way you can go. You'll just be worried the whole time anyway. You'd be a wet blanket.

Gabriela texts Dev a few minutes later. "Sorry, Dev. I just got a bad headache, so I think I'm going to have to pass after all. Let's get together sometime next week though!"

Gabriela is embarrassed of her fear and hopes her positive spin on the end of her text will make up for her lack of appearance. She collapses on the couch, throwing her phone on the coffee table. She ignores it as it vibrates wildly over and over again. She throws a blanket over herself and starts crying for being such a wimp. The rest of the night consists of her criticizing herself until she finally pulls out her laptop and starts buying everything she sees to quiet her mind.

Clearly, the belief that all dogs are dangerous is no longer doing Gabriela any good. If she chose to become aware of her programming, she could learn how to adopt a new belief about dogs—one that will not put her in harm's way but will also not dictate her social schedule around canines.

Most of us don't realize how we solidify a belief around past events and traumas, like Gabriela did. Can you think of any beliefs you may have adopted that are holding you back today?

To picture this, imagine your partner comes home from work and asks, "Why didn't you do the dishes like I asked you to?" Take a moment to notice and be honest with the way you would respond.

Does your response look something like this: "Why do I have to do everything?"

Most of us are blind to the underlying belief that makes us respond the way we do. For example, the belief driving this response could be: I'm irresponsible if I didn't do what I was asked.

Now imagine your partner comes home and asks, "Why didn't you call me back?" What's your response to this question? Are you feeling defensive? What are you feeling you need to defend? And what might be the belief driving your response?

When the price you pay for your previously adopted belief is your personal happiness and well-being, it's time to find a better way to look after yourself. In order to truly take care of ourselves, we need to be able to question the beliefs that appear to help us, but instead end up sabotaging our lives.

Chapter 6

OUR BELIEFS DETERMINE OUR EXPERIENCE

Many of us are raised in such a way that we believe that outside circumstances and other people can create our experience. Yet, it's evident that our beliefs *do* affect how we respond to a situation, because different people react differently to the same exact stimulus. Can you imagine how freeing it would be to know that you are the one in charge of your life? This is what you can achieve by addressing and releasing your self-defeating beliefs.

Let's take a look at an example of how a group of people may all have completely different reactions to the same scenario.

DIFFERENT PEOPLE, DIFFERENT RESPONSES

It's a wonderful summer night. Paula—Elizabeth's dramatic friend from the salon—and four of her friends have gathered at a chic new Chinese restaurant. They are sitting together at the same table, sharing the same food, talking with the same waiter, and listening to the same upbeat background music. They've known each other for years and always look forward to getting together.

Interestingly enough, while they're all sharing the same outer circumstances, each person is having a very different personal experience. Thomas is feeling quite happy, Lucy is feeling hopeless, Greg is feeling nervous, Paula is feeling extremely depressed, and Susan is feeling frustrated.

If the outer circumstances are the same for everyone, why are they having such drastically different experiences? This is because each person is viewing the events through a different set of beliefs.

Thomas believes there's nothing better than a meal with friends, so he's in a great mood. Everything he tastes and sees delights him. He can't stop talking and laughing.

Lucy finds the waiter gorgeous, but that stirs up internal drama from her recent breakup. She barely notices the food and is distracted from the conversation every time the waiter comes near. Her Monkey Mind reminds her, *You'll never be with anyone that attractive. You'll end up with some loser, if you end up with anyone at all.*

Greg can't move past Susan's announcement that she is getting a promotion. His jealousy is getting the better of him, and his Monkey Mind is reminding him of all the reasons why he won't get promoted anytime soon: *You're so slow—they'd never give you more responsibility.*

Paula is on her fourth cocktail. No one has complimented her on her new outfit, even though they commented to Lucy on how nice she looks today. Her Monkey Mind spouts, *Your friends don't even notice you. They probably don't like you anymore.*

Susan is on edge. Her perfectionist streak has come out, so she thinks the service is impossibly slow and the waiter is incompetent. Her Monkey Mind fuels this story. *At these prices, everything should be perfect. It's been ten minutes since the waiter checked on you. This is ridiculous.*

Each person has come to the same basic situation with a very different set of beliefs and, hence, a very different perspective. Each belief is creating its own reality from the same, very simple, raw material: a meal out with friends.

Imagine the last time you had dinner with your own friends. In your mind's eye, put yourself back into that restaurant. Look around. Notice what you think: ugly, pretty, good, bad, dirty, clean, matching, clashing—whatever catches your eye. Can you see how you can fixate on one thing and have a very different experience than your friend, who might be focusing on something else?

Let's take this a step further. Imagine that you're a ten-year-old child, who was raised your whole life in the wilderness with little contact with civilization. You're standing in this same restaurant, but most of the objects in this new environment are completely unfamiliar to you. Would you have the same responses and beliefs? Would those evaluations—good, bad, matching, clashing—even make sense? Can you see how different perspectives and the beliefs you hold create your experience?

We imagine that our responses are triggered directly by an outside stimulus, but in truth, we're being triggered by our beliefs. This is crucial to understand if we want to heal the Monkey Mind. Trying to change the outer details is usually a waste of time. It's far more efficient to confront our beliefs directly; this is the shortcut to changing the programming that sabotages our lives.

OUR PROGRAMMING INFLUENCES OUR RESPONSES

We have a lot of choices that we get to be in charge of in our lives—what to wear, what career to pursue, what music to listen to. We're accustomed to getting to choose how we spend our time. This means that when we don't have any control over a situation, we can often feel frustrated. We *want* to have control over the uncontrollable.

Despite what is happening in our outside circumstances, we *always* have control over how we respond. When we learn to be in charge of our responses, we become much more efficient and peaceful when life throws us a curveball. The trick to recognizing the deeper beliefs at play is to look *inside* ourselves instead of focusing on the *outside* factors.

Let's look at two people's nearly identical outside experiences to understand this by revisiting Patrick Smith and Charlie Walton as adults.

Patrick, Kevin's brother, was raised by very critical parents. Although he was well-accomplished in school and sports, nothing he did was good enough in his father's eyes. In contrast, Charlie was raised in the loving, accepting Walton household. His parents respected what he accomplished, while also encouraging him to learn more and grow.

Today, Patrick and Charlie find themselves in the exact same situation, although in different locations. Patrick is one of the top salesmen of a company in New York. Today, he has the most important meeting of his life: if he presents well and closes this deal, he will get a big promotion. Charlie is the lead salesman at a company in Los Angeles. He also shares the circumstances of a potentially life-changing meeting. Both of their meetings are at the potential client's office.

Patrick and Charlie both show up to their respective buildings a full hour before their meeting. To their surprise, they find the parking garage very full. So full, in fact, that neither can find an open parking spot. There is no street parking nearby, so they each drive in circles around the various floors, hoping someone will eventually leave. Before they know it, it's only fifteen minutes until their meeting starts.

Finally, they each spot a car leaving. They turn on their blinkers, relieved a spot has appeared. As each of them are about to turn into their respective spots, another car darts out of nowhere and takes the parking space.

Immediately, Patrick becomes irate. His Monkey Mind starts running, with more colorful language than I've included. *Are you serious? You clearly had your blinker on! What an absolute jerk! Who does that? Man, a guy like that deserves to have his car keyed.*

Charlie also feels a sudden onset of anger. However, instead of buying into his Monkey Mind's story, he takes a deep breath and allows himself the space to process these thoughts. Driving past the now-occupied spot to find another place to park, Charlie's Observing Mind plays a very different tune. *Well, apparently that guy needed the spot more than you. Let's just find another.*

By the time each of them finds a spot, it is now fifteen minutes after their meeting should have started.

When Patrick emerges from the elevator, he is sweating bullets. He can feel his boss's icy gaze from across the office as he rushes into the meeting room. Instead of quietly taking his place, Patrick decides to share the grand tragedy he just encountered. "So sorry for my tardiness, everyone! You won't believe what happened! I got here at eight and realized that there wasn't a parking spot anywhere! But then, nearly forty-five minutes later..." Patrick regales the room with his tale of woe, playing up the story.

Patrick's boss watches on in disbelief, his anger bubbling inside of him. He finally has to cut Patrick off and instruct him to start his presentation. Now off his game, Patrick gives a nervous, stammering performance that impresses no one.

On the other hand, Charlie walks confidently into the meeting room. Upon entering, his boss, Claudia, has the same look of anger that Patrick's boss had. Instead of going into a story, however, Charlie handles the situation very differently.

Charlie walks up to the front of the room next to his boss. He then proceeds to calmly say, "Sorry for my tardiness, everyone. Claudia, if we need to have a further discussion about this, I'd be happy to do it later. But right now, I'm thrilled to explain the new product we've been working on that brought you all here today."

Now, Charlie's boss eases up as she watches him self-assuredly deliver a stellar presentation.

After his work day, Patrick drives home through New York traffic with white-knuckled hands gripping the wheel. His Monkey Mind won't let up on him.

You are such an idiot! Why did you only get there an hour early? What were you thinking? You looked like a complete fool! Lou wouldn't even look at you the rest of the day. You're going to get canned tomorrow. And you should. Because you're a moron.

Patrick angrily careens into his driveway, slamming on the brake. When he gets inside, he digs his pouch of cocaine out of his dresser and quickly snorts a line.

On the other side of the country, Charlie enjoys his night with his boss and his new business associates, who invited Charlie out to dinner after finalizing the contract for his deal. The group has a lovely time getting to know each other, and they all look forward to the next time they can get together.

As you can see, Patrick and Charlie had very different end results from the same outer circumstances. The reason Patrick and Charlie reacted differently is that Patrick does not have confidence in himself because of the programming he received from his upbringing. He was trained that the way not to be scolded is to please others; by putting his focus on pleasing others, he learned to believe that they're in charge of how he feels. He developed the belief that "if they like who I am, then I feel good about myself." Conversely, he also believes that "if they don't like who I am, I feel bad about myself." Because of this, he wants to blame other people or outside circumstances for why he is upset.

Patrick was also raised to believe that it's not fair if something does not go his way. That guy shouldn't have stolen his parking spot. He *shouldn't* have been late to the meeting.

The truth is, we can't always control outside circumstances. We can't control if a restaurant is out of our favorite soup, or if it's raining on our wedding day. We can try to argue with the rain, which will get us nowhere. Or we can simply accept the situation and focus on changing our *belief* about the weather, which is something we can control.

Do you ever think this way? Imagine if you had been in a similar situation to Patrick and Charlie. Think of the ways your Monkey Mind would argue with what is happening when you couldn't find a parking space.

Say these judgments out loud: "I can't believe this. Why are there so many people here right now? Why didn't they build more parking for a building this large?" Notice what you are feeling. Does this improve your situation, or does it simply add more anxiety?

Now, think from the Observing Mind's perspective, and align yourself with the situation. Say these ideas out loud: "I'm not finding a parking space. There doesn't appear to be any open spots. I guess the parking lot is full." Notice how you feel when you align yourself with what is.

When we listen to the Monkey Mind, we launch into finding a reason why the circumstances aren't our fault, which doesn't resolve anything and aggravates the situation. With the Observing Mind, we take full ownership of our beliefs and have the power to change how we respond to any circumstance.

Chapter 7

THE CONSEQUENCES OF UNEXPLORED BELIEFS

Imagine that the day you were born, you were given a pair of red-tinted glasses to wear. You went about your childhood believing this was the way the world was. One day, when you are an adult, someone takes the glasses off your face. The world would look much different, wouldn't it?

In a way, each of us has our own unique red-tinted glasses—our beliefs serve as the lens through which we see the world. These glasses lead us to view situations in a certain way, sometimes even leading us to project our beliefs onto situations in which they don't apply. We're so engrained to see the world in red that sometimes we don't realize that other colors, or other beliefs, exist. This is true for how Elizabeth views the world.

∼

After her grandmother's funeral, Elizabeth and Ted continue to grow apart. Ted starts working longer and longer hours, and Elizabeth starts emptying more and more wine bottles. She has lost any traction she had made in being sober, and she's drinking even more than before.

While pouring her sixth glass of wine one night, Elizabeth sees a woman's name pop up on Ted's cell phone. Elizabeth's Monkey Mind views this as a dire situation.

Who is this woman? Why is she calling your husband at eight o'clock at night? Ted must be cheating on you. How could he do this to you?

Enraged, Elizabeth picks up the phone and storms into the kitchen, where Ted is making himself a cup of decaf coffee. "Who is Simone?" she demands, sliding Ted's phone across the counter.

Ted sighs and replies flatly, "Simone is my coworker. I've told you about her before; she's the one helping me with that workman's comp case."

"Oh? Why is she calling you after hours?" she alleges harshly, leaning against the counter for balance.

"Probably to tell me something about the case, Elizabeth! For once, can you not make something out of nothing?" Ted snaps, sticking his phone in his pocket and walking past her.

Elizabeth's Monkey Mind is deeply offended by this. *Make something out of nothing? He's trying to make you feel bad about this! How dare he!*

She follows him out. "Oh, don't act holier than thou, Ted! I've been right about plenty over the years," Elizabeth plops back down on the love seat. Feeling that anxious lump in her stomach, she quickly downs a gulp of Chardonnay.

Turning towards her, Ted's anger starts to rise in his voice. "No, Elizabeth! You haven't. Not about this. Have I ever done anything— anything —to make you think I would cheat? I've always been involved in our kids' lives. I've always been supportive of you." He pauses, rubbing his temples with his mug-free hand. "This insane jealously, Elizabeth, it has to stop. And when you drink, it gets even worse."

Elizabeth's Monkey Mind jumps in. *Of course he's blaming your drinking now. He always does. He doesn't want to take responsibility for what he's done.*

Elizabeth cuts him off. "Oh sure, let's just blame eeeeeeeverything on the alcohol!" she emphasizes loudly, finishing her glass.

"I'm not talking to you when you're like this," Ted mutters as he tries to leave the room.

"Because you have something to hide!" Elizabeth shouts after him, emptying the rest of the wine bottle into her glass and sinking down into the chair.

Upstairs, they hear their teenage daughter's door slam shut. Tiffany hates hearing her parents fight, especially after her mom has been drinking.

Spinning around, Ted takes a step toward her. "No, Elizabeth," he shouts back, "not because I have something to hide! Because you become a different person when you drink!"

Elizabeth rolls her eyes. Yet, internally, her heart sinks at these words. "Whatever. Go crawl away to your office and call your bimbo," she says, dismissing him with a wave of her hand.

Ted's face flushes with anger. "She's not my bimbo, Elizabeth! For God's sake, I am not having an affair! Not all men have to cheat—we're not all like your father!" he bellows.

Locking her jaw tightly, Elizabeth's eyes flutter closed quickly. As they reopen, the room seems unsteady. She can feel that knot in her gut growing, no matter how much she tries to stifle it. "Well, fine," she replies with a slur. "Maybe you aren't having an affair, Ted. But you're more in love with your job than you ever have been with me."

Ted shakes his head as he walks up the stairs. "You make it impossible to love you," he murmurs, just loud enough for Elizabeth to hear.

Just as she's about to take another sip, Elizabeth's son arrives home. "Josh! Come sit with me!" Elizabeth requests loudly, patting the armchair excessively.

Josh gives her one look, then uncomfortably says, "Um, I'm OK, Mom. I'm just going to go hang in my room." He then quickly heads upstairs, taking the steps two at a time.

Now, Elizabeth is alone with her thoughts. She feels an immense sadness and loneliness, and her Observing Mind takes this opportunity to try and push through the Monkey Mind's wall of words.

Elizabeth, you could go upstairs and apologize. You could connect with your family—isn't that what you really want to do?

Elizabeth recognizes this thought and starts to stand up, brushing away the newly-fallen tears from her cheeks. However, her Monkey Mind is quick to take the show back over. *You're a drunken fool, Elizabeth. You're a screw-up. You'll never get your family's trust again.*

Elizabeth decides to listen to the latter voice, slumping back down into the chair. Her tears grow stronger, so she flicks on the TV to drown out her sobs. She grabs her glass again to dull the pain.

Elizabeth wants to be able to trust Ted, but she can never shake that nagging Monkey Mind's comments about him cheating. So why is it that Elizabeth is unable to trust Ted, even when he's done nothing wrong?

After years of watching her father carry on illicit affairs, paired with his harsh criticisms, Elizabeth developed the deep-seated belief that men cannot be trusted. Now, she projects her disdain of men onto her husband. This belief has been a dark shadow for their entire marriage, and it is now the driving force behind most of their arguments. Unless she addresses her old programming, she will struggle to have a meaningful connection with men and will continue feeling the consequences from this unresolved belief.

Can you remember a time when you were completely absorbed in a story you made up, only to discover later that the story was completely false? What kind of experience did you create for yourself with that story? How many hours were consumed with that idea? How were your relationships affected? How was your work affected? How did your body feel?

Are you aware of the impact that occurs, both to yourself and to others, when these negative stories take over?

When we're able to take a step back and look at the beliefs that color how we view the world, we can begin to change how that perspective affects our lives.

CREATING SELF-FULFILLING PROPHECIES

When our beliefs shape how we see a situation, they often unknowingly set us on a path to prove that these beliefs are right. Sometimes, this leads us to influence the outcome of the situation into one that serves to reinforce the beliefs we already have. This can lead to a detrimental pattern of self-fulfilling prophecies in our life.

When Elizabeth believes "men cannot be trusted," she can no longer accurately see the person in front of her. As a result, she projects her perception of her father onto her husband; she only notices what matches her belief and misses the rest.

Elizabeth is not fully aware that she holds this belief about the men in her life—she is so used to thinking this way that she does not notice the subtle impacts her belief has on her overall behavior. Instead of being friendly with Ted, she holds back, asks suspicious questions, and cuts conversations short. She's reluctant to connect with him. This behavior drives Ted away, and her constant jealousy creates conflict in their relationship.

To start to identify the patterns in our own lives, let's explore another potential self-fulfilling prophecy.

Say that you believe that your business partner doesn't value your ideas. Because of this belief, you don't share any ideas with her. Now, your partner doesn't hear your ideas, so she gets inspired by and brainstorms with other people.

As a result, if you bring something up to your business partner, there is a higher chance she will not give it as much weight because you don't have a track record of sharing valuable ideas. Can you see how this would create a negative pattern in your life?

In order to stop the repetitive pattern of our self-fulfilling prophecies, we need to first be aware of our beliefs that are creating these cycles. Then we can begin to change our perspective on the situations that arise in our day-to-day lives.

Chapter 8

OVERCOMING OLD BELIEFS

As we've already seen, we adopted our beliefs from the experiences that were repeated over and over during our formative years, and we built our current identity off of those events. Yet, most of us are unaware that we even have those beliefs, let alone know where they came from. Let's see how Elizabeth's beliefs translate from thoughts in her mind to her current world.

~

Elizabeth continues down her self-destructive path for several more months. Occasionally she'll get a glimpse of the Observing Mind, but it is quickly squashed by the Monkey Mind. After more and more frequent arguments, Ted announces he has done as much as he can, but he can no longer stay in this marriage. He moves out, and the kids go with him.

After the separation, Elizabeth resigns herself to spending most of her time in her bedroom. The only time she leaves is when she goes to the office to do her freelance work. Even with that, she is starting to miss deadlines and her work is becoming sloppy. At night, she desperately tries to drown her sorrow in wine.

After coming home from a long assignment for her newspaper, one of the first things on Sarah's agenda is to go see Elizabeth. She has been very distant, even dodging Sarah's calls and texts. When Sarah surprises Elizabeth at home, she discovers her friend is in far worse shape than she imagined. Elizabeth has reached the point where she needs more help than Sarah can offer. So she gives me a call.

When Sarah brings Elizabeth to our first session together, Elizabeth's eyes are swollen from crying. She's tried to make herself as presentable as possible, but it's easy to see through her guise.

"J.F.! So good to see you," Sarah greets me with a hug.

"How are you doing, Sarah?" I brightly ask.

"Much better than when I started working with you!" Sarah turns to Elizabeth. "You remember how anxious I used to be at work, don't you? Now it takes a whole lot to throw me off my game," Sarah exclaims, turning back to me with a broad smile.

Sarah apologizes, "Oh, sorry! J.F.—this is Elizabeth. She's going through a hard time, and I think she could really use your help."

Elizabeth gives a small nod and reaches out for a handshake. She grips my hand weakly before quickly releasing my palm.

Slapping her hands together loudly, Sarah announces, "Well, my work is done. Elizabeth, I'll pick you up in a couple hours, OK? And remember to let your guard down—you can trust J.F., I promise." Sarah gives Elizabeth a small squeeze on her shoulder before walking out.

Looking around uncertainly, Elizabeth sits down on the chair across from my seat. I sit down as well and take a few deep breaths before starting our session. Elizabeth is watching me closely, as if she's trying to dissect my motives.

"What are you struggling with, Elizabeth?" I ask calmly.

"Well…" she begins, wringing her hands, "I'd say the first thing to look at would be my marriage falling apart. That tends to mess up a lot of people, right?" she asks somewhat sarcastically, looking me up and down with disapproval.

"Why don't you explain to me what happened," I invite kindly.

"He worked constantly and was always breaking commitments and canceling last minute. He stopped spending any time with me," she says, her voice breaking slightly. As hard as she's trying to put on this tough face, her true emotions are starting to trickle out.

Elizabeth clears her throat, "And to cope with that difficult situation, I… drank," Elizabeth admits, sucking her bottom lip into her mouth as a few tears start to well. Elizabeth stares out the window for a few seconds before suddenly looking me straight in the eyes. "Sarah told me to trust you, to open up to you," she quietly says, seeming to study my eyes for traces of malice. "Can I trust you, J.F.?"

"That is for you alone to decide," I reply with a soft smile.

Her eyes flutter closed. Dropping her head into her hands, she mutters, "What have I got to lose?"

She looks up, her tears now making their way down her cheeks. "I ruined my life. My husband left me, my kids don't want to be seen around me, and my dad would be happy never speaking to me again. I'm terrified that I'm going to end up alone for the rest of my life," Elizabeth states quietly, the tears continuing.

"Elizabeth, let's focus on one person at a time, and then we can start to track back to why you think you'll end up alone. Are you open to that?" I gently ask.

She nods slowly, her eyes closed.

"What's one specific thing your husband did that upset you?"

"He never did anything romantic. All he did was work and talk about work… and, criticize whatever I did," she responds coldly, wiping away a tear.

"Do you have a specific experience when you remember him doing this?" I inquire.

She half laughs before responding, "Oh, I've got a great one. For our anniversary a few years ago, I tried to do this big romantic dinner. I spent the whole day in the kitchen—an actual eight hours over the stove. I'm not much of a cook, so it was a big deal for me to put myself out there and try this for him, you know?"

She takes a breath, then continues, "So that night, when we're sitting at the dining table together, my husband—who *knew* I had spent all day working on this meal—had the nerve to say, 'You really should have just ordered takeout instead.' Can you believe that?" she explodes.

"And you took this as a criticism?" I prompt.

"Of course! It was an awful thing to say!"

"Elizabeth, can you take a moment to breathe with me?" I invite.

She agrees, though with some hesitation, and takes a few shaky breaths.

I continue, "Now, why did your husband's comment upset you so much?"

She swallows deeply and responds, "Because I had spent all that time putting together this special meal for him, and all he could do was criticize it." Her shoulders slouch and her head hangs low. "I think that's why I always accused him of having an affair... because I felt like he just wasn't interested in me," she whispers.

I inquire, "Why did his words upset you so much?"

"Because no matter what I tried or did, I was just never good enough for him. I'm just... I'm sick of that feeling," she replies despondently.

"When did you first experience this feeling of not being good enough, Elizabeth?"

"Well, my entire childhood. Nothing I did was *ever* good enough for my father. He was constantly criticizing me," Elizabeth recalls sadly.

"What's a specific instance of when you thought your father criticized you?" I ask lightly.

"There are so many to choose from!" she cackles. "I remember one time when I was on the softball team in high school, I had a great hit and got all the way to third base. That hit ended up winning us the game. Afterwards, everyone was celebrating and cheering. We were all so pumped up. Then I went to take a shower. When I got back out to the field to grab my glove, my dad was the only one still in the stands..." Elizabeth stops, closing her eyes tightly and squeezing her hands into fists.

"He started screaming at me for not getting a home run—saying I could have made it if I wasn't so scared to slide. Then... then he made me run the bases for the next twenty minutes so I 'would be better for next time.' Not only was it humiliating, but it also completely dissolved any pride I had about getting that triple."

I take a deep breath, leaving space for Elizabeth to do the same. "Elizabeth, how do you think criticisms like this affected you?"

"Well, I started to deeply resent my father. Then, when I found out about all the affairs... I felt like he had betrayed us. I hated him for a long time; I still kind of do, I think."

"Do you think you could be projecting your opinion of your father onto Ted?"

She sighs. "I don't know... I guess if I do, I'm not aware of it," Elizabeth acknowledges.

"There may also be another impact from your father's criticisms of you. Other than resenting your father, how else do you think your father's harsh words may have influenced you?" I inquire.

"Well, I think he stripped me of whatever self-confidence I once had," she responds with a shrug.

"Let's go back to Ted and the anniversary dinner—how does your father making you run the bases relate to Ted's comment about your cooking?"

"I guess they both made me feel bad about myself? I don't know, I always feel bad about myself, so I don't really keep track of what comments make me think that..." Elizabeth starts, drifting off into her own mind.

Before she gets lost in her thoughts, I point out, "Elizabeth, can you see that during your childhood, you adopted a belief that says you're not good enough?"

Elizabeth shifts uncomfortably in her chair. "You mean, because my dad was so awful to me, that's why I'm now so critical of myself?" She considers this for a moment. "I guess I've always known that in some way, how my dad treated me affected my self-confidence, or lack thereof. But I never thought about it affecting my marriage," she says, her eyebrows scrunched in thought. After a moment of silence, she thoughtfully asks, "So when Ted made that snide comment about getting takeout, I wasn't actually mad at him... I was upset because I was judging myself?"

I raise my eyebrows slightly and respond, "What do you think?"

She breathes, deeply this time. "That does make sense," she responds. "So... I don't trust Ted, not only because my father cheated... but also because he reminds me of how I don't think I'm good enough?"

"You've got it, Elizabeth. You've had so many experiences with your father and Ted criticizing you, that when you see Ted, you're reminded of the belief that you're not good enough." I pause for a moment. "How are you feeling now, Elizabeth?" I question lightly.

"I feel like crap," she scoffs. "No wonder I've been drinking so much. That's brutal."

"Most of us aren't aware of how much stress these judgmental thoughts cause us. It makes sense that we're trying to relieve ourselves from all the anxiety that this judgment produces. So, let's really take a look at where you stand with this belief right now. Think back to that dinner you made for your husband. Is it true that your meal wasn't good enough?"

"No, it's not," she says strongly. Her voice grows louder as she declares, "Sure, I'm not the best chef on the planet, but it was tasty! And more importantly, I put a lot of love into those dishes. I'm proud of what I made."

"And is it true that making it to third base wasn't good enough?"

"No, it's not," she says, getting a little choked up.

"It's great you can see that, Elizabeth," I note warmly. I then explain to her the concept of the Monkey Mind—how it works and the anxiety it creates in our lives. "Moving forward, you're going to have to be vigilant in putting this newfound confidence into practice. You're going to be challenged by the belief that you're not good enough over and over, and you'll have to remain strong to not fall into the Monkey Mind's story."

She nods along to my words.

I add, "Now that you can see how this relates back to your drinking, can you see how alcohol isn't the problem? It's merely a symptom. To help you kick drinking for good, we need to keep addressing these underlying beliefs. Are you ready to dive deeper into recognizing where those negative thoughts come from?" I ask.

Taking another deep breath, Elizabeth exhales slowly. "I'm ready to try."

Elizabeth unconsciously believed that her father's and husband's opinions were vital in determining her self-worth. Many of us also rely on outside sources to decide how we feel about ourselves.

Take a moment and think of someone in your life whose opinion you value more than your own. Perhaps it is your parent, your partner, or your boss. What do you really want from that person? And what is one way that you could achieve this on your own?

Once we're able to identify where our beliefs formed, we can start to understand how these beliefs lingered into our adulthood.

SHEDDING OLD BELIEFS

After identifying how a belief is formed, we need to challenge the validity of that belief. We do this by recreating the situation in which the belief was formed; however, this time we consciously question if the belief is true. By doing this, we create a *different outcome*. This new experience is vital in reprogramming our thought patterns and breaking the cycle we've been stuck in for so long.

$\sim$

When Elizabeth arrives to our next session, she still looks disheveled. Her eyes have heavy bags under them, and her exhaustion is apparent. She collapses wearily onto the chair.

"How are you doing today, Elizabeth?" I ask.

"Well, I was doing better. I even went five days without drinking! But then, two days ago, Ted called me and asked where I had put our son's saxophone. I said it should be in his room, and he suddenly became so angry and started blaming me for never knowing where anything is and saying how irresponsible I am…" Elizabeth rubs her eyes. "Then the argument escalated from there… after he hung up, I just felt awful. So I stayed up all night drinking." She bows her head down. "I'm sure that's not what you want to hear," she mumbles.

"Elizabeth, you've just begun your journey on overcoming the Monkey Mind. There are going to be some bumps in the road along the way—and that's OK," I reassure her.

She shrugs off my remark. "So last time I was here, we talked about how I developed my lack of self-confidence from my dad's criticisms, right? Well, I just got upset with Ted and drank. I'm sure it's related, but I'm not exactly sure how."

"How about if we try an experiment to help you figure this out?" I ask.

Elizabeth nods enthusiastically.

"Wonderful," I begin. "So I want you to name three specific criticisms your father said to you growing up that you can still think of to this day. After you name them, I'm going to write each criticism up on the whiteboard. Begin whenever you feel comfortable."

"Um, let's see… well, the first one that comes to mind is, 'Lizzie, stop biting your fingernails. It's disgusting.'" She recalls with a wince.

"What do you think was the underlying message behind 'stop biting your fingernails,' Elizabeth?" I ask.

She quickly lists off, "That *I'm* disgusting. That I'm not ladylike. That I should know better."

I write this all on the board. "OK, what's another?" I ask.

She bobbles her head back and forth slightly. "When I got to be a teenager, he started nitpicking what I ate. He'd say, 'You're not going to eat all that, are you? You're going to balloon up just like your Aunt Margie,'" Elizabeth says, mimicking her father's deep voice.

"What do you think was the underlying message behind that?" I inquire.

"I'm fat. What's wrong with me for eating so much."

I add this to the board. "One more?" I request.

Elizabeth exhales loudly as she thinks. "It's hard to think of a specific phrase… The only other thing I can think of is when I was in junior high. I was going through some bullying and was having a hard time in school, but he would always say, 'If you don't get your grades up, you're going to throw your life away. Why can't you be more like your brother?'"

"And what do you think the message behind this one was?"

"I'm stupid. I'm not as good as my brother. I should be better," she replies softly, massaging her sweaty palms.

"OK, got it," I say.

I write these final messages on the board and clasp my hands together. "All right, here is where we get experiential," I explain. "Now, I'd like you to read these three criticisms aloud, as well as their underlying messages, over and over again."

Elizabeth's puzzled face stares back at me. "What? Say them aloud?"

I nod reassuringly. "Elizabeth, these criticisms are already filed away in your mind—they're the self-judgments you hold about yourself. The problem is that you're repressing them. Right now, we're going to bring some consciousness to them."

"OK…" she looks over to the board and meekly reads the first statement. "Stop biting your fingernails. It's disgusting."

Pausing, Elizabeth looks over to me for approval. "That's great," I encourage. "Keep going, Elizabeth. And try to say the statements with the same attitude your dad would say them to you."

Taking a deeper breath, Elizabeth continues, "You're disgusting. You're not ladylike. You should know better. You're not going to eat all that, are you? You're going to balloon up just like your Aunt Margie." She stops for just a moment as her voice catches.

She continues, "You're fat. What's wrong with you for eating so much?" She blinks several times. "If you don't get your grades up, you're going to throw your life away. Why can't you be more like your brother? You're stupid. You're not as good as your brother. You should be better."

Her eyes move back up to the top of the board. "Stop biting your nails. It's disgusting. You're disgusting. You're not ladylike. You should know better. You're not going to eat all that, are you?" Now, Elizabeth is speaking very slowly, each word seeming to pack a powerful punch.

"You're going to balloon up just like your Aunt Margie. You're fat. What's wrong with you for eating so much? If you don't get your grades up, you're going to throw your life away." Elizabeth stops to take a shaky breath. She looks over to me. "Do I have to keep going?" she asks, a plea in her voice.

"What are you feeling right now?" I ask softly.

"I feel like I was kicked in the gut."

"What emotion would you say that is?" I clarify.

"Sadness. A lot of sadness," she whispers.

"Why do you feel sad?"

Elizabeth's tears now escape their barrier. She settles into deep, heaving sobs. Unable to answer for several moments, Elizabeth and I sit in silence.

"Just look how much these still affect me! It's been thirty years!" Elizabeth laments, grabbing a tissue from the box. She blows her nose loudly. "And those are only *three* things I heard, you know? No wonder I'm so messed up," she cries, folding her tissue delicately with shaking hands.

"Elizabeth, you're doing amazing. Keep letting your emotions be present—just like you are now. I'd like to continue with the exercise to help you experience how this impacts you today. Are you willing to do that?" I ask gently.

Sniffling, Elizabeth wipes a few tears away. "Yeah, I can try."

"Please read over the statements again, Elizabeth," I request.

"S...stop biting your nails," she stammers, the tears still streaming down her cheeks. "It's disgusting. You're disgusting. You're not ladylike. You should... you should know better.

"You're not going to eat all that, are you? You're going to balloon up just like your Aunt Margie. You're fat. What's wrong with you for eating so much? If you don't get your grades up, you're going to throw your life away. Why can't you be more like your brother? You're stupid. You're not as good as your brother. You should be better," she continues, her tears starting to slow. Her chest begins rising rapidly up and down, as if she can't catch her breath. She closes her eyes and bites her lip, allowing no more words to slip out.

Several moments pass, and Elizabeth remains quiet. I ask gently, "Elizabeth? Do you want to continue?"

Her eyes fly open and she snaps, "No! I don't! I'm done with this."

"What's going on for you, Elizabeth?" I calmly inquire.

Crossing her arms defensively, she bellows, "This isn't helping anything. It's just making me feel terrible about myself!"

"What do you want to do?" I bring up gently.

"I want to stop this ridiculous exercise! I want to go get a drink!" she shouts. Her eyes grow wide. "Did I really just say that?" she asks quietly.

I give her space to digest what just happened before asking, "What are you feeling right now?"

"I was irritated at first, but now it's this… knot in my gut. This tingling all over," she comments, looking down at her body as if it's an unknown vessel. She looks over at me, dumbfounded. "So *that's* what you mean about my drinking being driven by my beliefs. My dad's voice is constantly playing over in my mind, and I drink to…to shut it up," she reveals.

"That's it, Elizabeth. Deep down, you *believe* these statements and underlying messages that your father said to you growing up. You believe you should know better. You believe you're stupid. And every day, things in your life trigger these beliefs. Then your Monkey Mind replays these statements over and over in your head constantly. You desperately want to stop hearing these judgments—just like you do now. But you don't know how to make them stop. So you drink to drown out the voice," I describe.

"So my belief is there, but something triggers it… could that trigger be something Ted says?" Elizabeth asks. Her presence is very different—she is no longer depressed or angry. Now, she is curious and calm.

"Exactly. That's where the final piece of this experiential work comes into play. For the next step, I want you to name off three statements that Ted says to you that irritate you," I request.

With a small laugh, Elizabeth replies "Oh, those are easier to think of. He's constantly saying, 'Why do you always have to interrupt me?'" she says with a slight roll of her eyes. "Another one would be 'You're always making something out of nothing,'" she recalls, clenching her jaw.

"And one more?" I invite.

"He comments on what I wear all the time too. He'll say, 'Why are you wearing that? Why don't you want to show off your body?'" As she completes the last line, her cheeks flush.

"Now, I want you to read your father's statements and the underlying messages aloud again. But this time, after you say one statement, *I* am going to respond with one of your husband's statements," I describe.

Elizabeth looks surprised. "Oh? What's that going to do?"

"Let's try it out and see," I reply.

Clearing her throat and placing her palm on her chest, Elizabeth begins, "Stop biting your nails."

I respond with, "Why do you always have to interrupt me?"

"You're disgusting," she replies.

"You're always making something out of nothing,"

"You're not ladylike."

"Why are you wearing that?"

"You should know better."

"Why don't you want to show off your body?"

"You're not going to eat all that, are you?"

"Why do you always have to interrupt me?"

Blinking rapidly, Elizabeth continues reading, "You're going to balloon up just like your Aunt Margie."

"You're always making something out of nothing," I respond.

"You're fat," she recites. Elizabeth begins to tensely massage her scalp.

I stop the exercise. "What are you noticing, Elizabeth?"

Shaking her head, Elizabeth stares at the floor. "I'm not even hearing what Ted is saying. My dad's voice is so much louder," she reveals.

"Let's do it one more time," I request. "Pick up where you left off and muster all your energy to really try to listen to what Ted is saying."

She relents. "What's wrong with you for eating so much?"

"Why do you always have to interrupt me?" I ask.

"If you don't get your grades up, you're going to throw your life away."

"You're always making something out of nothing."

Elizabeth clears her throat. "Why can't you be more like your brother?"

"Why are you wearing that?"

"You're stupid."

"Why don't you want to show off your body?"

"You're not as good as your brother."

"Why do you always have to interrupt me?"

"You should be better."

I interrupt the exercise and ask, "How do you feel hearing these messages now?"

Elizabeth rubs her face before responding, "Everything we're saying feels like an attack, honestly."

"When you believe someone is criticizing you," I explain, "these deep-seated self-judgments are reactivated. They come right back up to the surface, just like if your dad was saying them to you today. So when Ted says, 'Why do you always have to interrupt me?' is he saying that you are stupid? Or that you should have known better?"

"Not those exact words, no…"

"And when he asks, 'Why are you wearing that?' is he saying that you're fat? Couldn't he mean that he actually thinks you have a beautiful shape?" I bring up.

"I guess he might…" Elizabeth admits.

I continue, "Can you see how you're not hearing the words Ted is saying? You're watching his lips move, but you're replaying the same messages your dad repeated to you so many times."

"So there's a chance that sometimes Ted isn't even criticizing me when I think he is?"

"What do you think?"

She sighs. "It's hard to believe that... but, yeah, I think there might be. If I actually heard what he was saying, I might respond in a totally different way." A moment of recognition flashes across her features. "You know what else I realized? When I kept repeating those terrible statements about myself? They're not even *true*. I'm not stupid! I'm not disgusting! Once I actually take a step back and look at those statements objectively, I can see how wrong they all are."

Elizabeth's story is a great example of how our programming will get reactivated in many relationships. Almost any time she feels she's being criticized, she's going to repeat the self-defeating beliefs she developed in her father's disapproving tone.

For most people, this reactivation is predominant in our intimate relationships, especially with the people we crave approval from the most. To connect with this experience, think of a few critiques you received in your own childhood growing up.

Now, think of a few interactions in the past year where you became very upset.

Ask yourself for each interaction: "Was I really upset by what the person said? Or did I hear what the person said through the perspective of the criticisms I received growing up?"

When we are aware of our programming, we can learn how to control our responses when our beliefs are reactivated and, ultimately, change the beliefs that are holding us back.

Chapter 9

WATCH OUT FOR
SHAME-INDUCING BELIEFS

Like Elizabeth, many of us harbor the shame-inducing belief that we are not good enough based on the experiences we went through in our childhoods. This belief eats away at our confidence over time until there is little self-worth left. To be able to change our shame-inducing beliefs, it is important to know how to identify them. One vital skill is to learn the difference between a shame-inducing belief and guilt.

THE DIFFERENCE BETWEEN SHAME AND GUILT

Think of guilt as being the rumble strip along the edge of the highway. When you're driving and become distracted or sleepy, you suddenly run over those loud, little bumps. They remind you to steer back into the center of your lane.

Guilt is our conscience's way of keeping us on track. When we intentionally lie, for example, we experience guilt. For a person with balanced mental health, our Observing Mind notes this feeling of guilt and then adjusts our course.

Shame is entirely different from guilt. With shame, the warnings never stop. The Monkey Mind gets stuck on autopilot, repeating the same accusations over and over. It's not trying to right a simple wrong—no, the Monkey Mind is focused on using shame to motivate you to change, just like many of our parents did, to the point where you believe that there's something fundamentally wrong with you. Shame-inducing beliefs don't create healthy, long-lasting change; they create stress, pain, depression, rage, panic, hopelessness, and addiction.

Kevin is a classic example of someone who was raised by a father who continually used shame to try and change his son's behavior. Let's see how this shame has affected his day-to-day life.

~

After our meeting at the farmer's market, Kevin starts lying awake at night as he contemplates what the *real* issue is behind his drinking. Finally, he looks me up and asks to have a session with me to see if he can stop drinking and begin to heal his relationship.

As Kevin walks through the door, I greet him with a bright smile. "Kevin! I'm so glad you came to see me."

Kevin nervously rubs his palms on the thighs of his jeans. "Yeah… I'm not gonna lie, I'm pretty nervous," Kevin admits with a swallow.

"That's to be expected," I reassure him. "Why don't we start off with an easy question? Then we can work up from there."

"OK," Kevin agrees, plopping down in the chair.

"Why have you decided to come and work with me?" I ask genuinely.

Quietly, Kevin responds, "Well, I want to salvage my marriage. And to try to get back on track to becoming a doctor, if that's even possible. I've just gotten to the point where I hate myself for how much I drink, especially after I had an, um, incident with my neighbor's dog."

"Let's pick one of those issues to tackle head on. What do you want to start with?" I ask.

Kevin pauses before saying, "Probably my relationship. I feel like that's where a lot of my problems stem from."

I open my mouth to speak, but Kevin cuts in, "And, just to let you know, I'm not really an *emotional* guy. I never cry or do any of that stuff. I thought you should know, so you aren't expecting some breakdown or something like that," he says, scratching his head uncomfortably.

"I have no expectations for our sessions together. However, it is interesting that you brought that up. I'm a firm believer that there's a reason for everything we do—so, what do you think is the reason you brought up not having any emotions?" I lightly question.

Kevin sits silent for a moment, a bit dumbfounded. "Um... I guess you've got a good point there. I've just never 'done' emotions, so I get a little nervous when I think someone expects to see them," Kevin admits, looking down. He grips the back of his neck and massages it slightly. "Maybe that's why I don't have the best track record with women."

I lean forward slightly. "What do you mean?"

"I've never been great at opening up in any of my relationships. Even with Jamie. I mean, we're married for Pete's sake! Why can't I let my own wife know how I'm feeling?"

"Why don't you tell me about your marriage," I kindly invite.

Kevin sits with this a moment. He lifts a well-worn fingernail up to his mouth, where he bites at the tip unconsciously. "Well, things were going well. Or OK at least. Not bad, I mean. Jamie is such an amazing woman," he shares with a loving smile.

Then Kevin's mood shifts. "But over the years, I've really put her through the ringer. I'm honestly surprised she didn't leave me a long time ago, but she stuck around for some reason. Then, a few weeks ago, my uncle died, and I… I froze up. It came as such a surprise that I didn't know how to process it. So I shut down and iced Jamie out." He pauses, inhaling deeply. "That was really tough for her. I think she almost left me over it," Kevin quietly admits, closing his eyes.

"Where did you learn to push down your emotions so much?" I inquire.

Kevin uncurls his fist and pulls his nail back up to his teeth. "Huh. I've never really thought about it," he admits, pausing for a moment. "I guess my dad? I remember him always being really strong, you know? He was never scared of anything. I don't think I've ever seen him cry either. But that man does have a temper," Kevin says with a small laugh. "If you disobeyed him, you'd get the belt. No questions. No excuses. We were the most obedient kids in the whole school!"

He continues, "Not even my mom can avoid his temper. I remember one time, Mom donated some of Dad's shoes without asking. I swear I saw steam coming out of his ears! By the end of it, they were both screaming," Kevin remembers, the smile slowly fading from his face. "But they got over it pretty quick. He didn't hit her or anything. They have a good marriage. It was just in the moment."

"How do you feel, thinking about your dad?" I ask.

"Well, he's a great man. He went through a lot, but he provided well for his family," Kevin replies with a quivering smile. He clenches his jaw to keep his lips in line.

I ask lightly, "Did your father push you to be strong like he was?"

Kevin considers this. "Yeah, I'd say so."

"Can you think of an example of when he did that?"

Kevin sinks down into his chair, his head falling back as he stares up at the ceiling. "Well, for some reason, I have this perfect memory of when I was six or seven," he recalls. "I fell and cut up my knee when I was playing with my brother. I ran over crying to my dad, and he told me to buck up or else I'd get made fun of by the other kids."

"Isn't it amazing how clearly we can envision those times from so long ago? Can you think of another time when he reprimanded you for not being strong?" I ask.

Kevin scans the room with his eyes, hoping something will spark a memory. Soon, a photo of me with my hockey teammates does. "I remember another time, in high school, I had worked really hard and tried out for the football team, but I got put on JV instead of varsity. I was pretty crushed, to say the least," he remembers with a huff. "When I came home I told my dad that I was upset about it. I wasn't crying or anything, but still upset, you know?"

Raising his eyebrows, Kevin's focus falls to the floor. "Well, instead of consoling me or saying, 'you'll get 'em next time,' he railed into me about not trying hard enough and how embarrassing it was for a sophomore to still be on JV. He said that if I put my energy into practicing more instead of feeling sorry for myself, I could have made the team.

"Then, since I didn't play in the Friday night games, he made me get a weekend job to 'learn a work ethic,'" Kevin says, his breath shallow. He wipes a bead of sweat off his forehead.

Pausing a moment before responding, I reply, "Kevin, how do you feel after thinking back to those incidents?"

Kevin clears his throat and shrugs. "I don't know. Kind of pissed off, but it is what it is," he responds blankly.

"Why do you think your dad said these things to you?"

"Because he was disappointed in what I had done," Kevin mumbles back, his jaw twitching.

I dig further, "Anything else?"

"Well, with football, he wanted me to be better so I would make the team next year. I guess he thought that tough love was the way to get me to work harder," Kevin recognizes, scratching his cheek methodically.

"And why did he tell you to buck up when you fell?"

Kevin releases a deep breath, which he'd been holding for longer than he realized. "I don't know… if I cried all the time, I probably would have gotten picked on at school. So he probably wanted to protect me from that."

Shifting his head up to look at me, Kevin adds, "You know, I've never really thought about it that way. I never thought about him trying to protect me. At the time, I just thought he was a hard-ass."

"Kevin, your father was using criticism and shame to try to make you into a tougher, more hard-working person. A lot of parents think tough words are what it takes to get their child to change. But when he told you these things, how did you feel?"

"Pretty terrible," Kevin mutters, looking away from me.

"Let's jump back to the present now, Kevin. What happens when you criticize yourself for not opening up to your wife?"

Kevin quickly replies, "I feel awful."

"So if you feel awful after criticizing yourself, why do you keep doing it?"

Kevin scrunches his thick eyebrows to the point where they are nearly touching his eyelids, "I don't know… I can't really help it," he states, clearly very confused by the concept.

I lean forward. "You've been programmed to believe that if you criticize yourself—if you shame yourself enough—you'll change. That's your Monkey Mind at work, Kevin."

"What do you mean?"

"Well, you think if you hate yourself for drinking, eventually that hatred will get you to stop. Unfortunately, that doesn't work," I explain. "For you to really understand how fruitless using shame to create change is, can you allow yourself to fully experience your self-criticisms for a few moments?"

"Oh, OK. If you think that'll help," he agrees hesitantly.

"Let's try it and see. Please spend a minute and tell me the judgments you have about yourself, and how you think you should be different," I instruct.

He sighs. "Well, I'm tired of driving my wife away and not letting her in on how I'm feeling. I should be able to open up to her more now after all these years. And I'm sick of the drinking. I'm *so* sick of it. If I could quit tomorrow, I would. But for some reason, I just always end up going back to it… God, I'm pathetic." He bows his head into the cradle of his hands.

I gently ask, "Is this voice helping you want to change? Do you feel motivated?"

"No," he responds, his head still buried.

"And how would you say you're feeling?"

"Well, honestly, I'm feeling pretty stressed out," Kevin admits, lifting his head up slightly.

I continue, "That's because when you hold these self-judgments, you create anxiety in your body. That anxiety is an overwhelming feeling, and all you want to do is get away from it."

Kevin cuts in before I can say any more, "Yeah, I know what you mean. When I get this horrible lump in my gut—I guess it's anxiety—I always go straight to the bottle. I know I shouldn't, and it's pathetic that I can't handle it, but… I just feel so much better," Kevin confesses sheepishly.

"The only way to fully release that anxiety is to *allow* yourself to experience it. Think of anxiety like a hot bath—at first, it's so painful that you yank back your hand after touching the surface. But, if you leave your hand in the water, it soon adjusts to the temperature and the pain fades away. Are you willing to try this idea out?"

Rolling his shoulders back, he replies quietly, "Sure."

"Kevin, we're going to do this by challenging a belief that creates a lot of shame for you—that showing emotion is bad. What would happen if you allowed yourself to feel sad, and *show* that you feel sad?" I ask.

His fingernail makes its way back to its post, and Kevin bites away as his eyes flicker around the room. "I… I don't know. I haven't done it in so long. If I even start to feel sad, I either shove it way down or I drink," Kevin replies honestly.

I nod understandingly. "You mentioned your uncle recently passed away. Think back to that day when you found out. How did you feel in the moment when you heard he was gone?"

Clenching his jaw tightly, Kevin doesn't respond for several moments. "It hurt," he whispers, eyes transfixed on a carpet fiber.

"Allow yourself to feel the pain, Kevin. Don't try to push it down. Why don't you tell me a little about your uncle?" I request.

Kevin remains still for a moment. The battle taking place inside his body is palpable. "He... he was a great man. He had three daughters..." Kevin takes a deep breath to try and calm his shaking voice. "He had three daughters, so he used to say I was his unofficial son." A smile breaks out on his face, but it is quickly stifled.

He clears his throat loudly and continues, "He would always come get me and we'd go do stuff that the girls didn't want to do. He'd take me to the amusement park to ride all the big roller coasters and then argue with the attendant when they said that I was half an inch too short for the ride," he says with a laugh, his eyes starting to well up.

Kevin carries on, "He just always looked out for me, you know? Whether it was giving me a few extra bucks or helping me with homework when my parents were busy, or even with girl trouble. He was actually the first person I went to after my first girlfriend broke up with me. And he told me, 'Kevin, you're a great catch. If she couldn't see that, you don't want to be with her.'"

Finally, a tear rolls down Kevin's cheek. A look of horror passes over his face as he quickly wipes it away. He clenches his jaw once more, seemingly refusing to speak again until he gets his emotions in check.

"Don't try to fight it, Kevin. This is a safe place to let your emotions really be present," I remind him warmly.

Nodding his head quickly, Kevin tries to take a deep breath, but his breath is broken and irregular.

"Kevin, allow yourself to really feel connected with him. Don't think about me or hiding your love for your uncle. Remember what a big part of your life he was, and how much he impacted you," I say sincerely.

Finally, Kevin's shoulders relax, and he closes his eyes. He loosens his grip on the armchair, and his breathing becomes more regular.

"He did so much for me. And I don't know if he ever knew how much I appreciated that," Kevin says, opening his eyes. When he does, another tear escapes. Again, he wipes it away quickly, but this time lacks the attitude of disdain.

"Is it true it's weak to feel emotion, Kevin? Do you feel weak right now?"

Kevin swallows and takes a breath. "No, I wouldn't say I feel weak. I actually feel better. Relieved even. Like I've been bottling that up so tightly for so long, and now I feel like I'm finally honoring my uncle's memory. Which is what he deserves."

Kevin looks at me, his mouth hanging open in uncertainty. "I just don't know what to think right now. I was always taught that the worst thing I could do was cry, yet I sit here with you, and I feel like a pressure has been lifted off my chest. But it still somehow feels wrong... does that make sense?" he asks in a worried tone.

"It does. For decades you've held onto the shame-inducing belief that showing emotion is wrong, so it's expected to feel unfamiliar or even uncomfortable at first," I explain. "Back when you were a child, this belief had a purpose. Do you know what that was?"

"I guess I didn't show emotion growing up because I didn't want my dad getting mad at me?" Kevin responds, his eyes widening slightly.

"Exactly. This belief served a purpose then, but what does hiding your emotions do for you now?"

Kevin goes to answer, then stops. He then lets out a sigh. "Honestly, it's holding me back. It's why I didn't tell my uncle how much he meant to me. And why Jamie is fed up with me. It probably plays into why I drink too, doesn't it?" he asks rhetorically. His eyes are brimming with equal amounts of fear and hope. "So how do I get over this?"

"What's your answer, Kevin?" I ask.

"Well, I'm going to have to keep working at this to find out."

"Great. I'll see you next week then."

Kevin learned from his father to use shame to change himself. Like Kevin, most of us have been conditioned to believe the Monkey Mind's story that judging is the way to motivate ourselves to change.

The promise of shame is that it will make you a better person; the reality of shame is that it makes you feel worthless.

To visualize this, think of a criticism you have about a loved one. How long have you had that criticism of them? How often have you expressed it in different ways? How does it feel when you judge them? Have your words ever made the person change their behavior?

Now think of a judgment you have about yourself. How long have you had this criticism? How often do you think about it? How does it feel when you judge yourself? Has this judgment ever motivated you to change your behavior?

To challenge the Monkey Mind's pattern, answer this question without overanalyzing it: What are you afraid would happen if you dropped this judgment of yourself?

Shame-inducing beliefs cause the war that promises peace, but instead creates constant, exhausting turmoil. We simply can't be happy and be damning ourselves at the same time.

Becoming aware of just how much our upbringing and beliefs influence us today allows us to finally shed those harmful beliefs. Before we can move towards letting go of this programming, however, we need to learn how to break the chain of these distressing beliefs.

BREAKING THE CHAIN OF SHAME-INDUCING BELIEFS

The problem with shame-inducing beliefs is that they keep piling up. One belief will lead us to do something that we later regret. Then we use this mistake as more fuel for another shame-inducing belief, without ever addressing the initial belief that caused the unfavorable action in the first place.

Let's look at Kevin's beliefs to illustrate this idea.

Kevin is struggling with the belief he inherited from his father: *it is weak to show emotion*. Let's call this **Belief A**.

Belief A has a lot of repercussions in Kevin's everyday life. One consequence of **Belief A** is when his uncle died, *Kevin argued with Jamie* because he wouldn't be vulnerable with her. We'll call this **Consequence A**.

After Consequence A *[arguing with Jamie]*, Kevin should look at **Belief A** *[it is weak to show emotion]* to understand why he fought with Jamie, as well as prevent future altercations fueled by this belief.

Instead, after **Consequence A** *[arguing with Jamie]*, Kevin moves straight into **Belief B** *[I'm a failure]*. Kevin bases **Belief B** on the evidence that fighting with Jamie makes him a failure.

Belief B *[I'm a failure]* gets reinforced with the thoughts "I shouldn't have fought with Jamie. There's something wrong with me for arguing with Jamie." Now, Kevin is busy judging himself and is sucked into **Belief B** *[I'm a failure]*, completely forgetting about the belief that created this all: **Belief A** *[it is weak to show emotion]*.

So, **Belief A** *[it is weak to show emotion]* creates **Consequence A** *[arguing with Jamie]*, which fuels **Belief B** *[I'm a failure]*.

Kevin starts experiencing a great deal of shame, created by the deeply-seated **Belief B** *[I'm a failure]*. He doesn't understand why he keeps fighting endlessly with his wife or why he feels terrible about himself. All this shame creates an enormous amount of anxiety within Kevin; he soon becomes overwhelmed with the anxiety and needs to numb it by drinking.

To begin to challenge and change **Belief B** *[I'm a failure]*, Kevin needs to get to the point where after **Consequence A** *[arguing with Jamie]* occurs, he doesn't get sucked into his self-judgments. Instead, he does some work around **Belief A** *[it is weak to show emotion]*.

If Kevin is able to get to the point where after **Consequence A** *[arguing with Jamie]* he is able to do work around **Belief A** *[it is weak to show emotion]*, he will begin to challenge and change **Belief A**.

After he has transformed **Belief A** *[it is weak to show emotion]*, Kevin will no longer have **Consequence A** *[arguing with Jamie]*. Now that there is no **Consequence A** *[arguing with Jamie]*, there is no trigger to set off **Belief B** *[I'm a failure]*.

By resolving **Belief A** *[it is weak to show emotion]*, Kevin will also feel more connected with Jamie; and **Belief A** *[it is weak to show emotion]* will no longer be the cause of any more of their disputes.

Like Kevin, many of us are stuck in this chain reaction of **Belief A—Consequence A—Belief B**. To illustrate the idea of the chain of shameful beliefs, imagine the following: Your partner says, "You always ignore me." Some of us would become agitated and start yelling in response to that statement. Now you have **Consequence A**: *arguing with your partner.*

From **Consequence A** *[arguing with your partner]*, you collect reasons to believe **Belief B**: *I'm a bad partner.* Now, you are experiencing the shame from **Belief B** *[I'm a bad partner].*

Can you name what was **Belief A** that created **Consequence A** *[arguing with your partner]* in this example?

By resolving the true belief in question, we can start to break free from the shame and anxiety the Monkey Mind has created and change all of the sabotaging beliefs that are holding us back.

Chapter 10

ADOPTING NEW BELIEFS

After dismantling a self-destructive belief, we need to spend some time solidifying our replacement belief. We need to find a new belief that takes us in the direction that we want to go. We have to engage with our life through this new perspective over and over again, until we can experience the change at a body level. The more we respond from this new belief's perspective, the more naturally engrained it will become. Elizabeth has been working hard to shift into seeing her life from a new set of beliefs, and she's ready to showcase this new way of thinking at an important event in her life: her niece's wedding.

$\sim$

Elizabeth and I work together intensively for several months to shed her shame-inducing beliefs. She learns to deal with many anxiety-inducing situations: her husband moving out, the subsequent divorce filing, acquiring joint custody of her kids, and—ultimately—overcoming her addiction to alcohol.

Now Elizabeth is feeling like a new woman. Her kids want to spend time with her, she's been doing more and more freelance writing, she isn't drinking, and she has the most self-confidence she's ever felt. While she does grieve over her old marriage, she has come to understand why Ted and her grew apart, and why he ultimately left her. Ted has found someone new; now, Elizabeth is ready to start developing her own authentic relationships, whether they be romantic or simply friendships.

Elizabeth's niece's wedding will serve as the first time many of her family has seen the "new" Elizabeth, and she has given herself two new beliefs to try out:

1. You *are* good enough.
2. Most men are inherently good, kind people.

Using these beliefs as her guidance, Elizabeth is going to assume the best of the men she meets tonight. She's hoping to reconnect with some distant relatives she hasn't seen for a long time, as well as make connections with some new, potential friends. While she realizes that not every man is going to be honest, she knows she has the self-confidence to determine if something feels wrong *after* she speaks with the man rather than assuming he is a bad person *before*.

When Elizabeth arrives at the reception, she quickly gets her first opportunity to test out her new beliefs. A man approaches her while she's getting a club soda from the bar. "What a great wedding so far!" he says happily, tapping his foot to the music.

"It really has been! How do you know the couple?" Elizabeth sincerely asks.

"I'm Nicole's second cousin. I haven't seen her for a few years, to be honest," he admits, grabbing a beer from the bartender. "My name's Carlos," he says, extending his hand out to Elizabeth.

Carlos's introduction sets off Elizabeth's Monkey Mind. *Oh geez,*

Carlos is here? The last time you saw him, he was trying to get your parents to lend him money!

Remembering her goals for the night, Elizabeth's Observing Mind quickly steps in. *That was many years ago. There's a good chance Carlos has grown since then. Give him the benefit of the doubt.*

Elizabeth takes a deep breath and replies, "Carlos! It's so good to see you again. I'm Elizabeth—Nicole's aunt. Remember me?" she says with a broad smile.

"Lizzie! Of course!" Carlos leans forward and gives Elizabeth a warm hug. "Wow, you look great. A lot different than the last time I saw ya," he mentions with a grimace.

Ignoring his comment, Elizabeth warmly responds, "Yes, I've definitely changed a lot. So how have you been? What are you up to these days?"

Carlos nods confidently. "Oh, you know. Been working on a lot of different projects. I'm actually working on a new start-up right now," he proudly states.

"Oh? What's it for?" Elizabeth asks, genuinely interested.

Straightening up, Carlos clinks down his bottle on the bar and claps his hands together. "You know when you're at your desk at like two o'clock, and you're totally drained and need some energy?" Carlos asks energetically. After a few moments, he nods his head toward Elizabeth.

"Oh, um, yes! I hate that," she responds quickly.

"Exactly! So that's why my business partner and I created— Electric Energy Power Bars! They're full of all these good nutrients and stuff to wake you up," Carlos concludes with a flashy, satisfied smile.

"Wow! That's… that's something else, Carlos," Elizabeth says kindly, trying to sound as supportive as possible. She takes a breath and much more authentically affirms, "Good for you for doing something you're obviously so passionate about."

"It is my life's passion, Lizzie. Thank you for saying that," Carlos says gratefully. "Are your parents here, by the way?" he asks.

"No, they couldn't make the trip," Elizabeth replies.

As Elizabeth takes a sip out of her club soda, Carlos adds, "Oh shoot. Well, then I guess I can tell you. Over at Electric Energy, we're always looking for investors. I'm sure you're interested—it's a really great opportunity to get in this early, you know!"

Elizabeth's Monkey Mind can't help itself. *And there it is! Of course, he's still only after money. Men are all the same—selfish and money-hungry.*

Taking a longer sip than she originally planned, Elizabeth gives her Observing Mind time to give its insight before responding. *He doesn't realize this isn't the place to discuss this. He's found something he loves to do, so wish him well in his venture.*

Finally, Elizabeth pulls the can of soda away from her lips. "You know, Carlos, I don't think Nicole's wedding is really the place to discuss investment opportunities. I would suggest that you probably don't do that for the rest of the evening," she kindly advises. "And while I love your passion, I think I'm going to pass on this one. But I wish you the very best of luck," she says with a genuine smile.

Carlos shrugs and rolls his eyes slightly, a hint of sarcasm making its way into his voice. "OK. Thanks for your support, I guess. It was good to see you again," he concludes, nodding his beer bottle at her and walking away.

Elizabeth goes into deep, continuous breaths to regulate herself before speaking with anyone else. Her Observing Mind is calming her down. *Great job at remaining centered when speaking with Carlos! Your belief of 'not being able to trust men' was being heavily triggered there.*

Elizabeth eases up a little as her Observing Mind continues. *Your belief of 'not being good enough' was also just triggered. You don't owe anything to Carlos. You couldn't have done any better. You did great.*

Closing her eyes for a moment, Elizabeth lets this idea sink into her bones. When she reopens them, she is full of excitement about getting back out there and meeting new people.

Tromping straight onto the dance floor, Elizabeth starts dancing alongside some of her cousins and her daughter, Tiffany. After a few songs, the DJ decides to slow the music down. Elizabeth uncomfortably starts to move off the dance floor to make room for couples when an attractive man approaches her.

"Would you care to dance?" He extends his hand with a smile.

Elizabeth hesitates for a split moment. Her Monkey Mind sees an opportunity to conjure up a grand tale. *He's going to think you're a bad dancer. You're going to embarrass yourself.*

Elizabeth's Observing Mind cuts the Monkey Mind short before it can make up any more. *Remember, you're exploring here. You're learning how it's safe to be your true self.*

She decides to go outside her comfort zone and agrees with an enthusiastic grin. The two start chatting over the music.

"I'm Bruce," he says, leaning in so she can hear him. Elizabeth's heart starts racing, but she tries to maintain her composure.

"I'm Elizabeth," she replies, a little louder than needed.

"How do you know the couple?" Bruce asks.

"I'm Nicole's aunt," Elizabeth responds, trying to ignore her niece giving Elizabeth a thumbs-up behind Bruce's back.

"Well, Elizabeth, you are a marvelous dancing partner," Bruce says with a warm smile, spinning her around. Elizabeth hasn't danced with a man since the early years of her marriage, and she's surprised how much she's enjoying it.

The two conclude their dance and step off the dance floor to chat some more.

"I can't remember the last time I slow danced," Bruce admits, wiping a bead of sweat off his forehead.

"Me either! I think the last time was when I was out in New York for a retreat," Elizabeth says, sticking an unruly piece of hair behind her ear.

"Oh? What kind of retreat?" Bruce asks.

"A writing retreat," Elizabeth says, her cheeks growing rosy.

"So you're a writer, huh?" he inquires.

"Yeah, I've actually been getting back into freelance work more now that my kids are older. Been trying to dust off the wheels!" she jokes.

"What kind of writing do you like to do?" he asks. "Poetry? Prose? Nonfiction?"

The two end up talking for the next hour. As the night comes to an end, they make plans to meet up the next week at Elizabeth's favorite Italian restaurant. Bruce bids farewell with a kiss on Elizabeth's cheek, and nothing more.

Elizabeth leaves in awe of the night's events. She didn't mean to actually meet someone tonight! As this thought passes, the Monkey Mind tries to latch on. *You're not ready. You're going to be a complete mess at that dinner. He's way too good for you.*

Elizabeth gets sucked into this idea for a moment, but then becomes aware of what is happening. She shakes off the Monkey Mind's story with the Observing Mind's wise comments. *See how well you did with Carlos and Bruce tonight? You're really catching on. You're doing great.*

When they get back home, Elizabeth is relaxing on the couch with Tiffany. "Man, it feels great to have those heels off!" Elizabeth exclaims.

"I took mine off when I was dancing," Tiffany says with a proud smile.

Elizabeth leans over and pats her head. "I've always said you were smarter than your mom," she says with a loving smile.

Tiffany laughs and nods in agreement. Then, trying to be as nonchalant as possible, Tiffany says, "So… that guy you were dancing with seemed pretty cool…"

"Yeah? You liked him? I'm supposed to have dinner with him next week," Elizabeth relays, trying to gauge her daughter's opinion.

Nodding slightly, Tiffany focuses on her fingers, picking away at her pink nail polish. Then she looks up to her mother. "I think you two would make a good couple," she states, her grin showing her dimples.

"Thank you, honey. It means a lot to hear that from you," Elizabeth whispers.

Elizabeth beams and brings her daughter in close for a hug. While embracing, Elizabeth thinks about what tonight would have looked like if she hadn't started changing her beliefs: her daughter wouldn't even be in her house, she would have felt alone all night, and she would be passed out from the wine by now.

Before working with me, Elizabeth had good intentions, but she couldn't seem to find happiness. No matter what she did, the belief of "I can't trust men" and, ultimately, "I'm never good enough" had only one destination: loneliness. The path she was on would never bring her closer to true connection. She had to create new beliefs in order to forge authentic connections in her life.

When Elizabeth went to the wedding, she admitted to herself what she really wanted. She made the decision to believe that happiness and connection are possible in her life. She chose, without any restrictions, a destination that she truly desires.

After she explored her limiting beliefs, Elizabeth consciously created a different path. Her new belief is, "No matter the intention or actions of men, I decide if I'm enough." By following this path, Elizabeth comes to a different destination with Bruce. She is now ready to venture onward and create even more authentic relationships. Even if things don't work out with Bruce, she's ecstatic to see where her newfound attitude is going to take her.

This new belief is creating a different reality.

Testing out new beliefs can show you the power that your beliefs have on your outlook of the world. For example, try going about your day with the belief "the world is unfriendly" at the forefront of your mind. The next day, try walking around with the belief "the world is friendly." How do your daily interactions differ between those beliefs?

Trying out a new belief can feel unfamiliar at first, but it is an incredibly rewarding process. If we are committed to repeatedly applying this new belief to our lives, it will quickly take the place of the harmful belief we used to hold.

Like Elizabeth, we can't arrive at destinations we consider impossible for us. If you think, for whatever reason, you can't get to the top of Mount Everest, you won't even try. Nor will you try to get to places you don't believe are real, like Shangri-La or Neverland. You won't drag out the map. You certainly won't seek a path or ask for directions. When we admit to ourselves what we want and give ourselves the proper tools to reach that end point, we open our lives up to what we may have previously thought was the stuff of fantasies.

Part 3

FEELINGS AS A
GUIDANCE SYSTEM

Chapter 11

THE IMPORTANCE OF EMOTIONS

How often do we get asked "What's wrong?" if we're not looking cheerful? If any resemblance of fear or anger or sadness is visible on our face, we often get bombarded with that leading question. But, why have we been conditioned to believe that if we feel certain emotions, something is "wrong"? There is such intelligence in our feelings, but most of us were not taught how to properly learn from our emotions. When we learn to use our emotions as a guidance system, we can continue to change the programming that sabotages our lives.

EMOTIONS ARE NOT "BAD" OR "GOOD"

Feelings are deeper than words; they are sensations in the body. Saying that you are upset at your husband is not a feeling; it's a story. Feelings are simple. They are the same basic emotions that every baby expresses, long before they have words to explain or describe them. You can be sad, happy, fearful, or angry; you don't need words for that. In fact, feelings are better expressed with movements and pure sounds like wailing or laughing or pounding the floor. This is different from the stories we give our emotions—the "why" of our feelings.

We use our emotions to relay back to our beliefs because they are far easier to track. We have thousands of thoughts every day—far too many to manage. However, an emotion is an experience we feel throughout our whole bodies, and typically we have fewer feelings than thoughts throughout a day. By being aware of a feeling and identifying it, we can easily see when a core belief is being triggered.

Right now, try paying attention to the emotions in your body. Your feelings are speaking to you, bringing you valuable information. Don't judge them or push them away. Don't sugarcoat them. Simply notice them as the Observing Mind might. *What am I feeling right now? Where in my body do I feel it? How intense is the sensation?*

Can you put a name to those feelings? Maybe you feel nervous, or irritated, or joyful, or hopeless. There are many names to call our emotions, but ultimately, they all boil down to five feelings: mad, sad, glad, afraid, and ashamed. When we can put our emotions into one of these five categories, we can more easily identify them and train ourselves to recognize when we are experiencing one of them.

For many of us, the idea of noticing our feelings seems foreign because we're so used to repressing them. We heard growing up things like, "Don't be a crybaby!" or "Watch your temper!" These, and the many other messages we received, were what established the idea that emotions are something to avoid.

Yet, in truth, all of our emotions are connected. We can't avoid one feeling while hoping to have another. Imagine your feelings as a water pipeline. Some people think that each emotion has an "off" valve. They believe that we can turn off an emotion, like anger, much like you would cut the water to the bathroom. However, our emotions don't have offshoots. There is only one main line—this means if you repress one emotion, you repress *all* of your emotions. Want to turn off anger? There goes your ability to feel happiness too.

No emotion is bad, and no emotion is good—they are all simply emotions that occur naturally in each of us. When we honor each of these feelings, we can start to learn what our emotions have to teach us.

Children are often the best teachers when it comes to emotions. They haven't yet developed any judgments around their feelings, so they fully embrace each passing sentiment. They feel one emotion, and then move on to the next. One minute a child is crying, and the next, she is laughing. She couldn't make them stick if she tried!

$\sim$

Six-year-old Molly is at the park with her father. She is joyfully chasing a butterfly around the playground, giggling incessantly as she follows after the winged creature in amazement. She isn't looking where she's going and trips over the curb. She falls down, scraping up her hands on the rocks. Immediately, she feels overtaken by sadness. She's soon sobbing rivers of tears as she stumbles over to her father for comfort.

"What happened, sweetie?" her father asks, leaning down to touch the little girl's auburn hair.

"I... fell!" Molly cries, barely being able to speak.

"Are you OK?" he asks, looking around her body.

"My hands!" Molly shrieks with a big lip pouting out. She sticks her hands in front of her dad, so he may inspect them.

"They look OK to me!" he says, trying to cheer her up.

This comment shifts Molly into acute anger. "I AM NOT OK! MY. HANDS. HURT!" she bellows, conjuring up the ferocity of a lion roaring.

"How about we go get a milkshake for you to put your hands against?" her father delicately offers. Again, Molly's emotion changes completely.

"Milkshake!" Molly yells in excitement, jumping up and skipping to the car.

We were all like Molly at one time, but at some point, we lost the ability to shift so effortlessly from emotion to emotion. We were introduced to the concept that some emotions are good, and some are bad. This judgment has made most of us afraid to let go and truly feel our emotions. Many people say:

"If I start crying, I'll never stop."

"If I really let my anger out, everyone will hate me."

"If I admit I'm scared, they'll think I'm a wimp."

Imagine having feelings without fighting to make them go away. Imagine having emotions without the Monkey Mind's story of whether they are right or wrong.

If you notice yourself suppressing your emotions, ask yourself, "What judgment do I hold about having this feeling?" It's the Monkey Mind's stories that make us suffer, not our feelings. When we embrace our emotions, they do not linger—they change as fast as we can feel them. It's only when we reject or resist them that our feelings get stuck, and our emotional suffering seems to go on forever. Be as free as a child with your emotions, and they will lead you into the present.

EMBRACE HOW YOU FEEL

Suppressing our feelings is not the only method we use to avoid our full range of emotions. We also sometimes discharge our feelings on others to avoid truly experiencing them. For example, when we're angry, we might yell at our partner in hopes that this shouting will release the anger. In this instance, we aren't owning and identifying the emotion—we're trying to get rid of it.

At the same time, we may also dwell in one emotion for a long period of time to try to avoid any other feelings that may be trying to come up.

Neither of these methods are healthy, and both drum up a lot of anxious thoughts. Most of the anxiety we have around emotions doesn't come from the feelings themselves—it comes from the stories our Monkey Minds create about why we shouldn't feel them. One way to make peace with our emotions is to accept the way we feel—whatever that feeling may be. This means letting the feeling take its course, without insisting that it should be any different. Call on the Observing Mind so it can become the witness of your feelings.

It is a gorgeous, sunny day. For our session today, Elizabeth chooses to enjoy the sunshine by walking around the lake.

"I feel so great today!" she laughs.

"I'm happy for you," I say. "How come you feel so great?"

"Well, not much has changed. My kids are still the same… and so is my ex-husband."

"So what's different then?" I ask.

"I think I'm not so self-critical anymore. Since we started working together, I've become much more accepting," Elizabeth says.

"How so?"

"Well, now I don't judge my sudden change in emotions," Elizabeth says, "I don't always blame being sad on PMS or being angry on not having had my coffee. I've stopped trying to keep every emotion under wraps. Now, I let myself feel whatever is coming up, and the emotions come and go before I know it!"

"Oh yeah? Tell me a little bit more about that," I request.

"All right, let's see. Well, yesterday, Ted texted me at the last minute that he was going to miss Josh's band concert that night. In the past, I would have just let him have it. But now, something different happens. I actually *notice* how angry I am. Then the thought, 'Don't react. Just keep with this feeling and see what it leads to,' pops into my head," Elizabeth explains. "It used to be that the instant I felt anger, I needed to blast it out of my body and get rid of that awful feeling. I never thought I would get to the point where I actually *appreciate* my anger! But I really do now, because I want to see what belief this anger is attached to."

She takes a breath and goes on, "So instead of exploding, I breathed through it and really felt my emotions. I became fully present with my anger. Then I was able to ask myself questions about why I was so angry."

"What did you learn?" I ask.

"At first, I kept putting the focus on everyone but myself. I was blaming Ted for not being a good father. Man, I could feel my anger bubbling up in me! Then I was making up the story that I felt sad for Josh because he isn't getting the attention he deserves. I could really feel the movement from anger to sadness," Elizabeth explains.

"That is often the toughest part for most people, Elizabeth: to be present with the ever-changing emotions they're experiencing," I agree.

"Yeah, it is. But now, I feel confident about my emotions. I'm not afraid of my anger anymore. I can simply appreciate and be present with it, and with all the other things I'm feeling," Elizabeth replies with a skip in her step. "So, when I did respond to Ted, I told him to remember that this concert meant the world to Josh. He had a saxophone solo and everything, so this was a big deal! I said that I would be there to support Josh, and I thought that it would mean a lot to him if Ted could rearrange his schedule to be there for him. And wouldn't you know it—Ted listened! He said he'd see what he could do. Then, when I got to the auditorium, there Ted was, saving a seat for me! It was just amazing to see how far we've come—that we're able to put our kids' needs ahead of our conflicting emotions."

As Elizabeth has discovered, feelings are meant to be felt. Enjoy them! We've become accustomed to stuffing them down, glossing them over, indulging in them, or using emotions to fuel a story. It's a huge relief when you learn how to welcome big emotions and still be in charge of your response to what caused them.

When you're not being whipped around by the Monkey Mind, feelings add a glorious richness to life.

Take a moment to walk through your feelings, like Elizabeth did. Think of something you're upset about. Now, say to yourself, "I am upset about this. It's OK to be upset. I welcome being upset. I'm safe with this feeling. I don't need to repress it or act it out on others. I know this emotion will bring me clarity and relief." Now you've opened the door to track this emotion back to the deeper belief.

To many people's surprise, it's easy to enjoy what is often feared to be a long and painful process of embracing our emotions. When we learn to love every step along the way, we're able to feel the relief in our own lives, as well as the lives of those around us.

Chapter 12

BE AUTHENTIC WITH YOUR FEELINGS

"I don't want to fake it and act like I'm happy."

This is a phrase that I hear a lot. No one wants to fake happiness. What we crave is a deep, abiding joy—a profound inner sense that life is wonderful, even when it's tough. And when we confront our beliefs, when we challenge the Monkey Mind, that's what we find.

Being authentic with our feelings is a vital step in achieving a healthy lifestyle. One of the reasons we have a tendency to ignore our uncomfortable feelings is that we believe we need to be perceived a certain way by others.

When we begin to discard fake feelings and welcome unfamiliar emotions, we greatly increase our emotional spectrum.

PUTTING ON A SHOW

Think back, for a moment, to when you were in high school. You probably believed you had to act a certain way, whether that be in the form of a peppy cheerleader, honor roll student, or punk rocker. While we've moved on from our high school personas, many of us still harbor the belief that we need to be perceived in a specific way by our peers.

To maintain this facade, some of us try to cover up our emotions by continuously chanting positive affirmations. "I am SO happy! I am SO happy! I am SO happy. Damn. I still feel sad. Maybe if I just say my happy affirmations ten more times, I'll be fine…" In actuality, this is a way to disconnect from authentic emotion and start an internal war.

This idea of putting on a show for others creates what I call "garbage cake."

Imagine having a bowlful of spoiled, stinking, week-old garbage that you blend into a thick brownish-green goo. You shape this goo into something resembling a little cake. You place the "cake" on a lovely plate, and proceed to frost it with delicious, white buttercream frosting. With special care and pride, you pipe lovely scrolled icing around the edges. You decorate it with miniature fresh flowers and set it in the center of your table.

Sound ridiculous? Exactly. Regardless of who admires this pretty creation, you can't magically turn your garbage cake into red velvet.

When we're not authentic with our feelings, isn't this more or less what we do? How many of us have stuffed our uncomfortable feelings into some hidden place, over which we frost our affirmations, our manners, and our attitude?

Eventually, the stuff we're trying to hide starts leaking through the frosting, and we can smell the stench. So can other people.

Then, we start shaming ourselves.

Instead of covering up our inner emotional chaos, the Observing Mind has a different approach. It assumes that it's always best to be aware of what we're truly feeling. Why? Because our feelings communicate with us. When we listen to this inner flood of information and attend to our own authentic emotions, something amazing happens: the very issues that we're most ashamed of bring us to our greatest wisdom, power, and compassion. Our feelings lead us to our core beliefs; from there, we can change our world.

Don't Get Fooled by Misleading "Feel-Good" Emotions

Comfortable habit patterns are just that—comfortable. Familiar emotions not only feel safe, they actually bathe our neurobiology in familiar and, yes, comforting hormones. But what feels good isn't always best for us.

Let's translate this concept to real life. Changing habits at first can seem awkward, unnatural, or even agitating. That's why people often fail at making meaningful changes in their lives; they get halfway into a change and think, "This feels so strange—I just want to feel better." So they retreat back to the familiar. Ah, here comes that comforting biochemical rush... and oops, what are these old habits doing here again?

Emotions. Unpredictability. Being a student again. That new, wobbly feeling of not knowing what comes next. These are all parts of change. And they are often uncomfortable.

Drinkers at social events will tell you they don't need to drink. But, when the next bit of anxiety comes up, they grab another glass. Smokers will tell you they enjoy lighting up. They'll tell you they feel better right after a cigarette. And nearly all of them will tell you they really want to quit—they're just not quite ready yet. Workaholics will tell you they enjoy what they do, or at least feel a sense of purpose, while stretching themselves to the breaking point. They'll tell you they have to do it. Some will even admit that it makes them feel important. They'll promise to get control of their schedules… as soon as the next project is done.

Compulsive shoppers love to hit the stores. They call it "stress management" or "retail therapy." For a few hours, they'll say, everything is perfect. After they get the goodies home, though, some will tell you they feel empty or even disgusted. They'd love a simpler life—but only if they first can buy the best of everything. People who misuse prescription drugs will tell you the pills ease their pain. The pain from a surgery or disease was so extreme that they got prescribed a medication, and soon they had to take more and more to keep the pain away. They'll say they hate being constantly constipated and forgetting where they are, but it's the only way they believe they can function and feel normal.

The social drinker, the smoker, the workaholic, the shopper, and the person misusing pills are all addicted to their own drug—the adrenaline, the dopamine, the slurry of chemicals rushing through the bloodstream, bathing their brains in temporary feel-good stress relievers. It's so tempting to think, "This must be good, it feels so good!" Except that it doesn't feel good for very long.

Think about your own tendencies. Answer this question spontaneously: "When I am really stressed out (sad, disappointed, worried), I typically . . . ." For example: "When I'm really stressed out, I typically shut down and grab a drink."

Breathe. Remember, it's OK. You've been trying to help

yourself feel better. What discomfort are you trying to resolve? What fear are you trying to soothe? Will avoiding discomfort truly resolve your stress?

When we try to change, and this change brings up unfamiliar feelings, it may seem like we're moving towards anxiety. *Wait! I don't like this feeling! Isn't this the wrong direction?* But it's not the wrong direction. These messy, uncomfortable feelings are exactly what we need.

Chapter 13

LET FEELINGS BE YOUR COMPASS

Lingering, painful feelings—ones that do not seem to resolve—are a signal that we are listening to the Monkey Mind. It will create the story that these emotions are caused by outside events and other people, but in truth, those lingering feelings are caused by the false, negative beliefs that we hold.

When we observe our feelings without judging them or trying to change them, they become valuable allies. Our painful emotions are like an alarm system: they alert us to the presence of a hidden belief. We need to learn from the Observing Mind (which uses our feelings as its guidance system) to change what we believe and, ultimately, create the life we want.

Imagine that your emotion—let's say anger—is a smoke detector. It starts beeping loudly one evening, letting you know that there's a fire somewhere (a hidden belief). If you rip the detector off the ceiling or ignore it, you've missed the warning. The fire hasn't stopped; all that's changed is your awareness of the danger.

If we pay attention to our feelings—if we listen to the smoke detector—we can discover the beliefs that are causing us pain. We can catch the fire when it's small and put it out before it spreads. Let's see how this concept applies to four emotions (anger, sadness, fear, and shame).

Chapter 14

TURNING ANGER AROUND

At its most basic level, anger can occur because we have an internal boundary that is being crossed. We often try to attribute our anger to other people or situations, but the truth is it comes back to some issue within ourselves.

For example, how many of us can relate to becoming angry if someone doesn't pay us back after lending them money? Most of us would blame the person for our anger, but in reality, we're mad at ourselves for lending money to this person in the first place. We might feel foolish or stupid for having trusted this person. We have unconsciously decided that we're not a smart person for having loaned money to someone who didn't pay us back.

Our anger is alerting us that there is something conflicting going on inside our heads. If we're able to stop letting other people's actions or outside situations affect how we view ourselves, we can shift away from anger and go about retrieving our money in a calmer manner. Then, when we track the emotion to our belief, we can learn to quickly assuage the anger before it gets unloaded onto other people.

~

Elizabeth and Ted are standing in Elizabeth's entryway. On the drive over, Ted found out some unsettling news.

"We've always said that I would teach them how to drive! I can't believe you did this," Ted says, shaking his head angrily.

"What was I supposed to say when Tiffany asked me, Ted? That she had to wait for you?" Elizabeth responds, trying to keep her voice down so their daughter doesn't hear them.

"Yeah! You could have done that! But you just have to have your hands in every little thing. It's so goddamn annoying!" he fires off before launching into a list of Elizabeth's offences.

As he rants, Ted watches his ex-wife take several deep breaths and listen to him patiently. Feeling confident that he has proved his point, Ted waits for her to explode back on him.

But she doesn't.

Elizabeth continues to breathe calmly until she finally says, "I'm sorry for the times I've done this in the past. I'm really trying hard not to do that anymore. I didn't realize this was that important to you, and I'm sorry if I overstepped my bounds here."

Ted stares dumfounded at the person who seems to have replaced the woman he had been married to for so many years. "God, it's like you're a new person," he bluntly says.

Elizabeth laughs, and the two go on to speak about Elizabeth's progression in her therapy, as well as her success in maintaining her sobriety. The two even touch on how hard the divorce has been on both of them, and Elizabeth states how healing it's been to work through her emotions.

After seeing the obvious change in his ex, Ted also decides to work with me on the challenges he has faced with the divorce, as well as his tendency to get angry in difficult situations.

Now, several weeks later, Ted finds himself feeling extremely impatient on the phone with a caterer. He has reluctantly agreed to host a dinner party for his visiting uncle and is already on edge.

"That's six orders of ahi then, correct?" the caterer repeats.

"Yes, yes. And you have the shrimp ready as well, right?" Ted confirms.

"Shrimp, sir?"

"The shrimp! For the shrimp cocktail! Pretty hard to have a shrimp cocktail without the main ingredient!" Ted explodes.

The caterer fumbles, "I didn't see any shrimp on the order, but I can double check."

"If there are not enough shrimp for a dozen people in my kitchen tomorrow night, I am going to come down there and demand a full refund!" Ted seethes. He hangs up before waiting to hear the caterer's response. His Monkey Mind senses the outrage and quickly starts spinning its web.

No shrimp on the order? Oh, c'mon! You triple-checked that order before sending it off. You know damn well shrimp was on there! You should tell everyone how awful this caterer is, and that they should never hire them.

The smoke alarm is going off—Ted is feeling angry. But what is causing his anger? At this point, Ted thinks that the caterer is the source of his emotion. He's furious at him.

At our next session, Ted begins to unload this story onto me.

"All right, Ted, take a deep breath," I interject between his expletives. "How are you feeling right now?"

"Well, I'd say I'm pretty pissed," Ted grumbles.

"Just take a moment to actually feel the anger. Bring your presence to it. It's OK to be angry, but begin by experiencing it in your body. Where do you feel it?" I ask calmly.

Ted takes a deep breath, closing his eyes so he can pay better attention to his body. "In my chest. In my gut. In my cheeks."

"That's great, Ted. Remember, if you allow yourself to feel your anger, you can learn from it."

"I know, but how am I supposed to learn if I'm so mad that I can't think straight?" Ted questions in a harsh voice.

"There's a difference between discharging your anger on other people and using it to gain insight," I explain. "The reason I'm asking you to feel your anger is not so you can dwell on it, but so you can learn to do something different with it. It all begins by allowing your emotions to take place. So, tell me what happened."

Ted dramatically goes into the story, painting the caterer as the worst kind of person. After he completes the story with a tumultuous cliffhanger, I respond, "Ted, you seem to be intensely angry right now. This caterer is a complete stranger, but you act like you've been mad at him for thirty years. Does your level of anger match this situation?"

"Well, when you say it like that, no," Ted reluctantly says, looking a bit let down that I didn't buy into his story.

"Who are you really feeling mad at right now?" I ask.

"I mean, the whole reason I'm hosting this stupid thing is because of… my mother! That's who I'm really mad at!" Ted relays, experiencing a sudden epiphany.

"Take a breath and feel that anger. Does it feel different than before?" I clarify.

Opening his mouth quickly to respond, Ted hesitates. He finally takes a deep breath and says, "Yeah, I feel more resentful rather than the blood-boiling anger I felt with the caterer," Ted discerns, seeming to surprise himself with this observation.

"Why are you mad at your mother?" I ask.

"Because I always cave in and do whatever she wants. Have I ever wanted to host a dinner party in my life? No! But Uncle Hans is coming all the way from Germany, and it'd be rude of me *not* to throw a party!" Ted goes off, quickly getting wrapped up in the story of his Monkey Mind.

"If you didn't want to do it, then why did you agree to your mother's request?"

"Because I never say no to her," Ted replies matter-of-factly.

"Why don't you say no to your mother?" I ask.

"Well, if I said no to her, she'd go ballistic," he responds, again, as if this is a commonly-known fact.

"Why wouldn't you want her to become angry?"

"Because she's the kind of person that might stop talking to me altogether if I don't do what she wants," Ted scoffs.

I take a deep breath, pausing for a moment. "Allow the anger you feel about your mother to just sit in your body."

He sighs out of annoyance. "It's getting too overwhelming. It feels like it's taking over," he notes, balling his hands into fists.

"You're doing great, Ted. Let's keep tracking your anger. So far it appears you won't express your anger to your mother, but you don't have a problem expressing it to other people in your life. Why do you think that is?"

"I… I don't know," Ted responds, racking his head for an answer.

"Why don't we take a breath?" I instruct lightly. Ted complies, taking several deep breaths.

He refrains from speaking for a few seconds, mulling this question over. "I guess with other people, if they end up getting mad back, I'm able to brush it off," he responds. "Who cares, you know? But with my mom, I get this feeling like I'm doing something wrong. Like a good son would just go along with what his mom wants."

"Do you believe you're doing something wrong if you say no to organizing this dinner party?" I ask.

Ted huffs. "Well when you say it that way, no. I'm not doing anything *wrong*. It's a party for Pete's sake—it's not like I told her she can't see her grandkids or something."

"So is it true that when you disagree with your mother, you're doing something wrong and not being a good son?"

"Huh," Ted quietly replies. "No, I guess there isn't anything wrong with it."

"Can you see how that's the real issue here? Not what your mom asks you to do or not do, but that you think you're doing something wrong and being a bad son by speaking up against her wishes?"

"Yeah, I'm starting to see what you mean," Ted confirms softly.

"Now that you can see that, Ted, where is your level of anger right now?" I inquire.

Ted pauses and takes a breath. He reflects, "I don't feel nearly as angry anymore. I actually feel a bit calmer, because I can see how it's not my mom making me mad. Or the caterer." Stroking his beard slightly, Ted asks, "So is that another reason I get angry so easily? Like I'm bottling up all the anger from not standing up to my mom, and taking it out on everyone else instead?"

"What do you think?" I prompt.

He bobs his head back and forth. "That would make sense, I'd guess. That would explain why I always get mad with Elizabeth at the drop of a hat too—she's been taking the brunt of this."

"That could well be, Ted. So right now, how do you feel about speaking up to your mom?" I propose.

"Man, I don't know! I do want to, but it's going to be tough that first time. But I know I need to do it," Ted acknowledges.

Now, Ted has seen the true source of the smoke. The Monkey Mind pointed a finger at the caterer, and then his mother, before the Observing Mind stepped in and brought Ted back inside his body.

Ted feels relieved and, unexpectedly, becomes grateful for his anger—the alarm that led him to the fire. The real reason for Ted's anger was his belief that he's doing something wrong if he speaks up to his mother.

Think of the last time you were really angry. What feelings were lingering after your anger blew off, like how Ted was experiencing fear about being a bad son? If you could get past your top layer of anger, what other emotions might you discover beneath it?

When it comes to managing our anger, it's very helpful to be aware of how we unconsciously doubt our own sense of self-worth. When you follow the anger back, you can change the disempowering belief before the coal sparks any other fires.

Chapter 15

TURNING SADNESS AROUND

Sadness often stems from the belief that we're losing something or someone, or that something has been taken away from us. For example, how many of us can remember that feeling of sorrow after a significant other broke up with us? Sadness can hit us so hard because it feels like we'll never find anything like what we've lost; in the case of a break-up, we feel like we're not going to find a connection like this again.

Oftentimes, the anguish can be so tough to handle because we are in some way letting this other person or thing define us. If we're able to identify the sadness before it becomes too overwhelming, we can follow it back to the belief causing the fire.

~

One day at the library, Elizabeth runs into Paula.

"Oh my God, wait until I tell you about what happened to me at the store—it's just *awful*," Paula quickly spouts off. Diving into the saga, Paula details how she had tried on a dress and noticed it was ripped down the seam. After getting a salesperson's attention, he had the audacity to accuse Paula of ripping the dress.

"Can you believe that?" Paula asks in a shrill voice.

Elizabeth compassionately replies, "That sounds like a lot, Paula. How are you feeling about that happening?"

Paula hesitates a moment. "Well, umm, it made me pretty upset," she uncertainly replies.

"Yeah, I can imagine. Do you want to talk about it?" Elizabeth offers.

The two sit down, and Paula notices that every time she tries to point out the horridness of the situation, Elizabeth always steers the focus back onto Paula. By the time they're done speaking, Paula feels much less stressed. She innocently asks Elizabeth where this newfound serenity came from, and Elizabeth shares about her work with me. A few days later, Paula calls to set up a session.

After sharing several sessions together, Paula has a curveball thrown her way that she needs help navigating. Paula's friend Robin put together a girls' trip to Vegas and didn't invite her. After the initial shock, Paula has been slowly sinking into a bout of deep depression. Over the past few years, Paula has been experiencing more of these dips into depression and has gradually been taking higher dosages of her anti-anxiety medication to numb these feelings. It's gotten to the point where her doctor won't prescribe her any more, and she's starting to feel desperate.

During this latest crisis, Paula's Monkey Mind is running rampant. *Robin probably invited all those women from her new book club. She's replacing you with them. You've got no friends, and who's going to become your friend at your age? Why can't you ever keep a friend? Why do you drive them all away?*

Paula hasn't left the house for days, which is not her usual habit at all. Her sadness is the smoke detector, alerting her to a much deeper issue. She finally pulls herself off the couch to come to our next session and regales the tale of Robin's betrayal. Soon, she is in tears.

"I just don't understand why Robin would do this to me!" Paula cries, with tears rolling down her face.

"Paula, what are you feeling right now?" I ask.

"Sadness. Immense sadness," she replies softly.

"Can you sit with me and just allow the sadness to rise up in your body?"

"I'm afraid... if I really let go... I won't be able to stop!" Paula cries between heavy sobs.

"We all have a tendency to repress our emotions, but when we do that, nothing changes. You're doing great, just take a minute to allow yourself to really feel the sadness," I encourage with a soft smile.

She begins to sob more. "It just really hurts to be rejected like that," Paula acknowledges, snatching a tissue from the box.

"That's the direction to go into, Paula. It's not comfortable, but it's how you're going to make things shift in your life," I point out. "What would you say is the reason you feel sad?"

"Because Robin went and made a bunch of new friends!" Paula anxiously responds.

"Try going deeper, Paula. Focus on how it feels and why it hurts so much. This will help you find the real reason you feel so hurt," I remind her.

She takes a breath and begins to cry again.

"This is just such a familiar experience for me," Paula begins, sinking deeper into her chair. "When I was in high school, I had this awful group of friends. For a whole year they pretended to be my friends, and then one night we all went to a bonfire outside of town. Or what *I* thought was a bonfire. We all got out of the car, and they told me to start walking down the path to where everyone else was. I remember walking for a bit, and then realizing that I couldn't hear anyone behind me. I turned around to see them peeling onto the road. I could hear their laughs over the engine. I ended up having to walk eight miles home that night. I was so embarrassed, I never even told my mom about it," Paula explains. More tears fall, creating a steady stream.

"Keep allowing your emotion to be there. Can you see how your emotions provide access to your past experiences?" I ask reassuringly.

She nods quickly, dabbing at her cheek with the tissue.

"Let's try to connect that past experience with Robin. How does this experience from high school relate to you being upset about not getting invited to Robin's party?"

"Robin is just like those girls. She's two-faced. She acts like she likes me, but really doesn't want anything to do with me," Paula exasperates, trying to steady her trembling hand.

"We can't know at this moment why Robin didn't invite you on the trip. That's something only she can answer. Yet, let's look at that possibility for a moment. Say that Robin doesn't like you. How do you feel about that?" I inquire.

"I feel bad!" Paula whips back, clearly offended by my question. This brings on a new influx of tears.

"Why do you feel bad if Robin doesn't like you?" I reiterate calmly.

Paula straightens up in her seat and raises her voice. "Because it feels like I haven't grown at all! Like I'm still that same loser from school without any friends. I worked so hard to redefine myself after high school, and it feels like nothing's changed!" Paula cries, her hands flying wildly around to emphasize her point.

"Look how much information we're able to access by allowing yourself to feel." I pause, giving Paula a moment to feel this. "Why do you feel sad about Robin not inviting you on the trip?"

"I mean, how would you feel if your best friend planned a whole trip for her friends and didn't invite you?" Paula cries, reaching for a new tissue as she balls her well-used one in her hand.

"Everyone has their reasons for how they respond to a situation. What's your reason for being upset with Robin right now? Remember to take time to breathe while you're working through this."

Paula bites her lip before responding. However, soon she relents and inhales deeply. In her breath, she seems to find a piece of clarity.

"I feel like I'm not wanted. Robin doesn't want to be friends with me. Those girls from high school didn't either." She sighs deeply. "I feel like I'm doing something wrong to have all these people in my life not want to connect with me… like there's something wrong with me," Paula reveals, new tears filling her ducts.

"It looks like you might be touching on the deeper issue now, Paula. Is your sadness really about Robin not inviting you?"

Dabbing at her eyes, Paula releases a heavy breath. "I don't think it is. I guess I was already believing that there's something wrong with me, wasn't I? So when Robin didn't invite me, it just… backed up that idea," she realizes, lost in a gaze. She shakes her head slightly, almost out of disbelief. "How is it that rejection *still* hurts as much as it did in high school?"

"You've held this belief a long time, Paula. This is a core issue you have with yourself, and when it's activated, it hurts just as much as it did when the belief was created. But now you're aware of this belief, which means you can start to question it. After you've begun changing this belief, you'll notice that your sadness will also begin to dissipate," I explain.

"It's amazing that I keep thinking she could have any power over me. I must be more insecure than I thought," Paula says quietly, wiping away her smudged mascara. "What's funny about all this is when I truly look at Robin, objectively, she's not treating me the way a good friend would treat someone," Paula recognizes.

"In what way?" I clarify.

"Well, she lies to me, thinks of herself first, loves to create unnecessary drama…well, honestly, I can't rag on her too much about that," Paula says with a sigh.

"What do you mean?"

"I mean, I tend to do that too. If I have the juiciest gossip, it gives people a reason to seek me out, you know?" she confesses, her cheeks flushing.

"After realizing this, about Robin and about yourself, what can you see?" I ask.

"I'm ready to start being real with myself. I deserve to be friends with people who treat me better than Robin does," Paula states strongly, her tears now completely gone.

"So can you see how allowing yourself to fully feel the sadness allowed you to reach this conclusion?"

"Yeah, it wasn't about her at all—it was about me thinking that I somehow drive people away," she admits.

"Is it true that something is wrong with you if she didn't invite you on the trip?" I ask.

"No, there's not," Paula powerfully declares, sitting up straighter in her seat.

This is one belief that Paula is now starting to break down. She can see how her sadness wasn't really connected to Robin's rejection; it was about how she was rejecting herself by thinking there is something wrong with her. Now, she feels empowered to continue finding the answers to her depression and anxiety. She can begin dropping friends that are holding her back, and—for the first time in a long time—she can imagine what creating new, authentic friendships would look like.

Take a moment to picture this kind of rejection in your own life. Imagine you just had an argument with a loved one, and they made a comment that really hit home for you. You're now leaving on a trip where you won't be able to communicate with them for a month.

Can you feel the sadness from being judged? Do you need this person's approval in order to change the belief that you're OK? Can you know that your self-worth doesn't depend on what they think of you?

Now, imagine yourself adjusting that belief to, "I'm OK even if that person thinks that of me." What happens to the sadness now?

When we are able to build up our own self-worth without being dependent on other people, experiences, or circumstances, we can begin to release the sadness that threatens to take over our lives.

Chapter 16

TURNING FEAR AROUND

When we're trapped in a fear-driven mindset, any given situation can result in an onset of worry or anxiety. This can be a debilitating way to live, yet many of us don't understand how this fear originates from a desire to control what we fear might happen.

We have this desire more often than we may be aware. At a job interview, for example, we may feel scared to be rejected by the employer. So we pressure ourselves into being perfect because we think that's what it takes to get hired. Then, if we're not perfect, the Monkey Mind berates us, and we fall back on our vices and addictions to numb the shame.

We also tend to project our fear externally, because it protects us in a way. "If I don't get hired, it was because the interviewer didn't like me." Now, we're not having to take responsibility for failing.

In reality, we can't control how the interviewer perceives us or what he or she is looking for in a candidate. When we try to perform to what we think they want, we only make ourselves more nervous.

Instead, if we were confident in our abilities and answered every question authentically, the interviewer would be able to see our mettle and, ironically, would be more likely to hire us. Once we recognize that we can't control everything and take responsibility for our roles in our own lives, we'll be able to track the feeling back to our belief and experience that pervasive worry slipping away.

Let's look to Elizabeth's coworker, Gabriela, to explain this idea.

~

After going back to work part-time at a small, independent magazine, Elizabeth notices that her new coworker, Gabriela, never seems to have the time or energy to socialize with the other employees at the office. She is always incredibly friendly, but it seems as if something is weighing heavily on her mind. Elizabeth tries a few times to get to know her better, but Gabriela leaves as soon as her shift is over and always declines invitations to dinners or parties.

One day, on her lunch break, Elizabeth gets into line behind Gabriela at the sandwich shop. She sees this as her opportunity to get to know this colleague more.

"Gabriela! How are you?" Elizabeth asks brightly.

"Oh, not too bad. Just getting a sandwich," Gabriela says with a small smile.

"Mm hmm. I'm starving! Do you have any big plans for after work today?"

"My son has a concert at school, so that's what I'll be doing," Gabriela quietly replies.

"Oh? I didn't know you had a son. How old is he?" Elizabeth asks.

"Ten. He's just a wonderful kid." Gabriela's eyes start to light up as her smile broadens across her face.

Elizabeth returns the grin. "I'd love to hear more about him."

The two get to talking, and Gabriela finally starts opening up to Elizabeth—mostly about her son, Steven.

"And he's so creative—I swear he has the biggest imagination of anyone I've ever met," Gabriela giggles. Then her face falls. "But sometimes that can get him into trouble with some of the other kids."

"Oh?"

"Yeah, he's on the autism spectrum, and some of his classmates don't really understand how to talk to him. It can be hard sometimes." Gabriela starts fidgeting with her straw.

"That's a lot to deal with as a mother," Elizabeth empathizes.

Gabriela scoffs, "Especially as a single mom."

Elizabeth shares her own hardships she's experienced with her kids, and the two soon start connecting on the level that only mutual mothers can. By the end of their lunch, Gabriela asks Elizabeth how she can be so open about discussing her personal troubles with someone she barely knows. Elizabeth smiles and begins to tell Gabriela about her work with the Observing Mind. After toying with the idea for a few weeks, Gabriela takes the leap and calls me to set up an appointment.

While driving to her most recent session, Gabriela receives a phone call from her son's school counselor; he wants her to come to a meeting to discuss Steven. Her stomach drops and her throat clenches. Her first reaction is white-knuckle fear; her personal smoke detector is blaring inside her body to get her attention. What is causing the alarm to go off?

Gabriela is fiercely protective of her beautiful, unique child, and her Monkey Mind quickly goes into defense mode. *Those teachers don't care about Steven. They just see him as another head in the bunch. They probably want to take him out of his program! No one is going to stick up for him. You're going to have to do this all alone.*

None of those fears, real as they may seem, are the primary cause of the smoke alarm that is now screeching so loudly. So what is?

After doing a brief check-in, Gabriela can't hold back her anxiety anymore.

"I have to go to Steven's school after this, and I'm freaking out about it!" she shrieks.

"Take a few breaths, Gabriela. What's going on for you?" I ask.

"Steven's school called on my way here and said they want to have a meeting with me, and I don't know what it's about! What if he got in trouble, or someone is bullying him, or a teacher doesn't like him, or..." Gabriela launches into a story, barely giving herself enough time to breathe between words.

"Gabriela, take a breath with me and allow yourself to feel the fear for a moment. Count to ten and breathe. Don't try to push the anxiety away, just let yourself feel it and your answer will come naturally."

We start counting together as she breathes. "One... two... three... four..."

I wait several moments, and then ask, "What are you noticing, Gabriela?"

Gabriela continues breathing deeply, closing her eyes before responding, "It's really amazing how worked up I am right now. My hands are trembling, and I have this deep pain in my stomach. I can't stop thinking about the worst outcome. My thoughts are firing off so fast, I can barely think straight," Gabriela observes, her voice still sounding shaky.

"You're doing great, Gabriela. Stay with that feeling. I'm going to ask you some questions, and I want you to imagine that you can answer the question from your anxiety, not from your overwhelmed mind. Imagine your feeling has a voice, and it's going to tell us what's going on."

"OK," Gabriela agrees, her eyes still tightly closed. "I'll give it my best shot."

"Let's count to ten one more time," I suggest.

We count aloud and allow space for the anxiety.

I pause a moment, and continue, "As you check in with yourself, why are you nervous about this meeting?"

Gabriela quickly loses her even breathing pattern and her eyes fly open. "Because every time I go to something with Steven or about him, it seems like it always goes badly! He's *always* being judged. The worst time was when he was only four or five, and we were in a grocery store before Thanksgiving. It was packed in every aisle, and Stevie started hyperventilating. Then he had a full-blown meltdown. I understand that isn't pleasant to listen to, but the way those people responded was horrible! Kids were pointing, and other moms were giving me glares and whispering to their husbands. One woman even told me, 'You know, you should really take him out of here if you can't get him under control.' What was I supposed to do, go home without any food because he was crying? I've seen time and time again that people just have no empathy when it comes to Steven," Gabriela responds, looking like she has the weight of a truck upon her shoulders.

I allow a moment of silence to sit between us, then respond, "Can you see how your anxiety is connected to a very specific moment in time that you are remembering?"

She resumes her deep breathing and nods slowly.

I continue, "Understanding that some people have been judgmental of Steven in the past, why are you afraid to go to *this* meeting?"

"Because of what I've always seen!" Gabriela says with a defeated shake of her head. "I'm afraid he's not going to understand what he needs."

"What's an example of his needs that you feel the counselor won't understand?"

Gabriela opens her mouth to speak but cannot produce any

syllables. "I… I don't know. Now that I'm thinking about it, I can't really come up with any examples. Honestly, this school has been a great help for him so far this year," she admits.

"Could this fear be attached to something else then?"

"Well, I kind of always feel worried in some way or another, so it's hard to pinpoint."

I ask, "Where do you think that worry comes from?"

Gabriela doesn't miss a beat. "Oh, my mom. She was *so* overprotective and always thought the worst was going to happen. I mean, one time I got bit by a dog, and she honestly thought they were going to have to amputate my arm."

"Do you think growing up in that anxious environment still affects you today?"

"Seeing how worked up I am, probably!" she responds.

"Well, let's go back to the meeting and see if we can gain a bit of clarity around this fear. If you can see that this school has been a good fit so far, why are you afraid?" I point out.

She closes her eyes and stretches her neck, trying to loosen up. "I think I'm afraid to trust others with Steven's care. I'm terrified to let go of the control."

"What do you think will happen if you let go?"

"Something bad will happen to Steven, and it will be my fault," she laments.

"And if something bad were to happen to Steven on someone else's watch, what would that mean about you?" I clarify.

"Well, it'd mean I'm a terrible mother. It's my job to protect him."

"Can you see how much pressure you're putting on yourself by believing that?" I ask.

"But what else am I supposed to do? That's the main job of a mom—keep your kid safe!" Gabriela cries.

"Is it realistic to believe that you can protect Steven every second of every day?"

"I mean… no." She sighs. "No, I can't."

"Now that you can see that, what if you considered a different perspective? What would happen if you allow yourself to believe that the counselor *does* have Steven's best interests in mind? Then, once you meet him, you can decide if you feel he is trustworthy or not," I suggest.

Now, Gabriela lets down her protective shield. "Yeah, it'd be great to think that way. It's just so hard to imagine! It's always just been him and me—I've fought for him by myself for so many years. If I trust the wrong person, then Steven suffers because of my mistake."

"Well, how is it working for you to have so much anxiety around Steven's care now?" I question.

Loudly blowing out a breath, Gabriela replies, "It's awful. I can even see how Stevie picks up my anxiety sometimes. I only want the best for him, but I think I've been protecting him to a fault. I mean, I'm treating his counselor as an enemy before I even know why he wants to meet! It would be really beneficial for Steven if I open him up to a bigger support system."

She closes her eyes and breathes deeply, quietly counting to ten. She stretches, this time reaching her arms high above her head.

"Actually," Gabriela says, seeming to surprise herself, "this could be really good for me too. My life has been so focused around Steven that I don't do anything else with my time. A few months ago, I met this other mom who also has a son who's on the spectrum. She invited me to bring Steven over to her house so the two could have a buddy. And she said she and her husband would be happy to watch the two of them, so I could have a little 'me time' away from Steven. When she first suggested this, I immediately shut down the idea, because I didn't know anything about her. I should really try to get know her a little bit and see if she would be capable of watching over Steven." Gabriela cracks her knuckles, seeming to get the last of the tension out of her body.

"How are you feeling now, Gabriela?" I ask.

She sits up a bit straighter in her chair. "Better. For once," she says with a slight laugh.

"Can you see how feeling your anxiety allowed you to understand how your need to worry constantly about his safety isn't serving you or Steven?"

"Yeah, I really can." Gabriela raises her eyebrows, impressed at what she was able to accomplish. "I can just feel how much anxiety is going away... It feels pretty weird, to let go of that control a little, honestly. It's unfamiliar... but good."

Courageously, Gabriela has allowed her anxiety to run its course and, for Steven's sake, agrees to drop her defenses and release her fearful beliefs. The smoke clears. The fear-alarm stops. She becomes excited and energized when she realizes what a difference this will make. No matter what the counselor might do or say, she will feel empowered.

Gabriela's meeting goes well, and she calls me back to report on what happened. I can hear the joy and enthusiasm in her voice and am delighted to learn that she now has a team of caring adults to help her support her son. Gabriela has reported a new ability to find loving and creative solutions to what she used to see as irreversible problems.

As part of her growth, Gabriela is teaching Steven to look for his beliefs when he's troubled by strong feelings—it's a game he's taken to with glee. So many of his previous behavioral issues were related to out-of-control emotions. Now when he's feeling something strongly, he comes to his mother and says, "The smoke alarm is going off." They stop and play detective, searching for clues. The two of them together are getting better at finding the fires and challenging each of their painful beliefs.

By seeing that her worry was connected to controlling every aspect of her son's life, Gabriela can recognize how she was putting unrealistic expectations on herself. While she will still try to keep her son safe as much as she can, she is no longer determining her success as a mother on factors outside of her control.

Can you relate to a time in your life when you were consumed by anxiety and trying to control a situation, like Gabriela? Think of a specific time this happened. Feel the anxiety it created in your body. What would happen if you allowed yourself to get to know your anxiety better?

To illustrate this idea, imagine being a parent to a child in a situation you can't control. For example, say your child committed a crime. In a few weeks, you're going to find out if your child is going to be sent away.

Can you feel yourself wanting to control the situation in some way? Are you experiencing some version of the belief "I'm a bad parent if my child goes to jail"? After doing as much as you can, what if you turn your attention to addressing your child and your own anxiety? Can you see how much more efficient you'd be if you weren't consumed with fear of what could happen?

When we let fear run our lives, when it constantly lives in our bodies, it becomes a problem. By developing the skill to walk through our fear and let go of what we're afraid might happen, we can become more confident in our own abilities and release the sense of overwhelming fear in our lives.

Chapter 17

TURNING SHAME AROUND

Once we have a heightened awareness about our beliefs and emotions, we begin to broach a new, unfamiliar issue: shaming ourselves for shaming ourselves. This type of double shame occurs only when we're conscious enough to notice that we are getting sucked into our Monkey Mind's stories.

As we've mentioned, we often unconsciously believe that shame is the way to make ourselves change. This idea is often so deeply engrained in us that we do it even when we're trying to *stop* ourselves from using shame!

Shame chips away at our self-confidence and self-worth. When we do something that makes us experience this feeling of shame, the Monkey Mind adds on a second level by repeating, *You should have known better.* We think that if we stop shaming ourselves, it means that we don't care about the issue and are simply going to let it continue instead of trying to change it.

When we feel ashamed about doing something, *combined* with the feeling that we should have known better than to have done it, we build up an overpowering amount of anxiety. Let's see how Kevin uses the Observing Mind to help navigate his shame around believing that he should know better.

～

Kevin and Jamie's relationship has taken a radical turn in the right direction after Kevin has worked with me for several months. Kevin is allowing Jamie to finally see his emotions, something she didn't think was possible.

One evening after work, the two are planning on meeting up to see a movie.

Since he started getting help, Kevin has been thriving at work. He is now the shift manager for the other nurses at the hospital. Earlier today, Kevin had to let go of one of the nurses, and it didn't go very well. Kevin feels bad for how he handled the situation and wishes he had said something different. He can't stop replaying the incident in his head, and he isn't in any mood to be romantic.

When they meet at the theater, all Kevin wants to do is grab some popcorn and silently watch the movie for the next two hours.

Jamie, on the other hand, had a wonderful day at the architecture firm. She had a surprise meeting with her boss, who explained how impressed she was with Jamie's last design. She wants to make Jamie the lead designer on a new, important client's project. Jamie can't wait to tell Kevin the good news.

When Kevin walks into the lobby, Jamie is waiting in the long line for concessions and eagerly waves him over.

"You're not going to believe what happened at work today!" she beams.

"What?" Kevin asks, noting how slowly the line is moving.

Jamie grabs Kevin's arm enthusiastically and exclaims, "They want me to be the head designer for the Johnson house!"

"Oh, that's great, honey," Kevin mumbles with a tight smile, keeping his eyes locked on the cash register.

"Really? That's the level of enthusiasm you can conjure up? I'm really excited about this," Jamie disappointingly says, taking a step back from Kevin and pulling her arm away.

"I'm sorry, Jamie. I've had a rough day and am pretty out of it. Can we talk about it more after the movie?" Kevin requests, rubbing his temples.

Jamie, still a bit upset, lets out a sigh. "Yeah, that's fine. You wait in line. I'm going to go grab a seat."

She leaves Kevin and heads into the theater. Now, Kevin's Monkey Mind starts in on him. *What just happened? You could see how big this news was and you just stood there, emotionless. What's wrong with you? Why didn't you hug her? What if she thinks you don't care? She deserves better than that. She deserves better than you.*

Kevin starts to feel ashamed of how he acted, and a pit starts forming in his stomach. But then, he takes a breath and gives his Observing Mind space to speak. *Yep, you did just revert back to not showing your emotions—either happiness for Jamie's big news or sadness for firing Todd. But that's OK. You did ask for space. Give yourself a chance to revisit this after the movie.*

Kevin buys a soda and popcorn, and spots Jamie in the crowded theater. He sits down just as the trailers are starting, and they don't speak for the remainder of the film.

On the drive back to their place, Jamie asks, "So what happened earlier? You've come so far with being open, and then all of a sudden, you have this huge wall up. Did I do something wrong?"

Kevin's hands tense up on the steering wheel. Again, his Monkey Mind's voice starts berating him in his head. *You have come so far! You know so much better than this! This is something the old Kevin would have done. You haven't made any progress. You're still locking yourself away, afraid to be vulnerable. You haven't changed at all. You're pathetic.*

Kevin breathes through these thoughts as they're being hurled toward him. Just as he's about to sink into the Monkey Mind's story, his Observing Mind pipes up. *You have a lot of shame building up right now. You need to look at this before you say something you'll regret later.*

Kevin pulls into the closest parking lot and looks at Jamie. He says, "I need a second to gather my thoughts."

To Jamie's surprise, Kevin hops out of the car and starts walking laps around the small lot. He focuses on maintaining an even breath and starts questioning his thoughts, as I showed him to do. Kevin's Observing Mind asks, *Why are you being so hard on yourself right now? You've been doing so well with her, and she's reaching out to you. What's the issue?*

"Wow, I'm really scared to tell Jamie how sad I feel about firing Todd today," Kevin silently replies.

Why are you afraid to tell her about that?

"Because I shouldn't *be* sad about it. He was a bad employee, and he needed to be fired. Period."

Why shouldn't you feel sad about that?

"Because as shift manager, I should be able to fire someone without crying about it!"

Why shouldn't you want to cry after firing someone?

"Because it's weak!" Kevin hears his Monkey Mind say, in his dad's disapproving voice.

Kevin stops his circuit, realizing he's reached the source. He calmly gets back into the car and clicks on the light button so he can see Jamie's face.

"I'm sorry, Jamie. I had to fire Todd today, and he didn't take it well," Kevin's voice breaks, and his eyes start to water. He takes a breath. "It's made me anxious all night, and I didn't even notice that I was closed off."

"Oh, Kevin, it's OK. What happened?" Jamie asks, rubbing her husband's arm.

"He started blaming me and saying I hadn't been giving him the direction he needed so he could do his job right," Kevin explains. "Then he went into how his family needs this job, and I'm basically putting him out on the street." Kevin bows his head low, and without hesitating, allows a few tears to fall.

"Hey, honey, none of this is your fault, OK? It's amazing how much you care for the other nurses, but you can't feel responsible for this," Jamie gently relays, leaning into her husband.

"Yeah… I know. It just still hurts to know that he'll be struggling, you know?" Kevin mumbles.

"He'll find his way. He'll be OK, Kevin. He will."

He looks over and smiles weakly at Jamie. "Thanks, hon." He leans over and kisses her forehead.

They sit in silence for a few moments, and Kevin slowly transforms his broken breaths into full inhales. Now, feeling much more regulated, he says, "I'd love to hear more about your meeting with your boss. You really do deserve this."

"Thanks, love," Jamie says, kissing her husband and giving his arm another squeeze before leaning up away from him. "So!" she says, becoming much more animated, "I was just sitting at my desk and…" She goes into telling Kevin about the meeting, her plans for the new home, and how she's going to utilize her team. Having acknowledged his own feelings, Kevin can completely be there for everything she is saying without the Monkey Mind deafening him with its judgmental voice.

Kevin went through two phases this evening that are important to highlight.

First, Kevin judged himself for not expressing emotions—joy for Jamie or sadness over firing his employee.

Second, and more importantly, Kevin judged himself far more

harshly for falling for the Monkey Mind's story yet again. He believed he has worked on his observational skills too long to still be listening to this disparaging voice. He thought that he should know better, and he shouldn't hear the voice of the Monkey Mind at all.

What's your "should"? Do you think you should be more responsible, less irritable, more honest, less selfish?

For example, say your judgment is, "I should be thinner." Now, look in the mirror and say your judgment aloud five times, as if you were saying it to another person. This would look like: "You should be thinner. You should be thinner. You should be thinner. You should be thinner. You should be thinner."

Can you feel the shame? Do you feel motivated to change?

Now, do this again, but add, "I'm sorry that I think…"

"I'm sorry that I think you should be thinner. I'm sorry that I think you should be thinner. I'm sorry that I think you should be thinner. I'm sorry that I think you should be thinner. I'm sorry that I think you should be thinner."

With this new level of compassion that you feel toward yourself, are you more inclined to want to change?

Being aware of the Monkey Mind doesn't mean being perfect all the time. The Monkey Mind's voice has been playing for many, many years, and it make sense for old patterns to resurface. Remember to cut yourself some slack when you notice yourself getting sucked into the Monkey Mind's story. Shame is never the answer to creating long-lasting change. The compassion you show yourself in these moments is the same thing that will help you ultimately overcome the Monkey Mind and change the programming that otherwise sabotages your life.

Part 4

THE TOOLS OF AWARENESS

Chapter 18

AWARENESS CREATES CHANGE

We are naturally wired to want to take care of ourselves. However, when we buy into the stories of the Monkey Mind, we're not aware that the way we are attempting to help ourselves is not working. Once we understand that beliefs and emotions are the keys to changing our programming, we need specific tools to shift fully into listening to the Observing Mind. This is where the tools of awareness come into play. In this section, we will explore how awareness can help us shift into a more efficient way of taking care of ourselves.

To start identifying the simple types of awareness that we experience every day, imagine putting a slice of bread in the toaster. The temperature dial is set to six. When your toast pops up, it's burnt. You now have a new awareness. The next time you make toast, you turn the dial to four.

Or let's say you're in a rush one morning, and you take the Tenth Street exit off the freeway. You end up stuck in construction traffic. Next time, you sail by that mess by exiting at Eighth Street.

Or say you get blisters from a particular pair of shoes. You stop wearing them.

We are inundated with various kinds of awareness all day, yet, we often don't apply this same concept of learning from our past experiences to our relationships with our loved ones and ourselves. We don't keep setting the toaster to six and expect perfectly-cooked toast—so why do we replay the same argument with the people in our lives, over and over again, and expect a different result?

When you have a heightened awareness, you observe and remember how you have expressed your irritation in the exact same way about a specific issue so many times before, and it never changes what the person does. Now, you understand that getting irritated is not the way to create the outcome you want. You can clearly see that you need to adopt a different strategy.

To start anchoring this idea of being aware, think of three things that you think "shouldn't" have happened in your life. Maybe you think you "shouldn't" have gotten divorced. Or you "shouldn't" have failed that test. Or you "shouldn't" have yelled at your child. Are you gaining any knowledge from that experience when you believe it shouldn't have happened?

Instead, say to yourself, "What do I now know about maintaining a successful relationship that I didn't know before?" "What do I now know about passing the test that I didn't know before?" "What do I now know about communicating with a child that I didn't know before?"

When we're aware, we notice what's working and what's not. We adjust our beliefs and our behavior naturally. With the right questions and the Observing Mind's compassionate outlook, we can create understanding, which naturally moves us to change.

Notice Your Thoughts

One of the first tools of awareness that often escapes people is becoming fully aware of the bombardment of thoughts that enter our mind at any given time and noticing the difference between the Monkey Mind's thoughts and those of the Observing Mind.

Inside your mind, notice the thoughts that are happening and practice making observations about what is transpiring around you. The Observing Mind would think in observations. *A motorcycle just drove by. There is an ant on the rug. The scent of freshly baked cookies is coming from the neighbor's house. This sweater is fuzzy. My partner is upset.*

Now, see how long you can maintain making nonjudgmental observations before the Monkey Mind starts trying to take over. More realistically, your thoughts will probably go like this.

A motorcycle just drove by. There is an ant on the rug... There's an ant in here! The exterminators just came by last week! Can't they do their job?

When you notice you're listening to your Monkey Mind, snap back into focusing on observations. *The scent of freshly baked cookies is coming from the neighbor's house. This sweater is fuzzy. My partner is upset. Why is she upset? Is she mad at me?* This is the Monkey Mind kicking back in.

Try to carve out a little time each day to actively practice the skill of observing. You'll start to develop the ability to ask yourself, "Where does the thought 'the exterminators can't do their job' come from?" Or, "Why do I instantly think something is my fault if my partner is upset?"

With each practice, you'll more easily be able to differentiate the Observing Mind's observations from the Monkey Mind's story and continue to change the programming that is sabotaging your life.

Chapter 19

EVOLVE THE MONKEY MIND

Most of us are caught in repetitive, reactive patterns, and we have difficulty recognizing where those patterns came from. One powerful skill that we can learn is to understand how we filter other people's comments through the Monkey Mind's voice. We often hear simple statements or questions negatively and react in the same way we would to a threat. However, these "threats" are nothing more than a product of our programming.

~

Paula plops down into a chair for our session and immediately clues me in on what's going on in her mind. "So last night, James and I were going to a show with some of our friends, and when I came downstairs, he asked if I was 'really going to wear that.' I said yeah, and snapped back, asking what's wrong with it. He said it looked pretty casual for this kind of event, and I just went off about how 'heaven forbid he's seen with someone in jeans...' but, after all that, I still ended up changing because I felt so self-conscious," Paula admits.

"Hmm. And why is that bothering you so much?" I ask.

"Well, I can see how out of proportion my response was to his comment," Paula explains. "Yeah, it kind of stung, but still. I felt like he was attacking me or something."

"Attacked is the perfect word, Paula. And not only verbally attacked—but the way you responded, you would almost think that you were experiencing a *physical* threat, wouldn't you?" I ask.

"Yeah, actually, that's how it felt!"

"So was James commenting that your clothes were casual a physical threat?"

"Not at all," she laughs.

"Isn't that interesting? Your reaction, like you mentioned, was out of proportion to the comment James made. It was as if you were perceiving the statement as a physical threat. And think how many other times you feel attacked by him..." I begin.

"Oh yeah, I feel like that all the time!" Paula interjects.

"Can you give me an example?" I request.

"Well, like the other day, he asked me why I hadn't cleaned the kitchen, and I snapped. I had been running around doing errands all day, and he focused on the one thing I hadn't gotten to yet."

"Do you know why you're caught in this cycle of fighting with James?" I inquire.

Paula shakes her head.

"We do this because it's engrained in us from our ancestors. In the days of early man, when there actually *was* a physical threat—like a tiger in the bush—we would either run or fight, right?" I question.

"Yeah, our fight-or-flight response," she agrees.

"Exactly. Our fight-or-flight response is what kept us alive back then. But now, we don't have too many tigers hanging around, do we?"

"No," Paula laughs.

"Yet, there is still part of our mind that has this survivalist instinct," I explain. "I like to call it the 'unevolved' part of the mind. This ancient part of our psyche still believes that there is an ever-present danger around us. While some people around the world do still have to deal with physical threats, most of us are relatively safe now. So over time, the unevolved part of the mind has shifted its focus to protecting something else: our self-worth."

"Our self-worth? So you mean when we think someone is criticizing us, we take that as the same kind of threat as a tiger about to attack?" Paula inquires curiously.

"Exactly," I reply. "When someone criticizes us, the unevolved part of our brain is triggered. 'Here's the tiger!' it warns—even if it's something as simple as your husband saying you look too casual. Now, you're reacting with the full weight of how a caveman would have defended his body against a tiger. You scream back and lash out. You're not satisfied until that threat—that critique—has been sufficiently conquered."

"That is what I did," Paula acknowledges.

I ask, "So Paula, when James said your clothes were too casual—how do you think that was associated with your self-worth?"

"Well, if I was wearing clothes that didn't look good, I was afraid that other people would think I look stupid."

"So that's one self-worth issue—that you're deciding if you're stupid or not based on the clothes you wear. What about cleaning up the kitchen? How does that relate to you?"

"Well, I told him I would do it, and then I hadn't done it yet," Paula responds.

"And what kind of a person doesn't follow through on their agreement?"

"An irresponsible person," Paula replies.

"Can you see when James makes those requests of you, you take them as a threat? With his statement about your clothes—the threat isn't about your clothes, it's about you looking stupid," I point out.

"I never thought about it, but yeah, I can see that," Paula responds.

"And can you see that when he asks you about the kitchen, the issue isn't about whether it's clean or not? He's asking why you didn't do it, but in truth you're experiencing the threat that you're an irresponsible person."

Paula laughs. "Geez, this is starting to look pretty ridiculous."

"When you really look at these perceived threats, you begin to see the absurdity of them. But, in the moment it feels like a real threat," I describe.

"It really does. Man, that's crazy," Paula says with a shake of her head.

"So how are you making the bridge that his comments should be taken as a threat?" I ask.

Paula whistles quietly as the realization hits her. "My Monkey Mind."

"Exactly. Your Monkey Mind thinks that this comment is threatening your self-worth, so it makes up the story that you need to defend yourself," I explain.

"So I need to start recognizing that my reaction has nothing to do with the kitchen or clothes—it's really about me believing that James' comments mean there's something wrong with me," Paula recognizes.

"You're spot on. And there's two steps to make this happen. The first is to be able to become aware of how many disproportionate reactions we have. You're already ahead of the game in that you're identifying these moments, like you noticed how upset you became from the simple comment about cleaning the kitchen."

"Yeah, for sure," Paula agrees.

"Now, you need to move into the next step: identifying what part of your self-worth is being threatened. You need to be able to distinguish which story your Monkey Mind is telling you. Then, all you have to ask yourself is if your self-worth is really dependent on this comment.

Is your value dependent on you cleaning the kitchen?" I ask.

"No! That's so crazy, how I've convinced myself that... it's really eye-opening," she responds.

Can you think of a time in your own life you felt attacked, like Paula did when James asked why she hasn't cleaned the kitchen? Notice how your response was out of proportion to what was said. Identify the aspect of your self-worth that was being threatened, like how Paula felt like James believed she was irresponsible.

Do you notice how simple it can be to be less reactive when you identify that your sense of a threat is not an actual threat?

PROTECTING YOUR SELF-WORTH

The concept of being attacked by the Monkey Mind is easy to identify when it comes to simple statements being said with out-of-proportion responses. But what about when someone is bringing up an issue that is directly hitting on a deeply held judgment you have? Let's see how Kevin is able to navigate this perceived attack when he's faced with one of his most shame-inducing beliefs.

Kevin and Jamie are sitting on their sofa, discussing the idea of hosting a game night at their house soon.

"Ooh, we have that new charades game we could try out! Who do you all want to invite?" Jamie asks.

"The Morgans would be a great time. And the Petersons," Kevin suggests.

"Yeah! And the Browns would be a blast too!" Jamie enthusiastically recommends.

Kevin can feel his heartbeat quicken at the mention of his neighbors' name.

"The Browns? Really?" Kevin scoffs.

"What?" Jamie asks defensively. "Oh, come on, Kevin. We've been through this so many times! You went through mediation with them. You acknowledged what you did. They see the change in you. They've said a hundred times that they forgive you!"

"You just don't get it. You weren't the one that ran over their dog, Jamie!" Kevin yells.

"This isn't fair—to me or yourself. The Browns are some of our best friends, and you're robbing us of that friendship by obsessing over the Max incident!"

"'Obsessing over the Max incident?' I can't believe you'd even say that. I can't do this right now."

Kevin angrily excuses himself to his den, where he tries to dissect the strong emotions he's feeling. As much as he tries to get to the underlying belief at play, all he can hear is his Monkey Mind. *You're such an awful person. No matter what you do, you'll never change the fact that you killed that dog. It's unforgivable.*

Kevin decides to table this subject and bring it up in his next session with me.

After he tells me about the argument with Jamie, I ask, "Why do you think Jamie suggesting the Browns coming over brought up so much emotion?"

"Because we're supposed to be on the same side, you know? She knows how hard that whole situation has been for me. And for her to bring up having them over so nonchalantly... It felt like she was picking them over me," Kevin says, rubbing his face.

"Do you remember when I told you that oftentimes when we feel criticized, we feel attacked? That our survivalist instincts become triggered?" I ask.

"Oh, right. And then we give a disproportional response, right?" He sighs. "That's what I did with Jamie, wasn't it?"

"Well, let's unpack that attacked feeling to find out. Picture the Browns coming over for the game night. How do you feel?"

Kevin closes his eyes and shifts uncomfortably in his chair. After a few moments of silence, his eyes fly open. "I can't even imagine it! I doubt they'd want to come over in the first place. Would *you* want to hang out with the guy that killed your dog? And god, did they love Max. They'd had him for almost ten years. He'd grown up with their kids and everything. Even if they say they forgive me, I can't really believe it. It's unforgivable what I did."

"Remember that you can't change what they believe. Whether they truly forgave you or not, you only have power over what you believe. So, the question is: have you forgiven yourself?"

"I'd say I have some more work to do around that subject," Kevin concedes.

"Well, let's go back to the feeling you had when Jamie brought up having the Browns over. Some aspect of your self-worth was being attacked when she said that, right? What do you think that could be?"

Kevin breathes in deeply. "Well, every time I think of the Browns and Max, I get this overwhelming feeling that I'm a terrible person. The worst kind of person, really. My Monkey Mind just goes off whenever I think about it."

"So you're basing if you're a good or bad person on killing the dog?" I clarify.

He sighs. "Yeah, I guess I am."

"Well, let's look a little closer at that. Think back to that night,

Kevin. When you decided to go to the bar, did you think, 'I'm going to get drunk tonight, drive home, hit the Browns' dog, and then pass out on the couch'?"

"Of course not," Kevin defends.

"What were you thinking when you left for the bar, then?"

"I don't know if I was really thinking about anything. I had lost us our chance at buying this amazing house, and I was just so pissed at myself that I needed to numb out."

"You're saying that you had no intention of killing Max then?"

"No!" Kevin shouts back.

"Then why aren't you able to treat the incident for what it was—a mistake? It looks like you're believing that you had a malicious intent, but you just said that isn't true."

Kevin ponders this for a second. "I didn't realize I was doing that."

"You keep telling yourself that you're a horrible person for hitting Max. But, we've just identified that a horrible person would've had the intention to kill him, wouldn't they?"

"Yeah, that's true."

"So again, let me ask you the question: that night, when you left for the bar, did you go out and get drunk to kill your neighbors' dog? Or, was it to relieve yourself from the shame and anxiety you were feeling?"

Kevin remains silent, processing this idea.

I continue, "Take this as an opportunity to shift into listening to your Observing Mind, Kevin. The Observing Mind knows you didn't mean to hit Max. It doesn't listen to all the stories the Monkey Mind is making up about you being a bad person. And it doesn't take the mention of the Browns as an attack on your self-worth."

I add, "Can you see how this isn't about the Browns at all? This comes back to you deciding your worth on one isolated incident. And until you're able to forgive yourself for that, you're going to keep feeling attacked whenever the Browns are brought up."

Kevin inhales loudly. "So, what do I do now?"

"If you took a guess, what would it be?" I respond.

"Well, from what you're saying, I need to observe that my reaction has nothing to do with the Browns or Max—it's really about me believing that what happened with the Browns means I'm a bad person," Kevin recognizes.

"And remember to ask yourself if your self-worth is really dependent on this event. Is your value based on killing the Browns' dog?" I ask.

"You know, I can feel myself getting there. But I still have a hard time saying no to that," Kevin says.

"Remember that one of the best ways to reprogram your beliefs is to put them into action. So, what do you think of agreeing to the idea of having the Browns over for your game night?"

"I mean, I have seen how powerful it is to try out new beliefs. But to have them over... you know what, yeah. It'll be tough, but I can do it."

"It only seems hard because you're still perceiving anything about Max as an attack on your self-worth. When you have the Browns over, remember to consistently ask yourself if it's true that killing Max permanently defines you as a bad man. Or, was it just a mistake?"

Think of something you have a hard time forgiving yourself for doing. Write down three or four comments that your Monkey Mind uses to attack you about this event.

For example, say you left your wallet at a gas station. Your Monkey Mind would say, *You're such an idiot. Why can't you just pay attention for once?*

For each statement your Monkey Mind makes, bring in the nonjudgmental awareness of the Observing Mind and name the truth about your self-worth. For example, with the lost wallet, your Observing Mind would notice, *When you went to the gas station, you were really stressed about getting to your meeting on time. Being anxious doesn't make you an idiot.*

Do you feel a shift in judgment when you consider all the factors that played into the situation?

Once we get to the point where we can quickly spot that we are in "attack mode," we can then track back what aspect of our self-worth we feel is being threatened in that moment. By doing this, we can make the Monkey Mind's control of our lives a thing of the past.

Chapter 20

TAKE OWNERSHIP OF YOUR EXPERIENCE

The Monkey Mind has convinced us that the sources of happiness and unhappiness are everywhere *outside* ourselves. This is no small issue. We are under a constant barrage of thoughts that want to blame situations and other people for how we are feeling. Most people spend a lifetime trying to control things that are out of their hands.

Focusing *outside* yourself is easy to identify: your daughter's whining voice, your husband's scattered clothes, your mother's disappointment with you, the traffic jam, the flooded basement, the ringing phone, the work piled on your desk. Any person (other than you), every event, and every situation—they're all *outside* you.

Conversely, when developing the habit of focusing *inside* yourself, you want to pay attention to your feelings, sensations, and thoughts about yourself. To do this, you have to first get in touch with the way you feel. Your feelings are inside of you. Your suffering and happiness are inside of you. There is no other place on earth where you can find your personal experience.

~

Imagine Paula jumps into her car only to find that her husband has once again left the gas tank on empty. She's already running late. Her frustration erupts into anger, and her Monkey Mind feeds the fire.

He is so inconsiderate! He only thinks of himself! How many times has he done this to you? And how many times have you asked him not to do this? He's hopeless.

The feelings of anger and frustration are boiling in her body. Can you see how easy it would be for her to blame her partner? She could easily get into an argument and unload her anger by having an outburst and accusing her husband of all sorts of things.

Paula could spend all of her energy trying to change outside factors. However, if she wants to turn the fire down, she must look inside herself.

The Observing Mind notices the empty gas gauge, and the anger, and the story. But it knows there is no value at this moment in focusing on anything outside of Paula. It's not going to let her slip into a melodrama. Wisely, the Observing Mind turns Paula's attention inward.

On the inside, only two things are happening:

1. The Monkey Mind is telling a story.
2. Paula is feeling frustrated.

These are the two things she needs to focus on. Paula can't undo the car being empty of gas, but she *can* notice and change her reaction going on inside her own body. Once she's done this, she can track back to her beliefs that are driving her irritation in this moment.

In actuality, her husband's absentmindedness has nothing to do with Paula, but that's not how she sees it. Unconsciously, she's making the leap that since she's told him not to leave the tank on empty before, and he still did, it means that she is not worth caring for.

Once she tracks back to the belief "I'm not worth caring for," Paula can see how this is not true. The gas tank being empty doesn't mean anything about her as a person. She can now let go of this belief in this moment. Even if her husband does end up doing this again, Paula will continue to remind him from a peaceful place, because she no longer is attaching her beliefs about herself to the gas tank or her husband's behavior.

Take a moment to reflect on Paula's example. Be honest—did you get a little upset reading about Paula's husband leaving the gas on empty? Were you thinking 'Well, sure, that'd make anyone mad'? Can you see how easy it is to get swept into the Monkey Mind's story?

Let's track back Paula's reasons for why she is upset and see what the deeper belief at play is here:

1. The car is nearly out of gas—Outside of Paula
2. My husband is so inconsiderate and needs to change—Outside of Paula
3. He doesn't care about me—Outside of Paula
4. I must not be important; I don't matter—Inside of Paula

Now we can see that the real reason Paula is upset is that she believes she doesn't matter.

We point the finger at others for our unhappiness so often in our everyday life. To experience this act of turning your focus internally, visualize being at the airport, and your flight just got canceled. Imagine the desk clerk for the airline is standing in front of you. Physically extend your arm and point your finger at them. Say aloud, "You are responsible for my frustration. Make me feel better now."

Sound ridiculous?

Now, drop your arm. Instead, shift your focus inward. Ask yourself, "What belief am I holding that is making me so upset about my flight being canceled?"

It's a tricky balance to keep bringing our attention back inside ourselves. It takes discipline to do this. The Monkey Mind is always ready to shift the focus to other people and outside situations. Focusing inward is often the most challenging aspect of mastering the tools of awareness. The key is to take ownership of our experience.

INSIDE MY SKIN OR OUTSIDE MY SKIN

Now that you're becoming aware of the concept of focusing inside yourself instead of outside, we need to break down exactly what that all entails. If we aren't able to look inward, we'll never be able to truly address the beliefs that form our negative perceptions. There is an endless amount of data within our own minds and bodies, and to become truly healthy, we need to learn how to tap into this pool of knowledge.

To better understand this idea of looking internally, let's look back to Patrick Smith. Last time we saw Patrick, he had lost his parking spot and had been late to his big presentation. He had butchered the meeting and went home and numbed his sorrow with drugs. The next day, he was fired.

Patrick began using heavily for weeks on end and couldn't stay sober long enough to go to another job interview. Kevin saw the oh-too-familiar path that Patrick was taking, so he sat his brother down and convinced him to go to a session with me to see if Patrick could start to uncover the underlying cause of his drug use.

Patrick and I spent a few intensive months together addressing the core beliefs that were driving his cocaine addiction. Slowly but surely, Patrick regained his sense of self and got his drug problem under control. Now, as he's about to start a new position, Patrick is determined to make sure this job experience is different than the last.

~

In one of our sessions, Patrick says to me, "J.F., I really want to understand why I crumbled under the pressure at my last job—I can't mess up again."

"Why don't I show you a tool to help you understand what happened? It's called 'Inside My Skin or Outside My Skin.' The principle is this: we fall into the Monkey Mind's fable that the real source of our problems is based on other people or outside circumstances. We can use this tool to recognize that the true cause of our issues is within ourselves—inside our skin. Let's start walking through it, and you'll see what I mean as we go along. To do this, we need to go back to the day you delivered that presentation," I explain.

Patrick takes a deep breath. "OK. I can do that."

"You've told me the story of how you were late to your meeting before, but let's start with when you first lost the parking space. How'd you feel when the guy took the parking spot?" I ask.

"Really upset," Patrick replies, his voice growing louder as he remembers the anger he felt.

"What's the reason you felt upset?" I ask.

Patrick is trying to remain regulated, but he's having a tough time with such a painful memory. "I was upset because that guy stole my parking spot."

"Now, notice that the Monkey Mind is telling you that the reason you're upset is because of this other person. As long as you're blaming your feelings on things outside yourself, you are not addressing the internal source for this feeling—your core belief," I explain.

"Oh, right. We've gone over that before. The real reason I was upset wasn't because he stole my parking space," Patrick acknowledges. He pauses and adds, "What was the reason then?"

"Let's use this tool to find out. So was the guy that took your parking space inside or outside your skin?" I ask.

"Was he inside my skin? Do you mean literally?" Patrick asks with confused eyes.

"Yes. Every time your focus is outside your skin, you're using an outside factor as the reason for why you're upset," I point out. "The key is to keep going until you reach the internal reason for why you're upset. The tool of Inside My Skin or Outside My Skin helps you to filter out any outside factors to quickly get to the underlying belief."

"OK, I get that outside factors don't determine our responses—I do. But at the same time, I don't quite see the deeper belief behind my anger in this situation," Patrick admits.

"Let's keep going, and it will become clearer. So was the man that took your parking space inside or outside of you?" I repeat.

"Outside," Patrick answers, more confidently now.

"Right. Another person is always outside of you and is always an external trigger. So since we want to get to the point where you're *inside* your skin, we need to go deeper. Now that you've lost the parking spot, what was the next challenge that upset you?" I ask.

Patrick's eyes start scanning the carpet, like he's looking for the answer within its threads. "Well, if I didn't get the spot, I was going to be late for my meeting."

"How did you feel about the possibility of being late?" I ask.

"I felt nervous about it."

"So you were nervous about being late for your meeting. Is a meeting inside or outside you?" I inquire.

"Outside," he quickly responds.

"You're getting it, Patrick. Let's dive in more. Say you're now late for your meeting. What challenge did you face next?"

"Well, I figured the clients and my coworkers were going to judge me for being late. Especially my boss," Patrick recalls, his mood quickly shifting into sadness.

"Is being judged by your clients, coworkers, and boss inside or outside you, Patrick?' I reference again.

Patrick pauses a moment, racking his head for a reason it could be internal. However, he takes a deep breath and admits, "Outside."

"Yes, these people's opinions of you are outside your skin. I know this can seem like a tedious process, but it's actually helping us shoot straight to the core belief at play here. Now that your colleagues could potentially be judging you, what challenge did you face next that upset you?" I ask.

"I was worried I would get fired," he concedes sheepishly.

"Is your job inside or outside of you, Patrick?" I ask yet again.

"Outside," he quickly admits.

"We're almost there. Say you do get fired—what's next?"

Patrick releases a frustrated sigh and shakes his head. "Well, I *did* get fired! I really can't think of anything else. I mean, what's worse than losing your job?" he asks, looking over at me with a grimace.

"This is often where people hit a roadblock, Patrick. It's difficult to move past this stage. When you get to the point where it gets tough to find any more reasons as to why you're upset, ask yourself: 'What does this mean about me?' So Patrick—what does losing your job mean about you?"

Patrick pauses a moment and closes his eyes tightly. "It means I'm a failure."

"Is you thinking you're a failure inside or outside you?" I ask gently.

"Hey, we finally got there," Patrick half-heartedly answers. "It's inside my skin."

"You're now reflecting on a deep-seated core belief you hold about yourself, Patrick: that you're a failure. You're no longer looking at something outside of your control," I explain. "I know that process can be a little overwhelming to go through, so let's recap all the different external focuses you named before getting to your internal beliefs." I pull out a dry erase marker and write:

Reasons for Being Upset:

Man who took parking space—Outside Your Skin
Being late to the meeting—Outside Your Skin
Being judged by others—Outside Your Skin
Getting fired—Outside Your Skin
I'm a failure—Inside Your Skin

"Can you see how many times your Monkey Mind convinced you that the cause of your distress was outside yourself, Patrick?"

"No wonder I get so swept up into stories sometimes," Patrick agrees with wide eyes. "And that's the exact issue we've been talking about for months—how my relationship with my dad affected my self-confidence. So the real issue was that I felt like a failure before I even went to the meeting," Patrick recognizes.

"Exactly. Did you see how fast we were able to reach that belief with this tool? So now, when you're facing stressful situations, you can use the same steps to question what these situations mean about you. Then you can ask yourself if it's true. Is it true that being late to a meeting makes you a failure?" I ask.

"Of course not! You know, this actually makes me feel better about starting this job next week. If I'm not taking everything personally, it shouldn't be nearly as stressful," Patrick responds with a small smile.

Sometimes, something as trivial as being late to a meeting can trigger our core beliefs. By using Inside My Skin or Outside My Skin, Patrick could map his responses to find his internal core beliefs. Now, he can understand what truly triggered his negative response and drove him to use drugs in the past, and he can feel empowered to identify what core beliefs are driving his responses in the future.

Try applying the tool of Inside My Skin, Outside My Skin to your own life. Think of a moment you became upset this month. For every reason you come up with about why this situation distressed you, ask yourself if that reason is inside your skin or outside your skin. As long as you're outside, keep going deeper, like Patrick did, until you find a reason that is inside your skin—a belief that is about you.

When we hone our focus inside ourselves, we let go of the outside layers and work down to the core of our issue. Only when we've reached the root cause of our behavior, our self-sabotaging core belief, are we able to begin making change.

Chapter 21

SLOW DOWN YOUR INNER RHYTHM

Now that your attention is focused inside, on your own feelings and thoughts, it's time to add another tool of awareness: slowing down your inner rhythm. This is something that your friend the Observing Mind might do, simply by being itself, when it arrives at the scene of an emergency. Through its calm, clear questions and alert, compassionate attention, the Observing Mind slows everything down. Panic subsides. Things stop spinning out of control. Slowing down offers the opportunity to remain calm and provide tremendous relief from anxiety.

∽

Elizabeth and I are walking and talking in a park. As we round the bend, we see Ted, sitting close to a woman on a bench. I can see that Elizabeth is becoming anxious and agitated, so we sit down near the fishpond.

"How are you feeling right now, Elizabeth?" I ask.

"Terrible. I knew he was seeing someone, but I haven't met her yet... What if they come over here? What am I going to say when I meet her? Has he introduced her to the kids? Did he not *tell* me that he introduced her to the kids?" she lists off, fidgeting with her bracelet.

"Elizabeth, can you see how fast your thoughts are firing off? Let's slow things down for a minute," I say calmly. "Close your eyes and listen to my voice. Together we will gently slow everything down. Start by taking a deep breath into your belly. Notice the sensations your body is experiencing. What are they?"

"I feel a fluttering in my stomach, and my heart is beating fast," she reports.

"Great. That's excellent observing. Right now, there's no need to resist anything. Breathe in again and let the feeling take its course without trying to control any of it," I instruct.

She takes a few deep breaths, and her shoulders relax.

"How are you feeling now, Elizabeth?" I ask.

"A little better," she relays, her voice still unsteady.

"OK, we're going to add another element to your breathing. I want you to think of a time in your life when you were completely peaceful. For me, I always imagine a big, roaring bonfire and the smell of the wood burning." I inhale deeply, then return my attention to Elizabeth. "Can you think of something?" I ask.

"Yeah... I remember being in a lawn chair at the lake, watching the ripples in the water and hearing the frogs croak," she relays with a small smile.

"Now, visualize yourself being there. Notice how you feel now. Notice what's happening in your body when you allow yourself to soak up that relaxation," I instruct in a gentle tone.

"My heart is slowing back down," Elizabeth responds slowly.

"Good. Keep thinking of that image of that lake. Come back to thinking one thought at a time. Be the witness of the thoughts you're having, like the Observing Mind."

"Wow, I feel a lot calmer already. Why is that?" Elizabeth ponders.

"Oftentimes, when you start to feel immense anxiety, it's because you're caught in the Monkey's Mind's fast-firing thought pattern. You aren't in the present moment anymore—you're transported to a specific time when you felt similar anxiety in the past, or you're thinking about what might happen in the future, based on a past experience. Your body is responding to that memory or possibility," I explain.

"What do you mean?"

"Well, right now, as you're seeing Ted, what are you most afraid of?" I ask.

"Geez, a lot is coming up. I haven't actually seen Ted with another woman before... it's just a lot to take in. Like, what if she's awful? How would I handle that? I don't want Ted to think I'm some jealous ex-wife or something," she quickly relays.

"Look at what you just said about not wanting Ted to think you're jealous—can you see how that relates back to how you were always trying to get approval from him during your marriage? And, ultimately, how you tried to get approval from your dad growing up?

"God, no wonder I'm so anxious," Elizabeth says with a small laugh, her breath starting to return to normal.

"The key is to come back into the present moment from what we were just doing. By focusing on the sensations in your body—your breath, your heartbeat, the feeling in your stomach—you brought yourself back to the present," I explain.

"Yeah, I can feel that."

"After that, you took the time to bring the imagery of that safe, relaxed memory you have. What happened to the overwhelming thoughts from the Monkey Mind when you did this?" I prompt.

"I am feeling less anxious now. My heart beat, my breath... I feel like I can breathe again. I feel like I should have grown past these spikes of anxiety by now, though," she concedes.

"Remember Elizabeth, this is all a learning process. You're still going to get triggered, but how you respond is what is most important."

We continue to bring presence to Elizabeth's feelings and thoughts. Her anxiety subsides, and the color returns to her face. We do some deep breathing together and continue to bring her body back into the present moment. By slowing down her inner rhythm, Elizabeth is able to continue her session and turn her focus into looking at what core belief was driving her anxiety.

Take a moment and breathe deeply. Can you remember a time when you felt completely safe and at ease, like Elizabeth's memory of being at the lake? Breathe and keep the focus on that memory. Really experience yourself being there. In your mind's eye, bring back the smells, the relaxation of your muscles, the breeze on your skin.

After you have that moment in your mind, think of a time when you were very stressed and allow yourself to feel the emotions and sensations connected to this memory. As you feel the anxiety building, go back to your safe memory. See if you can slow yourself down and become present and calm by focusing on that imagery.

Bringing our attention to our body is one of the most effective ways to ground ourselves in an anxious moment. Coupling this with a memory of a more relaxed time allows us to slow down the barrage of thoughts and objectively look at the situation at hand. By doing this, we open ourselves up to a calmer, more present experience uninhibited by the voice of the Monkey Mind.

Chapter 22

BE PRESENT IN YOUR BODY

The Monkey Mind has been dominating our thoughts for most of our lives. We now have several tools in our belt, but it doesn't mean the Monkey Mind is simply going to stop talking altogether.

When you learn the skill of being present in your body, you break the constant monologue of the Monkey Mind and can witness your thoughts without getting hooked into them.

This process starts by breaking the cycle of fight-or-flight responses we are constantly reacting to in our lives. When this fight-or-flight reflex is triggered, we go through three phases in lightning speed:

1. We hear the words a person says.
2. We listen to the Monkey Mind translate what it thinks those words *"really"* mean.
3. We respond not to the person's actual statement, but to the unspoken message the Monkey Mind has convinced us that the person really meant.

This whole process takes place in a matter of microseconds. It's so fast that we're often not able to track it. Let's look at an example of a fight-or-flight response in real life.

∼

Paula is filling in for her sister at her niece's soccer game. One of the moms, Kelly, comes over and says, "Oh, you brought pizza for your team snack?"

Immediately, Paula's Monkey Mind hears, *Wow, you really brought that for the snack? Didn't you hear you're supposed to bring something healthy? You're so irresponsible.*

Paula goes into the fight response and angrily replies, "Yes, I did. Sorry I didn't have time to cut up orange slices for everyone." Paula then abruptly turns away, her face red from embarrassment and anger. Kelly is stunned—she had actually thought that pizza was a great idea for a snack.

See how the Monkey Mind can trick us into interpreting what people say as negative? Even Paula, who has been working on using her Observing Mind, still reacted with her knee-jerk response.

However, if you turn to your body instead of your mind in a difficult situation, you give yourself one of the greatest tools to separate from the Monkey Mind: Conscious Breath.

When you focus on your breathing, you disconnect from the Monkey Mind's voice. This is because Conscious Breath creates space for us to observe our thoughts, something most of us lack. It teaches us the benefit of sitting with our discomfort instead of constantly running away from it. As we develop the skill to breathe through our distress, the most amazing thing happens—the discomfort subsides.

If Paula had taken a breath instead of snapping back with a response, she may have been able to regulate herself before jumping to the conclusion that Kelly was criticizing her.

Can you think of a time in your own life when you overreacted to someone's comment, or misinterpreted it completely? Think of what your response would be to the following statements: Your boss saying, "You're still working on that project?" Your mother saying, "You're moving in together?" Your partner saying, "You bought a new sofa?"

Can you use your breath to create the space you need to identify what's really upsetting you? Try to see how many times you can go to your Conscious Breath today before responding to someone.

Without developing the ability to leave space, we forever get caught into the Monkey Mind's lightning-fast judgment and continue feeding our reactive fight-or-flight responses. Conscious Breath breaks the pattern of fight-or-flight. Conscious Breath interrupts the Monkey Mind.

PRACTICING CONSCIOUS BREATH

If we really want to let go of our anxiety, we need to know that Conscious Breath is not a one-time fix. Creating a daily Conscious Breath routine and sticking to it is the best way to incorporate this tool of awareness into our lives.

This routine can be challenging, because our Monkey Mind will be very present throughout. Its stories will become loud, and it will be very tempting to stop practicing the breath to avoid these thoughts.

However, the more we practice sitting and breathing through this anxiety, the more we'll see the immense benefits it can have.

Kevin is about to learn how he can incorporate Conscious Breath into his life to support his continued sobriety, as well as keep his Monkey Mind even more at bay.

~

When Kevin arrives to his session with me, he's feeling quite anxious. He admits, "I'm really proud of how far I've come, but I still feel like I'm struggling some days."

"What are you struggling with?" I ask.

"I feel like I still have so many of these negative thoughts consuming my mind. Some days, it's so overwhelming…" Kevin rubs his forehead. "Last week, for example, I decided I'm going to apply to go back to med school. I really am excited, but I just keep thinking how hard it's going to be and whether I'll be able to do it, and whether I'll be able to stay sober through it. I've noticed when I get in that state of mind, I snap at Jamie a lot more."

"What is a specific example of when you felt you snapped at Jamie?" I ask.

"Well, the other day, she asked me to take out the trash, and I just went into this outburst about why do I always have to take out the trash and why couldn't she do it… it was pretty embarrassing," Kevin discloses.

"Can you see how aware you're becoming, Kevin? To be able to recognize a specific situation so quickly?" I point out positively.

"I guess… but I'd love to be aware more of the time."

"How about I show you a specific breathing technique which will allow you to change some of those knee-jerk reactions?"

"Yeah, that sounds great," Kevin agrees, leaning back into his chair.

"It's called Conscious Breath. When you do Conscious Breath, you continually breathe in and out. It's helpful to imagine there's a large, blue balloon stretched over your chest and belly. When you breathe in, you fill the balloon. When you breathe out, you release air from the balloon."

"My whole chest should be rising, right?" he clarifies, looking down at his stomach unsurely as he tries this technique.

"Yes. With Conscious Breath, you want to fill up the balloon with as much air as you can, then release as much air as you can. It's like the tide of a wave, moving back and forth. You're continually breathing in and out."

"Like this?" Kevin asks, demonstrating the breath.

"Almost, but don't hold your breath at all, Kevin. Let the air flow— continuously filling and emptying the balloon," I explain.

"Oh, I see," Kevin confirms, watching me and glancing down at his own body.

"While you're doing this, *observe* the thoughts you are having. Don't try to empty your mind of thoughts, don't judge your thoughts, and don't give in to the Monkey Mind's story about your thoughts. Simply observe, and breathe," I instruct.

Kevin asks, "Do I close my eyes?"

"Don't close them, but drop your gaze and relax your eyes, so you're focusing on the floor in front of you. We eventually want you to get to the point where you can use this breath whenever you're feeling anxious, and that may happen at times when you need your eyes open," I explain.

"Yeah, like if I'm driving or something. Got it." He gives me a thumbs up.

"We're going to do this for two minutes, OK, Kevin?" I ask, setting a timer.

"Sounds good."

The alarm soon goes off. "OK, Kevin, I'm going to jot down the thoughts that went through your mind just now on the whiteboard.

What was the first thing you thought of when you were doing your breath?"

Kevin relaxes his shoulders. "Um, honestly, I wondered if I was doing the breath right," he admits with a chuckle.

"What was the next one?" I ask with a grin, writing this thought on the board.

Kevin chuckles again. "I actually thought about if I forgot to turn my coffee maker off before I left home."

"Next one?" I request.

"I wondered how much time was left of the two minutes…" Kevin confesses, his face getting the slightest rosy tint.

"And then what?"

Kevin looks around, searching his brain. "Ah! Then I thought about how I need to check if Dr. Puri sent me her recommendation letter for my med school application."

"Next?" I ask, writing this on the board.

"Then I started thinking about how I still need to write my personal statement for the application. I actually kind of started writing it in my head," Kevin says with a shrug.

"After that?" I ask.

"Uh… then I thought about how hungry I am. Then I thought about what I wanted to have for lunch," Kevin says with a cheeky smile.

I nod and step back from the board. "Perfect. Why don't we go ahead and read your thoughts off?"

> **Thought 1:** Am I doing the breath right?
> **Thought 2:** Did I leave the coffee maker on?
> **Thought 3:** How much of the two minutes is left?
> **Thought 4:** I need to check if Dr. Puri sent me her recomendation letter for my med school application.

> **Thought 5:** I need to write my personal statement for my application.
> **Thought 6:** Started writing my personal statement.
> **Thought 7:** I'm getting hungry.
> **Thought 8:** What should I have for lunch?

After I've read off these thoughts, I ask Kevin, "Now, what happened to your first thought of 'Am I doing the breath right?' once you thought of the coffee maker?"

"What do you mean 'what happened to it'?" Kevin inquires curiously.

"Well, you had the thought 'Am I doing this right,' but then what happened?" I ask.

"Well, then I started thinking about the coffee maker… so, the first thought went away, I guess?" he uncertainly responds.

"Exactly. And what happened to your thought about the coffee maker once you started wondering how much of the two minutes remained?"

"I stopped thinking about the coffee maker."

"Kevin, can you see how easily our thoughts come and go? How easily they are replaced by other thoughts?" I point out.

"Yeah, I can see that," he agrees with a strong nod.

"I would also guess that you had a lot more thoughts during that two-minute period than you named. So often we aren't aware of how many thoughts we have in an hour, let alone in a day. That's why I recommend using Conscious Breath—it gives you an opportunity to be witness to your thoughts. It can also give you some insight into how much you might obsess over one thought. For example, how long do you think you thought about your med school application?" I ask.

"Hmm… not exactly sure how long, but it was a while. And then that thought sent me off into thinking about writing my personal statement, and then I started writing it."

"Can you see how you're now starting to become aware of which thoughts are being replayed in your mind?" I ask.

"Yeah," Kevin agrees.

"While you're observing these thoughts and repeated ideas, you can also notice what feelings are being created. For example, how did you feel when you thought about the letter for your med school application?"

"I started feeling nervous," Kevin acknowledges.

"And what happened to that anxiety when you eventually moved on to 'I'm hungry'?" I bring up.

"I didn't really notice... but, I don't think I was nearly as anxious. Actually, I got kind of excited because I remembered that there's that great burrito place right down the street from here," Kevin says, his eyes lighting up at this possibility.

"So your anxiety ran its course, and then it was replaced by another emotion—happiness."

"Huh. I guess it did," Kevin affirms.

"With Conscious Breath, you're developing the skill to let go of solving any problem that your mind brings up. You don't need to work on your med school application, or even decide what you're having for lunch. When you sit with your breath, you're simply giving yourself a designated time to sit with any uneasy thoughts, so you can become aware of them. This is important because the majority of the time, we've unconsciously developed coping mechanisms to avoid our anxiety—ones that don't work. Like how you started drinking to numb your anxious feelings," I explain.

"I mean, in a way, that's our mind trying to help us, isn't it?" Kevin counters.

"You're right. Its goal is to shield us from the discomfort of the anxiety. But, it doesn't work so well to simply ignore our problems. Let's look back at your drinking to see why. You drank because there were thoughts that the Monkey Mind always replayed in your head.

Every time one of those self-judgments would come up, you'd buy into it and feel bad about yourself."

"I... Yeah... Can you explain that a little more?" Kevin asks, stumbling over this concept.

"Well, think about how you felt when you heard your most common judgments: 'It's weak to cry. Don't show emotion. You're a failure. You'll never be a good husband,'" I rattle off.

Kevin breathes deeply. "Ah, all *those* thoughts. Yeah, I'd feel pretty terrible about myself all the time."

"Exactly. And when you obsess about these thoughts, you are creating a lot of shame and anxiety in your body. And when you do that, what do you do? Or rather, what did you *used* to do?" I clarify.

"I'd drink to numb the anxiety," Kevin replies.

"Conscious Breath works to bring awareness to those anxiety-inducing beliefs so you don't build up such an overwhelming amount of stress. So let's do it again. Two more minutes of breathing, OK?" I ask.

Kevin nods and focuses his eyes on the floor. After a couple minutes, the timer sounds off once again.

"Ugh, that one was really uncomfortable," Kevin announces, stretching his back.

"Oh? What thoughts did you have this time?" I inquire.

"My first one was that I have to pick up milk before I go home," Kevin shares.

"Next one?"

"Next was my back hurts. After that I was wondering if this is really helping. Then I thought about my application for med school again for a while—about writing that statement again. Then I just started worrying about what happens if they don't like my statement. Or my recommendation letters. Then I wondered what if I don't get accepted. Um... I went down that rabbit hole for quite a while. Then I remembered that I hadn't called my mom back yet and need to do that. Then I noticed I was starting to hold my breath a little and tried to adjust that," he lists off quickly.

"See how you're already becoming more aware of your thoughts, Kevin? Now, let's focus on the feeling. What was the primary feeling you were experiencing during those two minutes?" I ask.

Kevin responds without missing a beat. "Anxious. Quite a few of those thoughts made me feel anxious, actually."

I nod. "The reason I wanted to do this with you, Kevin, is to show you how our thoughts are creating our anxiety. Most of us aren't in control of how our thought patterns affect us—our thoughts are constantly coming in, and we buy into all of them without question. And then, when we do have those judgmental thoughts pop up over and over again—like 'I'm a failure'—we start to feel defeated."

"Yeah, I can definitely relate to that feeling," Kevin agrees.

"What you're doing now is building the muscle to sit with your anxious thoughts. You're not trying to change the anxiety or get rid of it—you're allowing space for it, which eventually allows the anxiety to move through your body. And it isn't a cake walk to do this, Kevin. It takes practice. That's why we time ourselves when we go to our Conscious Breath—if we didn't, we'd almost always quit early. Some really tough thoughts can arise when you do this breath technique for a longer period of time—the thoughts that you've pushed to the very back of your mind to avoid."

Kevin sighs, running his fingers through his hair. "Yeah, I could already feel a little bit of that with the med school application. All I wanted to do was quit the breath and do something else. Or go actually work on the application."

I nod empathetically. "Just remember: you're doing this breath technique to break your pattern of avoiding your discomfort. You need to make space for it if you really want to change how you think and feel. And if you want to make a long-term change, you need to make this a daily habit."

"So, two minutes a day?" Kevin asks.

"Not quite. I usually recommend twenty minutes a day—twice a day."

He gasps. "Twenty! Two was hard enough, J.F...."

"You work yourself up to it gradually," I reassure him. "And when you get to the longer times, you begin breaking the pattern of avoiding your anxiety. When you address your anxiety in bite-size portions every single day, your anxiety no longer builds up to that overwhelming amount where you have to drink to escape it. The more you repeat your Conscious Breath, the stronger your muscle becomes to sit with your anxiety. And now, your body will start to associate *anxiety* with *breath*. So next time you're in some stressful situation, your new default response is to go to your *breath*."

"What do you mean?" Kevin clarifies, cranking his neck.

"Well, say you get cut off in traffic. How would you normally respond?" I illustrate.

"Well, if it's really out of nowhere, I may say some, uh, choice words," Kevin admits.

"If you practice Conscious Breath consistently, your normal response will eventually shift to taking a deep breath instead of swearing," I explain.

"Wow, that would be great to get to that point," Kevin agrees.

I respond, "If you want to use Conscious Breath as a tool to support you in staying sober, you need to make it a discipline and a priority."

"So if I'm not busy running from my anxiety and I've learned to go to my breath instead, then this will be another way to help me stay sober?"

"It can be your biggest ally, Kevin. Just imagine if next time Jamie asks if you took out the trash, you breathe instead of snapping back. Can you see how little changes like that would start to add up?"

"Yeah, I can definitely see that. Jamie and I would have fewer fights, and then I'd have less things to feel ashamed about, which was usually the main thing that drove me to drink," he acknowledges.

"By the way, how are you feeling in your body right now, Kevin? Do you feel calmer than when you first got here?" I bring up.

Kevin arches his back, his eyes shifting focus as he assesses his internal response. "You know... I actually do! But I don't quite understand why that is," he admits.

"That's one of the wonders of Conscious Breath. You never *seek* to become calmer before going to your breath. Your only goals are to focus on your breath and be the witness to your thoughts and feelings. But ultimately, this process makes you feel calmer naturally when you're done," I illustrate.

"Yeah, I can see that. Well, if I want to get to the point where I do this for *twenty* minutes in a row, I'm going to need quite a bit more help, J.F.," Kevin says with a smile.

Kevin is learning how Conscious Breath can be a powerful tool in managing his addiction and relieving his anxiety. When you do your own Conscious Breath pattern, the goal is to build up to this level of awareness.

When you first begin, as soon as you notice a judgment or find that you're trying to solve a problem, say to yourself, "Monkey Mind." For example, imagine you're breathing and your mind brings up, "I'm too tired to do this right now." First notice this is a judgment, then label it by saying, "Monkey Mind."

Continue to breathe. As soon as you notice the next thought that's trying to solve a problem, label it as well. While breathing, can you experience how labeling a thought as "Monkey Mind" creates space to not immediately buy into that thought?

By allowing ourselves space to experience our anxiety, it's

only a matter of time until we more naturally shift from the Monkey Mind to the Observing Mind.

The tools of awareness we've explored in this section of the book are subtle yet powerful. We can use them to direct our attention inward to clearly see our thoughts and feelings, and also release anxiety. We can identify which beliefs are guiding us towards happiness, and which are causing us suffering and pain. Once we can become aware of these aspects of ourselves without being swept up in the Monkey Mind's stories, we are in a powerful position.

When we use the tools of awareness, it's much like shining a spotlight onto a darkened stage; suddenly, we can see everything clearly and the stage of our inner world becomes visible. As our beliefs dance in and out of the spotlight, we can examine their motives and decide which ones we want to keep in our production, and which beliefs we want to change.

All of this happens inside us; we're no longer focused on the outside world. It is here, on the inside, where we can seize control of our scripts and rewrite them to be whatever we desire. But seeing and rewriting are two very different activities. We need additional tools to actually change those beliefs—to eliminate the mind's nasty characters and promote the positive ones.

For that job, we will need a powerful tool we call Mindful Inquiry.

Part 5

MINDFUL INQUIRY

Chapter 23

QUESTION YOUR MINDSET

In this section, I'm going to show you how you can use Mindful Inquiry to further shift your unconscious programming. Throughout this book, you've already seen examples of how Mindful Inquiry is a powerful tool used by the Observing Mind to create awareness and clarity. By asking the right questions, you can release yourself from the anxiety-inducing grip of the Monkey Mind.

As we've discussed, most of us are stuck listening to the Monkey Mind's monologue, which sees the world through the lens of our programming. It insists that its narration of what's happening in the moment is the truth, and many times we automatically believe its stories, no matter how absurd they are or what kind of feeling they create.

Mindful Inquiry allows you to start a dialogue with your thoughts and put yourself in control of how you respond to life's outer circumstances. The process begins with the Observing Mind passively watching your thought patterns without taking action. When you notice a strong thought, the Observing Mind steps forward and begins to ask questions. *Why do you believe that thought? Is it really true? What words did he actually say? What are you feeling right now? Is it possible that this is a story?*

The Observing Mind listens carefully, then asks questions. It tests each thought, bringing new awareness. It doesn't assume that it already knows the answers. It knows that you don't have to believe these thoughts or be attached to them—you can simply observe and let them go.

No matter what personal challenges you may be faced with, whether it's alcohol or drug use, depression, anxiety, or relationship issues, you can use Mindful Inquiry to cut through the Monkey Mind's crippling perspective. Bless yourself with the gift of consciously questioning your thoughts, appreciate your honest answers, and create lasting presence and peace in your life.

BE CURIOUS

Mindful Inquiry begins by simply being curious and looking for what you don't know—this is where you will find your clarity and happiness.

For many of us, we don't always have this carefree approach to the unfamiliar. We tend to experience an uneasiness when it comes to things we don't know. Some people are even hooked into the belief that they should already have all the answers, so anything foreign can be viewed as a kind of threat.

Realistically, asking questions and maintaining a curious perspective is a sign of intelligence. The simple fact of acknowledging that there are things we don't know, and that we want to learn, raises our consciousness.

~

Jamie and Kevin are enjoying their six-year anniversary in their newly inspired and authentic relationship. They are celebrating by going to Paris and staying at a new hotel in the 16th arrondissement. On Sunday morning, as they dress for breakfast, Jamie realizes she is missing the necklace Kevin gave her Friday evening.

Her Monkey Mind launches into its trademark drama. *Someone stole your necklace! You just had it yesterday, and now it's vanished! That maid probably swiped it when you were at lunch. What kind of hotel is this? You better call the front desk right now and demand to speak to a manager. What is Kevin going to think? It probably was your fault—you're so scatterbrained.*

Jamie's heart instinctively starts to race. She erratically starts looking around the hotel room for the lost jewelry, and Kevin notices her peculiar behavior.

"Everything OK?" he questions curiously.

"I can't find my emerald necklace," Jamie frantically responds, ducking her head under the bed.

"Oh… OK, let me help you look for it," Kevin offers, running his hand through his hair as he scans the room.

"That'd be great. Ugh, I'm so sorry," Jamie ashamedly replies, pulling the covers off the bed. She can't seem to catch her breath.

"It's fine, Jamie. We'll find it," Kevin assures her with a warm smile, taking a deep breath.

Kevin's thoughtful breath reminds Jamie to go to her own Conscious Breath. This deep breath allows space for Jamie's Observing Mind to pipe up and ask, *Why is this making you so anxious?*

She stops her search and takes a few breaths before responding. Now, she's better prepared to have this conversation.

"Thanks for not yelling at me, honey. A couple years ago you would ice me out whenever I lost anything… I think I was still kind of bracing myself for that," Jamie admits.

"Well, that's the old me," Kevin replies lovingly, coming over to Jamie and giving her a kiss on the forehead. "So what do you think we could do to remember where you last put it?"

"Mindful Inquiry!" Jamie announces loudly, jogging over to the desk to grab a pen and paper. "Will you ask me some questions, Kevin?" Jamie requests.

"Of course, honey. Why are you anxious right now?" he asks.

"I lost my necklace."

"Why does that make you feel anxious?"

"I feel like it's my fault," Jamie says sheepishly.

Kevin walks over to his wife and takes her hand in his. "Even if it is your fault, why does that make you upset? Aren't you allowed to make mistakes?" he asks gently.

"I guess I am being hard on myself right now," she acknowledges with a deep breath.

As Jamie answers the questions, she can feel her anxiety lifting from her body. She decides to take over the role of the Observing Mind and begins to utilize it in a very practical way: by writing down every question she can think of that could lead to the necklace's hiding place.

Has it really been stolen? When was the last time you saw it? Were you wearing it when you undressed for bed on Friday night? Have you looked in the obvious places, like your purse or jacket pockets? Has it fallen behind the dresser or the nightstand? Did you hide it somewhere unusual for safekeeping?

"That's it!" Jamie cheers aloud.

She runs over to her suitcase and unzips an outer compartment. Inside lies a secret pocket, and sure enough, she reaches in and feels the necklace's chain.

"I put it in here to keep it safe! I can't believe I forgot that," Jamie says with a wide smile.

Kevin puts the necklace around Jamie's neck. He puts his arms around her, and they admire the sparkling jewelry in the mirror. As she looks at herself, Jamie is proud she was able to remain curious and maintain her composure to find this treasure. Now, the couple can appreciate this beautiful moment without those nagging comments from the Monkey Mind.

Take a moment and think of something you regret doing. Listening to the Monkey Mind, say to yourself, "You're so stupid. Why did you do that?" How does it feel? Do you even want to know the answer?

Think of something else you regret doing. This time, say, "You did the best you knew how. What do you think could have led up to this?" How does it feel this time? Can you see how you can't be judgmental and curious at the same time?

In everyday, stressful situations like this, the Monkey Mind is focused on rehashing the problem while the Observing Mind is looking for a solution. Its open-mindedness and curiosity will win the day and spare you from unnecessary anxiety.

Chapter 24

ASK GENUINE QUESTIONS

When you use Mindful Inquiry to ask questions, make sure to notice if you're coming from a place of judgment. If you are, the questions will only strengthen the Monkey Mind. Angrily shouting "WHY DIDN'T YOU CALL ME?" is not a question. It's an accusation that ends with a question mark. This is just a judgment in disguise.

When you're in judgment, you're coming from the Monkey Mind's point of view. It is not interested in the answer; it's just making its point. It has already decided what the correct answer is, and it's trying to trick you into agreeing with it. This will never lead to a new solution. The real focus is not on a missed call, or on starting a real conversation, but on proving the Monkey Mind's judgmental story.

At the same time, our Monkey Minds are so predisposed to judging that it's hard to let go and listen to a question for what it is. Instead, we hear genuine questions as accusations and become defensive. If we can release our self-loathing and shift our focus to genuinely asking and listening to questions, we can create stronger, deeper connections with the people in our lives.

Let's look at how Kevin's brother, Patrick, uses Mindful Inquiry to avoid falling into a judgmental perspective.

~

After being at his new job for several months, Patrick has already been promoted and is loving what he's doing. One day, he receives an email that an important client had not yet received the shipment they ordered a week before. Patrick goes into his tracking system and realizes that his employee Mason hadn't sent out the order. His Monkey Mind furiously goes directly into blame.

What are you paying him for if he can't even do his job? This was a huge contract, and now it's all in jeopardy because Mason couldn't make sure this got done. This is the third order he hasn't sent out on time in the last two months. He doesn't deserve to work here. You should fire him. You could find someone much more efficient.

Fortunately, Patrick's Observing Mind takes over and instructs him to take a deep breath before speaking to Mason. Then it reminds Patrick to ask Mason a question rather than accuse him of doing something wrong.

Patrick approaches Mason and kindly asks, "Mason, I just found out that you never sent off the Wilson order last week. I'm starting to see a pattern of you dropping things. Is anything going on for you?"

"This job is very stressful—that's what's going on for me! I'm expected to juggle a hundred balls, and then I'm scolded when I can't. I'm sorry I'm not a superhero, Patrick," Mason shoots back angrily. His defensive Monkey Mind is clearly in full force right now.

Mason's comments trigger Patrick's defensiveness, but he remains calm and fights the urge to run to his Monkey Mind. He focuses on remaining open-minded.

"Mason, three other people have the same position as you, and they are all able to keep their orders on track. How would you explain this?" he asks in a calm tone.

"I'm sorry if I don't want to work sixty hours a week like they all do! I actually enjoy having a life!" Mason scoffs.

Patrick is about to call out Mason's excuses, but the memory of the last employee he fired at his old position pops into his head. Patrick had become very reactive, engaging in a yelling match with this employee in the middle of the office. Not only did this relationship end very poorly, but everyone in the office had a lesser opinion of Patrick because of the experience.

This time, Patrick decides to stick with a loving attitude. "They each work forty hours a week, with very minimal overtime. Now let's switch the focus back to you, Mason. Why do you think you keep missing orders?"

Mason doesn't give up that easily. "Because I'm not as fast? I'm not as smart? Sorry I can't be like the other stars on your team, Patrick. I'm doing the best I can."

"When you first started working here, you didn't miss any orders. Have your abilities changed since then?" Patrick points out nonjudgmentally.

"Seriously? You know I had less orders to keep track of back then!" Mason shouts back.

Patrick takes a deep breath, trying to call upon all the compassion in his body. He keeps his Monkey Mind at bay and remains centered.

"Mason, can I point out an observation I've seen with you?"

Mason nods slightly with a shrug of his shoulders.

"Before these last few months, you've always done an excellent job. But lately, I don't see the spring in your step anymore. When I've seen this shift in employees in the past, it meant their heart wasn't in their work anymore." Patrick pauses and rests his arm against Mason's tan cubicle wall. "There's nothing wrong with that, Mason. We all change and want different things from our careers. I just want to make sure that you're still enjoying what you're doing."

Mason takes a deep breath and lays his face in his hands, rubbing his temples. When he lifts his head, there is a much more relaxed man looking back at Patrick.

"I didn't realize it was so obvious. A few months back, I started helping one of my friends with some photography gigs on the weekends. I had no idea how interesting it would be. Now, it's all I think about. Even on my breaks here, I'm looking up different techniques and cameras… I've been so distracted. I think that might be what's been dragging me down lately. Especially after my friend offered me a full-time job with him last week…" Mason states, looking down at his feet.

"That's nothing to be ashamed of, Mason. I fully believe that everyone should pursue what they're passionate about," Patrick says, staying nonjudgmental and giving Mason a confidence boost.

"Man, that's pretty terrifying though. I've never done anything like this! I mean, I want to, but it's just so daunting. And you'll be without a worker," Mason points out, his Monkey Mind threatening to squash his dream.

Patrick gives him a reassuring smile. "Don't worry about us. You leaving allows space for someone else to join our team who *is* passionate about the work we do. How about this to make the transition easier: for the next month, we'll taper down your hours and have you switch to part time in a few weeks. This gives us time to find your replacement, and also gives you time to get your ducks in a row. What do you think?"

"That's really nice of you to offer that, Patrick. But this is such a big leap for me… is it OK if I sleep on it?"

"Of course. But I do want you to consider what you'll do if you don't take that leap. You'll keep working here and keep wishing you were out there with a camera. Is that something you really want?"

"I know. I'll be sure to give you an answer by the end of the week, one way or the other," Mason quietly responds, spinning his wedding ring around his finger.

"Sounds like a plan. Have a great night, Mason," Patrick says, lightly patting Mason's shoulder as he walks away.

When Patrick gets back to his office, he's filled with pride in himself. Instead of a disastrous firing situation, Patrick was able to listen to his Observing Mind to help Mason discover what he really wanted. Additionally, Patrick was able to let go of any judgments he had about Mason, and he wasn't shaming himself about how Mason's behavior reflected upon him. Instead, Patrick remained present and genuinely connected with his employee, which resulted in a mature conversation.

Think back to the last argument you had. Did you ask any rhetorical questions that you didn't really expect the person to answer? Name the judgments behind the question. When you name them, imagine someone is saying these judgments to you. How does it feel to receive those judgments?

Now, rephrase the question in a non-judgmental way. How does it feel this time?

When faced with an uncomfortable situation, use these tools to ask genuine questions and release your judgments about the other person and yourself, and you will more effortlessly find a resolution.

Chapter 25

WHAT QUESTIONS TO ASK

When learning the science of what questions to ask during Mindful Inquiry, the ultimate goal is to address and change the core beliefs we hold about ourselves. But how exactly do we go about asking the right questions to reach those deep-seated beliefs?

What questions to ask will depend on what indicator we are using to alert ourselves that a core belief is at play. For example, if we notice we are extremely sad, we would want to question that emotion to get to the deeper belief at play. Other times, we may notice that we're tapping our foot incessantly during an uncomfortable conversation. In that situation, we would want to use questions centered around that physical response.

When we're already quite aware, we may notice when we're experiencing an external belief about someone else or a situation, like "He's so rude when he smacks his gum." Then we would follow this outside belief until we track it back to an inner-focused belief.

Finally, once we've done a great deal of work on our programming, we'll be able to identify the coping mechanisms we use in difficult situations. Maybe we make a joke when someone talks about something we're uncomfortable with, or we smoke cigarettes to unwind after an extra tough day. Once we recognize these strategies within ourselves, we can begin to notice them and ask deeper questions to see what was making us feel uncomfortable or anxious in the first place.

In this chapter, we will explore each of these indicators, so we know how to address them as they pop up in our daily lives.

QUESTION THE WAY YOU FEEL

As we've seen, emotions are a compass to lead us back to our beliefs. In Mindful Inquiry, we question all of our emotions to quickly cut through the mind's chatter and get to the underlying issues at play.

One of the main focuses of Mindful Inquiry is to consistently question the way we feel. For example:

How do you feel about Susie yelling at you?

How do you feel about being relocated to Dallas?

How do you feel about putting your father in a nursing home?

When we question our emotions, we now have an opportunity to address the limiting beliefs behind them.

To picture this, imagine you're at a restaurant waiting for a friend to arrive, only to receive a call that they aren't going to make it. How do you feel in this moment?

Many of us might respond to this situation with a feeling of sadness. After questioning this emotion and recognizing the Monkey Mind's story, we find the belief, "I must have done something wrong." Now with a clear belief in hand, we can check and see if this is our old programming being triggered. Is the belief that we did something wrong a common belief that tries to sabotage us? If so, we can now clearly see how our sadness doesn't actually have to do with the friend being unable to join for dinner, but rather stems from this negative belief we hold about ourselves.

Many people don't believe they should have feelings at all, so questioning them can be difficult at first. However, when you do question your emotions, it's important to always hold the nonjudgmental attitude of the Observing Mind. Remember, emotions are the smoke detectors that will lead to your deeper beliefs—that is how you will ultimately change your behavior and self-defeating programming.

Question Your Physical Responses

In addition to our feelings, Mindful Inquiry questions every physical response we have to a situation—something we often ignore when we're caught up in a reaction. However, our physical responses can give us valuable clues as to what is going on inside our minds, the same way our feelings do. Once you've developed the skill to notice your physical responses, it's a shortcut to get to your beliefs.

Let's see what knowledge we can gain from observing our bodies' red flags.

While returning his rental car after a business trip, Ted is informed by the desk clerk that he's going to be charged for a small dent on the hood. In response, Ted raises his voice. His Monkey Mind goes after the worker. *Who is this guy? Why does he think he can con you into paying for this? You show him you're not going to back down!*

Red flag/Physical response: loud voice

Ted's Observing Mind notices this physical cue, so it asks Ted, *Hmm, you raised your voice just now. What emotion is that linked to?*

Now that he's aware of his anger, Ted can start to get to the belief that is feeding this fire.

Let's look at another example. In a meeting at work, Gabriela's boss asks if anyone has graphic design experience for a new project. Although she enjoys working with graphic design, Gabriela remains silent and avoids eye contact with anyone. Her Monkey Mind starts berating her. *Are you seriously not going to say anything? You love to design! You're wasting a huge opportunity. You're so pathetic.*

Red flag/Physical response: avoiding eye contact

Instead of punishing herself more, Gabriela's Observing Mind comes on board and takes her lack of eye contact as a red flag. Her Observing Mind tracks this physical clue to connect to an emotion—fear—and then uses the fear to find the deeper core belief at play.

Sometimes, physical responses are automatic, like when the physician taps your knee at the doctor's office and your leg goes up. However, more often than not, your physical responses are linked to beliefs.

Paula is at her parents' home eating dinner. Her father brings up a recent election and her mother slams her palm on the table. Paula's body flinches in response.

Is her body simply reacting to a loud noise? Or is there something of bigger meaning hiding here?

Paula's Monkey Mind's comments soon reveal the answer. *Don't say anything else about this. She'll find a way to blame you for this. Just change the subject.*

Red flag/Physical response: flinch

Paula's Observing Mind picks up on the flinch and uses that physical signal to hone in on to an emotion—fear. Now, she can start to uncover the core belief that is being triggered in this moment: the belief that she's doing something wrong.

Can you think of your own default physical responses that occur when you get triggered? Do you become quiet? Do you walk away? Do you nervously laugh? Do you bite your nails? Do your cheeks flush? Did any of these responses show up during your last argument? What about after the argument ended?

The next time you become upset, try to keep your physical red flags at the forefront of your awareness and question them. By doing so, you get a direct path to finding the emotions behind them, as well as the core beliefs that created the emotions in the first place.

QUESTION YOUR EXTERNAL BELIEFS

Earlier, we looked at the many different types of beliefs we can have: beliefs about ourselves, or a particular person, or what's right or wrong, or about the world in general. Most of our beliefs are external—about other people and circumstances—and when we focus on these, we get stuck repeating the same patterns over and over again. With Mindful Inquiry, we question our external beliefs so we can get to our core beliefs and, ultimately, regain control of our lives.

Let's see how questioning external beliefs can lead us to a core belief.

After embracing the perspective of the Observing Mind, Paula has been more authentic and vulnerable with her husband than ever before. However, she finds herself getting frustrated when she opens her heart to him, only to get short, one-sentence answers in return.

Paula is believing that her husband should be more open with her. This is an external belief she holds about someone outside herself. When using Mindful Inquiry, she questions this belief: "Why do I believe James should be more open?"

Through this questioning, Paula realizes that she is assuming her husband is rejecting her if he doesn't open up. After questioning why this perceived rejection is triggering her, she eventually gets to the core belief: "I'm not important."

We start by questioning external beliefs, because they're easier to identify than our deeply held core beliefs. Most of us don't realize how deep our pool of beliefs is until we start examining it.

Think about something that you want to change about someone else, like how Paula wanted her husband to open up more. What is the belief you hold about yourself that makes you want to focus on the other person?

When we use Mindful Inquiry, it puts us back in charge. When we no longer base our importance on other people's behaviors or on outside circumstances, we can fully enjoy and connect with those around us. On the outside nothing has changed, but the internal shift is enormous.

QUESTION YOUR COPING MECHANISMS

We've all developed different coping mechanisms for dealing with problems. We think these strategies are benefiting us in some way—and perhaps they did help at one time—but now they're only sabotaging our behavior. It's amazing how often we limp along in life with coping mechanisms that create just as much damage as they do success.

Remember when Paula had lunch with four friends at the Chinese restaurant? Susan was feeling irritated by the waiter's incompetence, Greg was nervous thinking about the rejection of a promotion, and Lucy was feeling heartbroken after a recent breakup. They were all having very different experiences based on the exact same situation, for a variety of reasons.

However, one variable that heavily influenced each of their responses was how they learned to cope with stress. Let's take a look at the coping mechanisms Paula's friends use and see what happens when we question them.

~

Susan, an analytical woman who handles the investments at a large firm, receives a call from her financial management company. Because of a computer glitch, they weren't able to make the complicated stock transaction she had ordered. She's furious and spends the next fifteen minutes unloading her anger over the phone to a person whose name she doesn't even remember. When Susan doesn't get her way, she gets angry. After growing up with a controlling mother who gave her little say in her own life, Susan views this strategy as positive, because she at least has a voice in the situation.

Greg is tight-lipped and conservative, especially about money. He never discusses finances where anyone might overhear and learn too much about his situation. When growing up, Greg often witnessed his parents arguing over money. His father was driven by the anxiety that came from his high-pressure position, and he would act out that anxiety with his wife. Today, Greg is no different than his father. He believes that his worry and fear keep him focused and aware of his own financial situation.

Lucy, a very image-conscious woman, is depressed. She hates her life. She stays home night after night, trapped in a cycle of destructive shame, listening to the Monkey Mind tell her what a wimp she is. She hates her domineering mother, yet feels obligated to smile and pretend that everything's OK. Every night, when the discomfort gets too intense, Lucy finds relief by taking a few sleeping pills.

The Monkey Mind believes that these strategies are working just fine, and that the problems they are facing are caused by the world around them. The Observing Mind, though, wants to question these coping mechanisms to see how well they are delivering the desired result. It doesn't put much stock in what other people do or don't do. Its emphasis is on what *you* do and what *you* feel.

This is worth repeating: the Observing Mind wants to question the strategies to see how well they are delivering the desired result. This is extremely valuable information. Be honest with yourself, and you're halfway home.

If I were to sit down with each of these three people, I would bring awareness to their coping mechanism and question its effectiveness in their life.

I'd ask Susan, "Is it true that the very best way to take care of yourself is to be angry? Honestly, what happens when you get angry?"

Susan would reply, "Sometimes, I get what I want, and I enjoy that victory. But lately, I've been feeling ashamed afterwards, which makes me want to jump even harder at the next person who crosses me. When this doesn't work, I get really pissed off—excuse me, miffed—and feel frustrated for a while."

I'd ask Greg, "Is it true that the very best way to take care of yourself is to be scared about money? Honestly, what happens when you do that?"

Greg would reply, "I do keep on top of my finances, but there are emotional consequences that bother me. I often feel unhappy and uptight, and I've been told I'm cold with people. I worry a lot. Everyone seems to be having fun but me. And now my wife claims I'm smothering her."

I'd ask Lucy, "Is it true that the very best way to take care of your depression is to misuse drugs? Honestly, what happens when you do that?"

Lucy would reply, "I feel a temporary reprieve while I'm asleep. But each week, I have to keep increasing my dosage to fall asleep. And now, I've started sleepwalking down the stairs, and that scares me. I'm even hiding it from my mom because I know she'd make me stop. Then, in the morning, I'm still depressed about my life. Most mornings I don't even want to get out of bed."

By questioning the result of an established coping mechanism, you start to dissect the benefit —or harm—that strategy is providing.

These mechanisms are always tied back to a core belief. For Susan, the belief she holds about herself is that she is weak if she doesn't get her way. By reacting out of anger, Susan is trying to mask this belief. If she wants to balance her anger, she needs to address this core belief and see that her strength as a person is not dependent on getting her way.

For Greg, the belief he holds is that if he's not anxious, he is irresponsible. Worry and fret are the strategies he has developed to keep his life in order. When he questions this belief, he'll start to see how he can be calm, yet still keep track of his finances.

For Lucy, she believes that she's never good enough. The strategy she has created to stop herself from feeling this belief is to numb her mind with drugs. If she addresses this core belief and learns to be accepting of herself, she'll feel less compelled to continue her drug habit.

Think of something you do repetitively that doesn't work and consistently leaves you frustrated, like how Greg was always anxious about money or how Susan used anger to get her way. Then think of a few examples of what happens when you utilize your strategy.

What feeling are you left with? How do the people around you respond to you? Do you get the result you're looking for? How efficient is your strategy? What is the hidden belief that is keeping your ineffective strategy alive?

It's helpful to write down the answers to these questions, because oftentimes we brush off our coping mechanisms—putting them on paper helps us become conscious of the pattern.

When we question our strategies and address the hidden beliefs that are fueling them, we empower ourselves to toss out the hurtful coping mechanisms we've developed over the years. From this place, we can start to develop new, beneficial strategies to help us maintain healthy and authentic lives.

Chapter 26

THE MINDFUL INQUIRY PROCESS

Now that we've learned about each phase of the Mindful Inquiry method, let's see how the process unfolds when we combine all the pieces together.

I'm going to walk you through the Mindful Inquiry process, using a session with Paula as an example, so you can learn why we ask the questions we do. In this dialogue, I will be acting as Paula's Observing Mind, and I will show the steps I take to remain focused to move through the different tools of Mindful Inquiry. After witnessing the specific questions asked and reasoning behind these questions, you can begin to apply this inquiry method to your own life.

∾

Although Paula is starting to use her Observing Mind more often, her Monkey Mind is so strong that she still finds herself getting sucked into its story. She has managed to stop taking her anti-anxiety pills, but the anxiety from the Monkey Mind makes her worry that she might start using again.

Paula walks into our session with a huff. She exclaims, "No matter how much I try, James *always* knows how to push my buttons!"

I don't get sucked into the Monkey Mind's story; I am simply curious about the event. "What happened?" I ask.

"Well, yesterday, I went shopping and found this *beautiful* Persian rug with these maroon accents—it's just gorgeous! I was so excited for them to deliver it and see how it looked in the family room. And after they did, James got home from work and started yelling at me for not talking to him before buying it and how he didn't like it, and I need to return it! It was so inconsiderate of him!" Paula shoots off.

I now have a picture of the situation, so I shift my focus to Paula's response. "Imagine you're back in the moment where you're fighting with James, Paula. What was your first reaction to James yelling at you?"

"At first, I tried to ignore him," Paula replies.

"How did you do that?"

"Well... I wouldn't look at him while he was going off on me," she explains with a huff.

I recognize a physical response and question it to uncover her emotion. "Why wouldn't you look at him?" I clarify.

"I couldn't look at him. I couldn't talk to him. It's no use trying to reason with him when he's like that. So I just stormed off," Paula scoffs, looking out the window at the rain.

I question her strategy to see how well it is working. "How come?"

"I was just so mad. I couldn't think of anything else to do," she defends.

Ah, now we have a clear emotion. I question it and stay focused on Paula's response, rather than buying into the Monkey Mind's story. "What's the reason you were so angry with him?" I ask.

"I was angry because James is such a control freak!" she announces.

I recognize an external belief about someone else that distracts from Paula's own internal beliefs. I question the judgment by first clarifying, instead of quickly agreeing.

"A control freak. What exactly do you mean by that?" I ask.

"Everything has to be exactly the way he wants. I feel like half the time he doesn't even want to hear my opinion," Paula insists.

I question the emotion instead of buying into the story, looking for the belief that is causing it. "I hear that you don't like his behavior. But let's go back to the original situation for a moment. Why are you upset if he wants you to return the rug?" I inquire.

"Because I don't like it when he tells me what to do!" Paula argues.

"Oh, yes, that can be hard for anyone to hear. But let's go a little deeper now. Why don't you like it when James tells you what to do?" I ask.

"I feel less-than when he does that. It's like he's telling me I did something wrong," Paula admits hoarsely.

"And if you think you did something wrong, what does that mean about you?"

"That I'm a bad wife," she says, closing her eyes sadly.

I see that we're getting to a core belief, so I take my questions in that direction.

"Stay with that emotion, Paula. There's a leap you're making that may or may not be true. Listen closely: if he's telling you to return the rug, why do you believe that this means you're a bad wife?" I ask.

"Oh, that sounds so stupid," she quickly dismisses.

I look for clarity. "How so?" I ask.

"How is it stupid? I mean, me thinking I'm a bad wife for him not liking a *rug* is insane!" she persists.

I see that Paula is refining her core belief, so I ask her for verification. "Look, Paula, on one hand, we have his remarks about the rug. On the other, we have the assumption that you're not a good wife. You seem to have linked those two things together. Why do you believe that if he tells you to take the rug back to the store that you're a bad wife?"

Paula has put the source of her value outside herself, where she has no power, so I am seeking the internal belief that is within her power to change.

"The more you say it, the more ridiculous it sounds," Paula scoffs.

I make space for further exploration. "How is it ridiculous? What are you thinking right now?" I ask.

"Well, I'm thinking about what you've been teaching me... the rug can't really be the reason I feel this upset. It's just a rug after all! Somehow, I must have been believing I was a bad wife even before James said anything about the rug..." Paula reflects, getting lost in her thoughts.

One of the major causes of suffering is the core belief that we are good or bad, so I question that self-judgment.

"That's quite an insight, Paula. Let's set aside James' opinion of the rug for a moment and come back to you. How do *you* decide if you are good or bad?" I inquire.

Paula laughs. "That's a good question."

I gently repeat the question until there's a clear answer. "What's your answer?"

"Wow! I can't believe this! I guess I always let other people decide. If people don't like what I do, I think I'm doing something wrong... it's all going back to that feeling that I don't fit in, like I felt with Robin and those girls in high school. If they thought I was doing something wrong, I thought I was doing something wrong," Paula says, releasing a frustrated breath.

Now, Paula is really getting some clarity about her core beliefs. She's seeing right through the stories. The focus is in the right place now. I shine the light of awareness here to take a closer look.

"In this particular situation with the rug, why did you decide that you're doing something wrong?" I further question.

"Honestly, anytime James yells at me I feel like I'm doing something wrong," she says with a sigh.

This is a clear belief, confidently stated. I am curious to test it out.

"You think that your husband yelling at you means you've done something wrong. Why do you believe that?" I inquire.

"I can't stand this! My husband would probably say I'm great if I did what he wanted... Hmm. That means I only feel like I'm good when he's happy with me," Paula observes, her eyebrows furrowing.

I encourage her to look at the same belief from different angles, checking it out. Is it solid? Is it true? Is it useful?

"Let's examine this more closely: why do you believe that if your husband is happy with you, that means you are a good wife?" I continue.

"This is so frustrating!"

"It might be easier to picture it like this, Paula—if you ask me for an apple, and I don't give it to you, does that mean I'm doing something right or wrong? Or that I'm a good or bad person for not giving you the apple?" I illustrate.

"Well, no, that's stupid." Paula says more confidently, sitting up straighter.

Paula is realizing that "good" and "bad" don't actually apply here. She's questioning her own beliefs now.

She huffs. "Can you believe that I have lived most of my life thinking this way? Looking for approval from my husband? If *he* likes me, *I* like me. Yuck!"

This is the moment of realization. The old belief cracks and crumbles.

"That's the belief that creates your suffering, Paula—'If he likes me, I like me.' How does it feel to see that?" I ask.

Paula looks directly at me. "It's hard to digest."

I look for more clarification. "How so?"

"Because I've been looking for his approval for so many years..." Paula says, biting her lip once more anxiously.

Paula realizes how long she's been suffering with this core belief. I shift her back into the present.

"It takes however long it takes, Paula. Let's stay focused on the present for right now. It still comes back to the same question: why do you believe that you're bad if your husband is angry about you buying the rug?" I inquire.

"This is just plain nonsense. If my husband is happy or unhappy, it's because of his own reasons—not because of me," Paula confidently states.

When the old belief is released, often a new and refined belief spontaneously rushes in to take its place. I help Paula explore how this new thought affects her emotions.

"How does it feel to see that?" I bring up.

"I feel relieved," Paula emphasizes, taking a deep breath.

"Now, Paula, close your eyes. Imagine the scene with James again, where he's really angry with you, and he says, 'Take that rug back to the store!' How do you feel now?" I ask.

She keeps her eyes closed for several moments. "When I imagine James being mad at me, I *still* feel like I'm bad somehow," she admits with a confused shake of her head.

I continue to question assumptions of good and bad.

"How does James being angry about the rug make you bad?" I question.

Paula has a distressed look on her face. "It's the *way* he says it to me. It's so accusatory."

Another replay of that old belief; I question it again.

"And you believe that? How come?" I ask.

"Ugh, I feel like I'm going in circles! I guess I am pretty attached to what he thinks about me," Paula admits with wide eyes.

We're getting closer; I stay focused on what's happening inside Paula.

"It seems like you have a pattern of defining yourself based on your husband's and friends' opinions of you, Paula. Why is this your way of deciding whether you're good or bad?" I ask.

"I think I've just always done that," she quickly relays.

"What do you mean?"

"Well, even when I was little, I would seek my mom's approval for everything I did. And a lot of times, she didn't approve of what I wanted to do… Like I remember one summer, I wanted to go to this science camp, and my mom wouldn't even entertain the idea. I remember she physically ripped up the permission slip I had gotten from school. She signed me up for this dance camp instead, even though I really didn't want to do it. After that, anytime I thought about wanting to do another science thing, I just felt so embarrassed about it that I'd get this awful knot in my stomach, and I wouldn't even bring it up to my mom. I truly thought that there was something wrong with a girl liking science." Paula takes a deep breath. "I haven't thought about that in a long time."

"Given that this happened to you with your mom growing up, how come today, when your husband asks you to take back the rug, you feel like you did something wrong?"

She closes her eyes and pauses. "You know, when you ask me that, I feel that same knot in my stomach."

I notice and question the re-occurring feeling.

"Why do you think that is?" I inquire.

"I think it's because that feeling of wanting others to like what I do is so engrained in me. Almost every day I feel the knot in my stomach, but I've never really thought about it. When I do… I feel like a child. Like I'm still constantly looking for Mom's approval. But James isn't my mother. Robin isn't my mother. I don't need anyone's approval but my own," Paula responds firmly.

"How do you feel to see that?" I inquire.

"I feel angry," Paula quietly acknowledges, clenching her jaw.

"How come?"

"I'm angry that I have been holding on to this for so long! No wonder I feel like I need anti-anxiety pills to relax! Why can't I love myself? Why can't *I* decide who *I* am?" Paula shouts.

I stay calm and patient as Paula goes through her emotions.

"What's your answer?" I ask.

"You know what, I can! I love my husband, but I can't let him define me. I get to do that myself!" Paula triumphantly declares.

Breakthrough! Paula is dropping old beliefs and generating empowering new ones.

"How does it feel to see that?" I point out.

"Good. No, great! I'm not bad. I'm. Not. Bad! I can't believe I have kept this up for so long! I'm a caring and loving woman. I may have some quirks, but I'm not *bad*," Paula repeats strongly.

I am looking to see what emotions are created by each belief.

"How does it feel to say that?"

"Awesome!" Paula breaks out into a radiant smile. "I can do this. I get to decide who I am!"

Paula feels a deep sense of relief. Her life will adjust itself to accommodate this new belief. She won't be triggered in the same way when her husband is unhappy. The relationship is already shifting, because she's changing herself.

After witnessing the step-by-step process of the Mindful Inquiry questioning, can you see how the Observing Mind's sharp focus on Paula's core beliefs allowed her to identify and dismantle a self-destructive belief? When we listen to the Observing Mind's wisdom and guidance, we won't find ourselves getting sucked into the Monkey Mind's story.

It takes practice to perfect the skill of what questions to ask with Mindful Inquiry, so I invite you to read this dialogue a few times through to catch all the nuances the Observing Mind picked up on during Paula's session. Once we've trained our focus in the right direction, we can continue shifting away from our old programming. Then we can experience the immense relief and excitement that comes from taking our identities back into our own hands.

Part 6

BECOMING THE MASTER OF YOUR MONKEY MIND

Chapter 27

NO LONGER RULED BY
THE MONKEY MIND

Once we've learned the primary tools on how to move away from the Monkey Mind's stories, there are additional ways we can specifically apply these skills in our everyday lives. We can learn how to look for gratitude in situations we previously would have thought were hopeless. We can shift into accepting what is, no matter the circumstances. We can learn how focusing on the facts about our lives is a strong method for combating our Monkey Mind's stories. There are so many opportunities to incorporate these ideas into our lives, and in the following chapters, I've included several of the specific ways we can apply these methods to our daily rituals. These further tools will be illustrated through my sessions with Kevin and Elizabeth.

KEVIN'S AND ELIZABETH'S TRANSFORMATION

Kevin and Elizabeth have each been heavily applying the perspective of the Observing Mind to their lives. Overall, Kevin's and Elizabeth's lives have taken radical turns since they first started working with me, and they both have been sober for many months now.

Kevin began studying vigorously and was recently accepted into medical school. He continues to work at the hospital as a nurse, and his deep compassion is well-known across the floor. His marriage is happier and healthier than ever, and Jamie and Kevin are expecting their first child. Kevin has even been able to reach a place of self-acceptance where he has finally forgiven himself for the action that sent him spiraling down his dark path: hitting Max.

Elizabeth has reconnected with her kids in a deeper way than she had ever thought possible. Her relationship with Bruce is filled with authenticity and trust. With support from Bruce and her children, Elizabeth shifted into working full-time at the magazine, having rediscovered her passion for the written word.

They have both become incredibly conscious of their own programming and have successfully changed their most harmful core beliefs. They're effective at managing the Monkey Mind's stories, and their new default responses come from the perspective of the Observing Mind. By taking the next step and applying these skills to their day-to-day lives, Elizabeth and Kevin will demonstrate the even deeper levels of change that the Observing Mind can offer.

Chapter 28

LET YOUR LIGHT SHINE

Kevin and I start our session by walking around the park. As the sun warms us, I ask, "Kevin, how are you doing at not building up shame?"

Kevin shrugs. "Definitely better, but I feel like I still get sucked into it sometimes."

"There's an old Hawaiian story I'd like to share with you that I think could help you understand how harmful this shame really is."

"Sounds interesting. Go right ahead," Kevin agrees with an enthusiastic smile.

"Imagine that each person is born with a perfect bowl of light. This light represents their self-worth and self-identity. If this child grew up in a world where he never felt shame, this bowl would stay full of light. Unfortunately, in society today, children often receive thousands of criticisms."

"Yeah, like how my dad taught me that I shouldn't cry," Kevin chimes in.

"Exactly. So every time this child feels ashamed, he drops a stone into his bowl. There is only so much space, so for every stone he drops, he loses some light. By the time this little boy becomes an adult, his bowl has become filled with stones—to the point where there is very little light left."

"That's a dark image to imagine," Kevin says. "No pun intended, I promise," he jokes.

"It's a great story, but I really want to show you a visual of this. So, I brought a bowl for you," I explain, pulling a beautiful, large Koa wood bowl from my backpack.

"If you wouldn't mind, can you help me gather some stones? Then just scatter them up and down this part of the path here," I say, motioning ahead.

Once we have found and spread the stones, I continue, "Now, as we walk up and down this path, I want you to tap into your bowl of light. An easy way to do this is to tell me about your greatest passion. Just explain what you love to do and how you do it."

"So I love to help people heal… you want me to explain how I do that, right?" Kevin clarifies.

"Yes. And then, after you've talked about your love for a while, I'm going to cut in with a comment that might sting. I'm going to pull from what you've told me over the time we've worked together, and I'm going to be pretty ruthless—like the Monkey Mind is. Are you OK with that?" I ask.

"Yeah," Kevin says with an energetic nod of his head.

"OK, just wanted to make sure. When you hear me, try to stay focused on what you're saying and keep talking. However, whenever you really resonate with something I'm saying, stop and pick up a stone and place it in your bowl," I say.

"Let's do it."

"Begin whenever you're ready," I instruct.

"OK. Well, I really love meeting new patients and being able to connect with them to calm their nerves. At hospitals, everyone is a little on edge, so I try to be as understanding as I can be," Kevin says, his voice livening as he talks.

I cut in, "You? Understanding? Hmph. You can't even show emotion—how could you be understanding toward these people?"

Kevin slows along the path. "Wow... that took me by surprise a little. I'd say that one hit," he says, looking over at me.

"Pick up a stone," I invite, motioning toward the ground.

Surveying the choice of rocks before him, Kevin chooses a medium-size rock and plunks it in the bowl.

"Continue, please," I request.

"Um, man, I don't remember where I was. Well, I really like to work with former patients too. Because then I have a bit of a rapport with them already," Kevin's voice returns to its levity. "And they know my style—like, I don't just want to hear about their symptoms. I want to hear about how their diet might play into this, or their surroundings or..."

I cut in, "How do you know what you're even talking about, Kevin? You aren't a doctor yet—why are you acting like one?"

"Um, I think they appreciate this because a lot of doctors and nurses are so stressed about meeting their quota that they don't spend the time to really get to know their patients, but I understand how important it is to build that trust..." he explains, his speech slowing considerably.

"*You?* Building trust? Oh come *on*, Kevin! No one trusts you! Who would trust a drunk?" I hiss.

"That one hit home," he mumbles. Kevin stops along the path and silently picks up the closest stone and places it in the bowl.

He takes a deep breath, closing his eyes for a moment. Then he continues, "I also really enjoy following up with patients and making sure they got the care they needed," he quietly says, his pace much slower than when we started. "And sometimes I find out that a test wasn't ordered or checked, and I'm able to help it along on my end. I really try to make every person feel cared for..."

"If only you could do that for your loved ones! Jamie doesn't really feel cared for. You're always working or studying—you're making her take on the stress of pregnancy all on her own!"

Closing his eyes once more, Kevin stops. He takes a moment, then reaches down and throws a stone into the bowl.

"How are you feeling, Kevin?" I ask calmly.

"Awful," he blankly replies.

"This is what we do to ourselves every day. We collect the stones of shame along the path of our lives. And did you notice how much harder it felt to speak about your love and passion when you kept getting knocked down?" I ask.

"Definitely," Kevin quietly agrees.

"The good news is that these stones aren't permanent. We do have the ability to remove them from our bowl," I bring up.

"How exactly?" Kevin asks with furrowed brows.

"Well, let's look at the times when you picked up the stones. What was the first one again?" I inquire.

"Um, after you said that I wasn't understanding."

"So which is truer in this moment—that you aren't an understanding person? Or that you now try to share emotion as much as you can?"

"I try to show it," he says with a shrug.

"Once you can see that, Kevin, you've become aware that this stone does not hold any truth and you can remove it from your bowl."

"Gladly," he snorts, tossing it onto the path.

"Next one?" I ask.

"Next was that no one could trust a drunk," he says, exhaling deeply.

"Is it truer that you're a drunk? Or that you haven't drank in a long time and have worked hard to overcome your drinking?" I ask.

"That I haven't drank and am working hard," he repeats, a little calmer.

"Ditch another stone then."

He acquiesces and tosses the second stone out with a flick of his wrist.

"The last one?" I prompt.

"That Jamie doesn't feel cared for because I'm never around," Kevin mumbles.

"And is it truer that you're never around and you don't care about your family? Or that you're working hard and deeply love your family?"

"That I'm working hard and love them." Kevin picks up the last stone, gives it a long look, and then throws it behind him.

"Can you see how healing it is to remove that shame from your life?" I ask.

"Yeah, I can," Kevin replies strongly.

"Can you see that you're in charge of putting stones into your bowl, and at the same time, you're in charge of taking the stones out?"

He nods in agreement.

"This is the process of life, Kevin. If we begin to recognize that this is the real journey, we can see that we're not meant to be perfect. It's OK to drop some stones into your bowl sometimes. The truth is, when you become conscious of the darkness of the stone, you allow yourself to become aware of the light. Then, when you remove it, your light shines even brighter."

"Shame has been such a big part of my life for so long, and I can see how helpful it'll be to imagine this little bowl inside of me getting filled whenever I do shame myself for something. But when I do notice that, I know I have the power to throw the stone out," Kevin replies confidently.

Get a bowl and gather some stones and put them around you.

Think of a criticism you have about yourself, such as, "You're such a procrastinator." For each criticism, put a stone in your bowl. To keep track, write down what this judgment was.

After you've done this several times, take a stone in your hand that represents one of your criticisms. Ask yourself, "How am I trying to take care of myself by being this way? Can I love myself enough to take the stone out of my bowl?"

For example, "Which is truer: that I'm bad because I procrastinate? Or that sometimes I get overwhelmed, and that's OK."

Once you see which is truer, remove the stone from your bowl.

Chapter 29

BE PRESENT

The fall has brought with it a nip to the air, and Elizabeth rubs her hands together to warm them as she scans the street. Soon, she spots me and jogs over, giving me an embrace before we start our session.

"It's a little colder than anticipated today," I say with a laugh as we walk down the chilly city streets.

Elizabeth whistles in agreement.

"Why don't we talk about remaining in the present moment today," I suggest. "Let's use one of your main triggers to illustrate this. What's something that's been weighing on you lately?"

"Well, I was just assigned to write this pretty important story, and I've been getting writer's block more than normal—I just keep doubting myself."

"Why do you keep doubting yourself?" I ask.

"I don't know... I'm always just a little worried that my writing isn't going to stand up to the stories on the other pages. Or what if this story isn't what the editor was looking for, and they get mad at me? That actually happened, many years ago at a newspaper I worked at." She sighs. "There's just a lot riding on this one," she says with a far-off look.

"Elizabeth, did you notice how many times you were looking ahead to the future or focusing on your past when you made those statements?" I bring up.

Elizabeth remains silent for a moment, keeping in line with my steps as she considers this. As we walk, we approach a woman who is struggling to balance six grocery bags.

"Do you need some help, ma'am?" Elizabeth politely asks, rushing over to her side.

"Oh, that would be wonderful!" she exclaims. Elizabeth and I both help the woman unload her car and carry the bags up to her front door.

"Thank you so much," the woman gushes, giving Elizabeth's arm a squeeze.

"No problem at all," Elizabeth replies warmly with a wide smile.

We bid our new friend farewell and continue down the sidewalk.

"What are you noticing about how you feel right now, after helping that woman with her groceries?" I ask.

Elizabeth arches her back as she responds joyfully, "I feel great!"

"What's different about how you feel now and how you felt talking about the article you have to write?" I inquire curiously.

"Well, thinking about the story made me feel stressed... and helping out this woman made me feel really good," she responds with a shrug.

"Yet before, when you were thinking about your story, you were anxious. Did the fact that you still need to write this article disappear when you were helping that woman?"

Elizabeth chuckles and replies, "Of course not. But I wasn't thinking about the article when I was helping her with the bags."

I loudly clap my hands together. "Exactly! You were focusing on the present moment. Imagine if, instead of spending so much time worrying about the future or kicking yourself over a past mistake, you simply stayed in the present. Are you willing to dive deeper into this idea, Elizabeth?"

She smiles back at me, raising her eyebrows. "Sure, I'm game. What is it?"

"For the next hour, you and I are going to go back and forth and merely name something we're observing. So if I were to start, I'd say 'a pigeon with two spots on its belly,'" I explain, pointing to the bird nibbling on some garbage. "The more specific you are, the better."

"OK... you said an *hour* of this, though?" Elizabeth clarifies dubiously, leaning backward as she considers the task ahead of her.

"Just try it out, and then we'll see what you think. So you go next," I request.

"OK, let's see... I spy... a broken fire hydrant!" Elizabeth yells enthusiastically.

"Let's call it the 'I Spy' experiment then," I respond with a chuckle. "But really put your attention on the objects themselves, rather than the act of choosing what to say. My next one is a birdhouse-shaped mailbox. Now you."

Elizabeth looks around, more seriously this time. "A Dalmatian with a blue collar."

I fire back, "A purple, knitted beanie."

"A plastic bag flying in the wind."

"A weed growing through the crack in the sidewalk."

We do this for another twenty minutes. I turn suddenly to Elizabeth and ask, "How are you feeling right now?"

Surprised by this question, Elizabeth stutters a moment before responding, "I...I don't know. I feel pretty good I guess."

"How long do you think it's been?" I ask.

"Oh, I'd say ten minutes or so," she guesses.

"Twenty-two, actually," I respond with a slight nod towards my watch.

"No way! Wow, it's really easy to lose track of time when you do this," she notes, her eyes still scanning the street for another object to name.

"Shall we continue?" I ask.

"An umbrella with tulips on it!" Elizabeth energetically replies. We continue this until we reach the end of the hour.

"All right, time's up," I announce, clapping my hands together.

"No! Already? That is really something else," she remarks, shaking her head in disbelief.

"Elizabeth, what would you say are the benefits of staying in the present?"

Hopping over a puddle, she answers, "I mean, during that whole hour, I didn't have any time to think about my story!" Elizabeth exclaims, looking at me in amazement. "But now, already, I can feel the anxiety creeping back in. If I could do this more—not focus on the anxiety, I mean—I would be so much more productive! Like when I'm writing, instead of spending half of my time freaking out about if I'm going to write the story well, I could simply focus on what's in front of me and start typing. I have a feeling I'd get a lot more written that way," she recognizes.

Before I can respond, Elizabeth continues quickly, "Man! I just keep thinking of other times this would be so helpful. Like when I'm with Bruce, I could focus one hundred percent of my attention on him, and not think about bills or the kids or work or any of that. Then he wouldn't call me out for not listening to him!" She picks up her pace, enlivened from this discovery. "This is great."

I respond with a smile, "I remember when my kids were little, I would do this with them on long drives. It was amazing how much fun we'd all have enjoying our surroundings."

"Well, I'll definitely have to try this with Josh and Tiffany," Elizabeth says, returning my smile.

Set a timer for fifteen minutes and go for a walk. Focus on silently naming what you're observing around you. A bird flying. The smell of roasted coffee. A truck backing up.

If you have a friend who wants to join you—even better!

When the alarm goes off after fifteen minutes, ask yourself: "When I'm fully present, is it possible to be stressed at the same time?"

tell anyone you want to go to Bora Bora. What do you think are the chances you'll end up going?" I ask.

Kevin shrugs his shoulders. "I'd guess I'd never go."

"Exactly. Unless you focus on achieving your goal, you'll never go. The same is true with choosing the Observing Mind. If you want to live by the Observing Mind's outlook, you have to make a conscious choice to put your attention on that perspective. When you wake up, you have to think, 'Today, I'm going to observe my thoughts. I'm going to stay an observer as much as I can throughout my day.'"

Kevin nods along to my words. "I can understand that. But isn't it easier said than done? I'm so busy with school and work and Jamie... there are so many thoughts constantly racing through my mind. I feel like I have the *intention* to listen to the Observing Mind, but I get carried away by the Monkey Mind sometimes," he admits honestly. He stops along our walk to look at the grand hibiscus bush next to us.

"This isn't always an easy thing to do, Kevin. It takes practice to consistently listen to the Observing Mind's voice over that of the Monkey Mind. When you choose to listen to your observational perspective, your day is full of all these little awarenesses where you're observing the negative thoughts from your Monkey Mind. Then you use the Observing Mind to *reverse* these negative thoughts," I explain.

Kevin cocks his head to the side. "Reverse the negative thoughts? How?"

I look over to Kevin with a smile. "What's a negative thought you've had today?"

Kevin mulls this over a moment as he looks up at the tree branches, his face shaded from the sun for a moment. "Well, one thing that keeps running through my head is that I'm not smart. I keep hearing that critical voice tell me that I'm not going to pass my boards in a few months," Kevin openly admits, without any shame.

"Would you say that the Monkey Mind is reinforcing the story that you're not smart, and that's what is creating your anxiety?" I ask.

"Yeah, I would agree with that."

"When you choose to listen to the Observing Mind, you allow yourself to see the facts and observations of your life and use them to guide your experience without listening to the unnecessary drama drummed up by the Monkey Mind. So let me ask you this: what are a few things that you *were* smart enough to do?" I request.

Kevin laughs warmly. "That's a new idea! Hmm, the first one off the top of my head is that I was smart enough to stop drinking," he says with a proud grin.

"What all did that involve?"

"Well, first I had to admit I had a problem, which was a big step in itself. Then I had to have the courage to really open myself up to you, and then to Jamie and my friends and family. And then I had to grasp the idea that my beliefs were driving me to drink," he notes.

"You should be really proud of yourself, Kevin. What's another thing you were smart enough to do?"

"Getting into medical school is pretty tough, so I had to be pretty smart to do that," Kevin says, a red tint appearing on his cheeks as his humbleness is being threatened.

"Tell me a little about how you were smart enough to get accepted into med school," I request.

"Um... I had to spend weeks and weeks studying for the MCAT. Then I had to get my application in order and make sure that it was unique and written well. And I had to interview well," he explains.

"And how many people can say they did all that *and* were accepted into med school at the end?" I encourage. "Can you name off one more thing you were smart enough to do, Kevin?"

"Oh geez," he says, rubbing his neck. "I did just get 'Employee of the Month' at work, which was a big confidence booster," he says with a shrug.

"So what did you have to do to be up for that award?" I ask.

"Well, I try to be as proactive as I can be and plan ahead. And at the same time, I really care for our patients. Like I always try to have some coloring books in my office for when parents come in with their kids. I like to focus on the little stuff, you know? Because that's what can make the biggest difference," Kevin tells me more confidently.

"There you go! Now, after naming these facts about yourself, is it true that you're not smart?" I ask.

Kevin stands a bit straighter. "Actually, no. It's not. I don't feel the negative pull of the Monkey Mind nearly as much. Even if I feel like I'm bragging a little, they *are* all true," Kevin reports brightly.

"Acknowledging your success doesn't make you arrogant, Kevin. It's a vital part in choosing the Observing Mind and seeing the world for what it is."

"It's so interesting how difficult it is to be accurate about who I really am."

"It's something we've never learned to do," I affirm. "But the Observing Mind can help you see yourself accurately—it's not embellishing who you are or discrediting you. The Observing Mind is using data from your life to see yourself candidly. When you're able to take a step back and see how your Monkey Mind is repeating the story that you're not smart, you can refute that story with factual evidence. Then it's easier to break free from any judgments the Monkey Mind has created."

Kevin adds, "And what I like is that doing this isn't the same as just repeating a positive affirmation either. I'm not saying, 'I'm smart!' just for the heck of it. I now have *proof* that I am smart. And that's eye-opening to see."

Let's look at Kevin's situation. First, he believed he was not smart enough to pass his boards. Second, he made a list of several things he was smart enough to do. Third, after looking at this evidence, he questioned the belief that he's not smart enough to pass the boards.

Come up with a belief you consistently hold about yourself, such as "I'm a failure because I can't stop drinking."

List five situations where you were able to avoid drinking.

Ask yourself, "Why do I focus on the first statement 'I'm a failure because I can't stop drinking' instead of acknowledging the five times I was able to stop myself from drinking?"

This is the beginning of seeing yourself more accurately.

just happened. It doesn't want to judge it—it wants to learn from it."

"So how does this apply to something other than slipping on gravel?" Elizabeth inquires, adjusting her helmet.

I pull over to a patch of grass. Elizabeth follows my cue and pulls up next to me, keeping one foot balanced on the pedal.

"Can you think of a time recently when you were aware of your response to a stressful situation?"

"Well, a few weeks ago, my boss told me I was a shoe-in for this promotion. Then I got to work on Monday and they announced that they were giving the position to another woman instead!" Elizabeth takes a deep breath. "But I was able to do some Mindful Inquiry around it and ended up being really OK with it."

"I have a feeling that when you did that process, you were more aware than you even realize. Why don't you walk through what went on in your head when you processed not getting the promotion, and then I can help point all the different types of awareness you had," I offer.

Elizabeth places her other foot on the ground. "OK. At first, right after they broke the news, I kind of stormed off. I didn't make a scene or anything, but I definitely caught my boss's eye. I knew I was really worked up, so I decided to take my break. I sat on a bench in the courtyard and started using my Conscious Breath to identify what thoughts and feelings were coming up."

"What did you notice?" I ask.

"The most prevalent feeling I noticed was anger. I felt like my boss had misled me," Elizabeth notes.

"So what did you do with that?"

"I didn't try to fight it at all. I embraced the anger. I started questioning it, because I knew the anger was going to lead me to a deeper belief," Elizabeth explains.

"So you were *aware* that you needed to question the anger. What did you ask yourself?" I inquire.

"I asked myself why I was feeling so betrayed about not getting the promotion. Then I noticed my first response was that my boss had lied to me. I immediately realized that my boss was outside my skin, so I kept questioning—why was I feeling so betrayed? Then I realized if I had gotten the promotion, I would have had more freedom in choosing the topics of my articles, which I was looking forward to. But getting to choose articles is still outside myself, so I kept going."

I identify, "You were *aware* that external things can never be the cause of your emotions. What next, Elizabeth?"

She scratches under her chin strap. "As I went deeper, I noticed how my anger was shifting into some pretty strong fear. So I allowed myself to sit in that fear for a moment."

"You were *aware* enough to allow the different emotions to flow through you. What about after that?" I ask.

"Then I asked myself why I felt so afraid. My first response was that I must have done something wrong, and then my thoughts really got away from me for a few moments. I started wondering what I possibly could have done, and how could I not even be aware of it?" Elizabeth breathes deeply.

She adds, "Then I let go of that idea and went back to questioning my thoughts."

"So you were *aware* enough to observe your thoughts, notice when you were getting hooked into them, and let those go so you could go back to questioning. What'd you do after this?" I ask.

"Well, I was definitely looking inside myself now, so I continued down this path. I asked what it meant about me if I had done something wrong to not get the promotion. Pretty quickly, I could hear my dad's voice in my head criticizing me—saying that I'm not good enough. That belief just never fails to jump up in these kinds of situations," Elizabeth says, with a small laugh and shake of her head.

"You were *aware* to track the feelings all the way to your core belief. Then what?" I inquire.

"After I saw that, I noticed how attached I was to the belief that I had done something wrong, and that this was the reason I didn't get the promotion. A few seconds later, I noticed how I was using the fact that I didn't get the position as the *reason* for why I am a failure. I recognized pretty quickly that I needed to first look at the belief that I had done something wrong before getting caught any further in this story," she describes.

"You were *aware* that one belief was creating the basis for another. What next?" I request.

"Then I questioned if it was even true that I had done something wrong. I thought back to the previous weeks and couldn't think of anything that would overturn getting a promotion. So I quickly dismissed the belief that I had done something to cause this," Elizabeth says, swatting away a mosquito.

"You were *aware* that you should question the accuracy of your beliefs. What did you do after that?" I prompt.

"Once I saw that I hadn't done anything to jeopardize the promotion, I knew it had to be something else—something that may not even have anything to do with me. Maybe Shirley had gone above and beyond in her role, and she deserved the title even more than I did. Who knows. I had to accept that I did not get this promotion, and there was no changing that decision."

"So you were *aware* that you likely had no control over this decision, and you accepted that. What about after that?" I ask.

"I could still hear my dad's voice criticizing me for failing to accomplish this—it just wouldn't go away. So I started asking myself what it meant about me if I didn't get this promotion. Was I truly a failure if I didn't get this? Of course not! Shirley is an extremely hard-working person, and she's been here several years longer than I have. Just because I'm not at Shirley's level doesn't mean that I'm a failure. So I decided to shift my energy into feeling really excited for Shirley—she did deserve this. I respect her so much, and know I can learn a lot from her," Elizabeth continues.

"You became *aware* of what the impact was for you, and you used facts about Shirley's accomplishments to shift your focus into happiness for your coworker. What happened next?"

"After seeing all that, I could see how the belief that 'I'm a failure' didn't apply to this situation at all. Shirley getting the promotion over me doesn't define me," Elizabeth relays with a sharp nod of her head.

"So you were *aware* that other people's decisions don't determine your self-worth. What next?"

"Then I thought back to how I had reacted to the news—by walking off. I could feel the shame start to come on board for reacting in such an immature way. But I stopped it. So what if I stormed off? This was extremely surprising news to me, and I responded the way that I needed to in that moment. I don't need to keep replaying it over and over in my mind. It happened—it's done," Elizabeth strongly states.

"You were *aware* of the double shame building up, and you kept it at bay. What about after that?"

"I made a plan to go talk to my boss later in the day to discuss why he had chosen Shirley over me. I was going to strive to put the focus on learning from this and turn my attention to how grateful I was for how much he has helped me during my time with the magazine."

"You were *aware* to choose gratitude over resentment. What next?"

"Then, when I did go and speak with my boss, I was completely calm. I was really proud of myself for being able to keep a level head! In the past, I would have been an anxious mess—I probably would have avoided my boss at all costs," Elizabeth says, staring off at the trees as she recalls this.

She resumes, "So when I walked into his office, I said that I totally respected his decision and would love to know how I can continue contributing to the team. He thanked me for coming to talk with him and did explain that Shirley's longer history with the company was a big factor in the decision. I agreed that she's going to do great, and I'm looking forward to learning more from her. Then he said if I keep doing what I'm doing, there will a lot more opportunities coming my way."

"Can you see how much you were aware of the way you felt all the way through? You honored your emotions. You allowed them to take place. And then you were able to use those emotions to track back to your beliefs, and easily identify whether something was externally or internally focused. And did you see how quickly you shut down the belief that you're a failure? It's incredible!" I applaud.

"By you naming the different things I was doing, it really opened my eyes to see how many tools I was using, even in that short dialogue. When I do it so fast, I don't take the time to appreciate how much I've learned, or how much I've grown. It just comes so naturally now that I do it without a second thought," she acknowledges.

"When you hone your awareness as much as you have, Elizabeth, change comes easily. And this skill will only grow as you keep using it. You're definitely on the right path," I assure her.

"And why don't we hop back onto *that* path?" Elizabeth asks, nodding her head toward the bike path.

We continue our bike ride, remembering to be aware of the little things that enhance our experience along the way.

Remember a time when you really wanted something, and it didn't happen—like how Elizabeth really wanted that promotion.

Looking back at this event, see how much awareness you can have by asking the following questions: How did you feel? How did you respond? Did you feel ashamed for not receiving/achieving this? What did you think not doing this meant about you? Is that belief true?

Notice how easy it is to create change when you simply observe the truth.

Chapter 32

EXUDE GRATITUDE

Kevin and I have our next session in my office. After the initial pleasantries, I ask him, "How often do you think about gratitude in your life?"

"Well, I thank Jamie a lot for all she does, but I don't give it much more thought than that," he replies.

"Another way the Observing Mind takes control away from your Monkey Mind is by using gratitude as a tool. The Observing Mind observes a negative thought the Monkey Mind has created, then thinks of something to be *grateful* for about that thought," I offer.

Kevin scrunches his brow as he tries to process this. "I don't quite understand."

"For you to really understand this idea of using gratitude, and to see the power that it can have, I want to show you the impact of consciously receiving gratitude. Are you open to trying that?"

He nods quickly.

"OK, Kevin, what are two things that Jamie doesn't like that you do?" I ask.

"Hmm…" Kevin begins. "Well, she hates it when I throw my jacket on a chair instead of hanging it up in the coat closet. And a second one… oh! She gets mad when I leave my lunch bag on the counter after work. Sometimes I even leave dirty dishes in there… it can get a little gross," he confesses.

"Perfect. And what are two compliments that you wish your wife would say to you? Maybe about something you do around the house or with her that she doesn't acknowledge all the time?"

"That's a bit harder to think of," Kevin replies, rubbing the back of his neck. "I would like her to acknowledge all the yard work I do. It's kind of a given that I'll do everything outside, so it doesn't get brought up much unless she's telling me to do something. And for the other… it'd be nice to hear her say thanks for all the little ways I've gone out of my way to help her with the pregnancy. Like, I'll go the long way home so I can pick up a meatball sub from this bistro she loves. Little stuff like that," he says, breaking eye contact with me as his cheeks grow a little pink.

"OK, Kevin, I'm going to start by repeating the criticisms Jamie has of you. As you're listening, really imagine that this is Jamie saying them. OK?"

"Go ahead," he says with a wave of his hand.

"Kevin, you didn't hang up your coat *again?* How many times have I asked you to do that? And you didn't put away your lunch bag! There's still a dirty bowl in there. That's disgusting, Kevin!" I harshly accuse.

Kevin's eyes start to glaze over, and a scowl starts to grow on his face. He is using his Conscious Breath, but I can see that it's hard for him to continue a level breathing pattern.

I stop and ask, "How are you feeling, Kevin?"

"A little angry," he admits curtly.

"All right. Now move around for thirty seconds and release all that anxiety," I instruct.

"Gladly," Kevin replies, jumping up and shaking himself out.

"Wonderful. Now, I'm going to tell you her compliments. Imagine Jamie is saying these things, OK?"

Giving his arms one last shake, Kevin nods and takes a seat.

"Thank you so much for mowing the lawn and trimming the hedges. I don't say it a lot, but I really appreciate how much work you put into making our home look beautiful. And thank you for always going the extra mile for me. It's so thoughtful that you remember how much I love those meatball subs, and you go out of your way to make me feel good during my pregnancy. I'm so appreciative of you, Kevin."

Sitting with his eyes closed, Kevin is taking in the full effect of the words.

"How do you feel now?" I gently ask.

He opens his glistening eyes and looks back at me. "It feels really good."

"So as we go through this, keep in mind that *this* is the response you're creating when you focus on gratitude. Now let's put the idea of choosing gratitude into application. What's a challenging situation you've been in recently?"

Kevin pauses a moment. "Hmm... well, one thing that Jamie and I have gotten into arguments about for years is her leaving her mugs of half-drunk tea all over the place. She doesn't like cold tea, so she just forgets about it after she's stopped drinking it. She knows how much it bugs me, but she just keeps on doing it. And now, she's drinking twice as much tea because there's this kind that is supposed to be good for the baby. Last week, she left a mug out for so long that by the time I found it, it had attracted a bunch of fruit flies! So J.F., how do I find gratitude in this?" he asks with a mischievous smile, clearly enjoying giving me what he thinks is an impossible example.

"Why does your wife drink the tea?" I ask.

"*Why* does she drink tea? I don't know. I guess to relax?"

"Don't you want a relaxed wife?" I counter.

"Well, yes, of course I do."

"So can you be grateful that your wife has created this tea ritual for herself so she can relax?"

"Well, sure I can appreciate that she wants to de-stress. But she could be more considerate about it," he disputes.

"Kevin, how long have you been focusing on Jamie leaving her tea cups around?" I ask.

"Since we first moved in together. So, six years."

"And has it ever changed?"

Kevin shakes his head disappointedly.

"Can you see how the Monkey Mind focuses on the idea that you have to be in control of where the mugs go?" I ask.

"Yeah, you're right. And it's even worse than that... it's like I need to be in control of Jamie's behavior." A look of embarrassment flashes across Kevin's face at this thought.

I nod. "Exactly. The Monkey Mind thinks you need to control Jamie's behavior. Yet, when you try to do this, nothing changes, and you both get aggravated. You need to shift your attention to the *attitude* in which you address the issue. What would happen if instead, you choose to be happy that your wife drinks tea to relax? And even praise her for it?" I suggest.

"I think both of our lives would be a lot happier," he replies with a chuckle. "It amazes me how much I try to control things that I have no control over," Kevin says with a shake of his head. "So I need to focus on my own feelings and focus on gratitude. I think I can do that."

"And at the same time, this doesn't mean you have to abandon discernment entirely. You can still want to keep the mugs put away. You just have to remember to always come from a perspective of gratitude," I explain.

"That sounds a lot more doable. I really don't want to just focus on gratitude and then have a bunch of mugs laying around." He looks up at the ceiling, imagining this in his mind. "Man, even when

I think of the mugs everywhere, I still get a little upset!" he admits. "It's going to take some practice to get this down."

"Let's try one more thing to really cement this idea," I suggest. "I want you to tell me every single thing you're grateful for about Jamie drinking tea. Don't be afraid to really overdo it too!"

"Um, OK…" Kevin clears his throat. "Well, I love how much she cares about the pregnancy and our baby, and that she takes the time to relax and keep herself healthy. I mean, every day people are pestering her about wanting to rub her belly or ask her how much weight she's gained or if she has any stretch marks—if people did that to me all day, I'd probably handle it with a lot less poise than she is. And, you know, some women get so stressed out while they're pregnant that they can actually make themselves sick! But she's been a rock through this whole thing, and if drinking tea can help her maintain that, good for her."

"Now, take a deep breath, Kevin."

Kevin inhales loudly.

"What are you noticing? How are you feeling?"

"Wow. I feel a lot more appreciation for her. So this is what I miss when I focus on the mug, huh? This connection?"

"That's it, Kevin. You see, gratitude is rooted in the truths about your life. When you become close with the Observing Mind, you not only feel more connected with those around you, but you can also see how much you have to be grateful for."

Think of someone whom you have a tendency to argue with in your life and what those arguments are about. For example, it could be your partner repeatedly telling you to wash the car.

Instead of thinking, "I've been working hard all week. I'm

exhausted. Why do I have to do more?" ask yourself, "What am I grateful for about that request?"

Name these gratitudes. "I'm grateful to have a partner who likes to maintain what we own and keep things beautiful. I'm grateful to have a partner that doesn't bow down to my mood swings. I'm grateful for my car. I love it, and I love the idea of keeping it nice."

Now repeat this process with the person you had in mind.

Chapter 33

WELCOME WHAT IS

We were supposed to do an outdoor session, but Elizabeth calls me and requests to meet at my office instead. When she shows up, I realize why.

Holding a tissue in one hand, Elizabeth raises her hand to refuse my greeting.

"I caught a bug," she groans, her nose obviously quite stuffed up.

"Yes, I can see that," I joke with a snicker.

Elizabeth tries to inhale but ends up going into a coughing fit instead. "Ugh, I just hate being sick. Like right now, I'm so jealous that you can breathe out of your nostrils," Elizabeth bemoans, dabbing at her nose with the tissue.

"Why don't we take a look at why we spend so much time arguing with what is, Elizabeth? Almost everyone does it, but we're rarely aware that we're doing it. Like right now, why are you unhappy with being sick?" I ask.

"Well, being sick sucks. No one *wants* to be sick," Elizabeth argues with a sniffle.

"What happens to you when you're frustrated about being sick?"

"I don't know. I guess it doesn't help me feel any better."

"I wonder if you realize how it might actually make you feel *worse*. To show you this, I'd love for you to start complaining to me about all the reasons why you don't want to be sick," I request.

"Just name off why I hate being sick, huh? OK," Elizabeth agrees. "Well, for one, I have to carry tissues with me everywhere because my nose somehow manages to be stuffy and runny at the same time. Then, when I try to go to bed, I can never get a good night's sleep because I wake up feeling like I can't breathe. And then I get this sinus headache that just pounds away in my head..." she rattles off, her words not quite able to catch up to her thoughts.

"What are you noticing right now, Elizabeth?" I ask.

She reflects a moment. "Honestly, I can feel myself getting worked up a little. And then the more I listen to myself, the more I'm like, 'Look at all this terrible stuff you're dealing with! You've earned the right to complain a little!'"

"So you feel like you've earned the right to complain... does complaining change anything? Has it made your nose clear up? Or your headache go away?" I point out.

"No..." Elizabeth agrees with a sigh.

"And when you complain about these things—how does it affect those around you?" I ask.

"Probably makes them kind of annoyed," she confesses.

"When you choose to welcome what is, Elizabeth, everyone wins. The Monkey Mind doesn't like to bless what is because it wants to argue with what's happening instead. It makes you think 'I don't like this. I don't want this. This has to change right now.' I'm guessing you can start to see where this kind of thinking leads you."

"To a bar, I'd imagine," Elizabeth huffs, coughing into her elbow.

"Can you feel how much you *want* to stay upset about being sick? Why do you think that is?" I ask.

"I don't know. Because I feel like I *shouldn't* be sick?" Elizabeth replies, a high inflection appearing in her voice.

"Hmm. That's an interesting idea, isn't it? That something *shouldn't* be the way it is? What if we think about it another way? Picture an overzealous dad at his kid's football game. He's screaming at the referee—red in the face—about a call he made. Why do you think he's doing this?" I question.

"I'm sure he thinks if he yells enough, he'll get the ref to reverse the call," Elizabeth shrugs.

"Exactly. And how often do you think that actually happens?"

"Oh, hardly ever," Elizabeth responds. "Maybe one in fifty times?"

"Mm hmm. The reason this man continues yelling at the ref, game after game, is because his Monkey Mind has convinced him that if he becomes upset, he has some control over this situation," I explain.

"Yeah. Because one in fifty times, his complaining actually does affect the ref's viewpoint," Elizabeth responds.

"That's true. Very rarely his yelling does change the call. But the funny thing is, the Monkey Mind is blind to the result of its narrations. It doesn't see whether the referee changes his call or not—it's too focused on its own story to see the result."

"Huh. So the Monkey Mind isn't seeing the reality that its story creates… this is kind of like how the Monkey Mind pressures you to change by using shame, isn't it? Like how I used to tell myself if I hate myself enough for drinking, it'll get me to stop. But in reality, all that did was make me feel worse and drink more." Elizabeth illustrates, sniffling.

"That's it exactly! On the other hand, the Observing Mind notices how often you don't get your way by becoming upset. It notes how forty-nine out of the fifty times, the referee doesn't change his call. And, more importantly, it observes the repercussions that occur from yelling at the referee—how his son becomes embarrassed by his loud dad, how his wife becomes angry at her husband for making a scene, and most importantly, how he ends up feeling frustrated with himself," I explain.

"So when I get upset because, say, I'm stuck in traffic, that's because the Monkey Mind thinks that if I get upset, there actually is a chance that I will be able to *stop* being stuck in traffic?" Elizabeth asks.

"Yep. Since it never witnesses the results of its actions, the Monkey Mind doesn't know how ridiculous that sounds. It applies the concept 'getting upset will fix this' to everything that it doesn't like—even when it's completely outside of our control," I reply.

"Huh. That's really trippy," she squeaks out before erupting into another coughing episode.

"Isn't it funny how easy it is to recognize how ridiculous it is once you take a step back? But I'd guess that you do this every day in your life, and you aren't even aware of it," I bring up.

"I'm worried you're right…" Elizabeth admits, scratching her nose.

"Why don't we find out? Think back to the last time you had a flat tire. What was your response?" I inquire.

Elizabeth shrugs. "I was really frustrated. I ended up being late for my appointment."

"So did being frustrated stop you from being late for your appointment?" I ask.

"No," she acknowledges.

"And did being frustrated make the wait any more enjoyable?"

"Not at all. I was just anxious the whole time I changed the tire," Elizabeth says with a shrug.

"OK, can you think of another time recently where you weren't happy with a situation?" I inquire.

"Hmm… well, I asked an intern to set up an interview with a source, and the next day I found out she hadn't."

"What was your response?" I ask.

"I was pretty annoyed at first. *But* I caught myself on this one!" Elizabeth proudly announces. "I noticed how much anger I was feeling and took a few deep breaths before responding. I remembered that we all make mistakes and didn't hold it against her. Then I just sent the email myself." Elizabeth smiles widely as she dabs at her nose.

"Well, look at you! So can you see how being annoyed didn't change that the interview hadn't been set up?" I bring up.

"Yep, definitely."

"And did letting go of your annoyance make the situation more enjoyable?" I ask.

"Oh yeah. It saved headaches for both of us," she recognizes.

"You can see where I'm going with this, Elizabeth. You couldn't control if you got a flat tire or if the intern didn't set up the interview."

"Sometimes I wish I could! But you're right," Elizabeth agrees.

"So let's go back to you being sick. Why do you think you're arguing with it?" I ask.

"Well, based on what we just said, I'd guess my Monkey Mind thinks that if I'm frustrated about having a cold, there is some chance I can change the fact that I'm sick," Elizabeth responds.

"And is being frustrated changing the fact that you have a cold?"

"Not at all," Elizabeth replies with a strong shake of her head. "I'm just thinking back to when I was naming off those reasons for why it sucks to be sick. And I can *still* feel myself getting pulled into that story that I *should* be mad about this! It's so easy to get drawn in that it's hard to notice the absurdity of trying to stop a cold by being mad," Elizabeth concludes with a cough.

"Why don't we start to shift away from that voice then? I want you to name off the things you said earlier—the things that sucked about being sick. But now, say 'I welcome' before each of them. See how you feel after that," I suggest.

"OK... I welcome having to carry around tissues all the time. I welcome not being able to sleep at night. I welcome—what was the other one again? Oh yeah, I welcome this sinus headache," Elizabeth recites.

"How do you feel?" I ask.

"Huh. On the one hand, I feel much lighter. But I can still feel that voice saying, 'No! Why would you ever accept a sinus headache? That's ridiculous!'" Elizabeth turns to me. "But I get what you mean. I can still feel sick, but I don't need to get upset about it. If I can stick with this, it's going to make this whole cold a lot less miserable."

Write down three situations where you were upset because you wanted it to turn out differently than it did. For each situation, write down, "This shouldn't have happened because… (fill in the blank). Keep coming up with reasons and writing them down."

Then ask yourself: Am I in control of the situation? Does arguing with the circumstances change the situation? How do I feel when I'm arguing? Does it improve my life, or anyone else's?

Now write, "I welcome (fill in the blank)."

Can you feel your perspective start to shift?

Chapter 34

ACCEPT YOUR MISTAKES

The scent of freshly baked bread wafts towards me as I walk through Kevin's front door. We had decided to have this session at his house, and Jamie baked a loaf of brioche for us before heading off to work.

As soon as we get settled, I can tell something is off. He sits in a wingback chair opposite me, and his shoulders sag into the backrest.

"What's on your mind, Kevin?" I ask.

He sighs and shakes his head. "Jamie and I got into a big fight a few minutes ago."

"What about?"

"Well, her mother offered to come stay with us for the first couple months after the baby is born. Mind you, I said *months*, not weeks. I can barely stand to be around her mom for a weekend, let alone having her live in my home for months on end! So I told this to Jamie... As you can imagine, it didn't go well. It quickly escalated to her saying I don't care about her needs," he huffs, rubbing his temples.

"So why are you feeling upset right now?" I ask.

"I just feel ashamed for reacting that way… I really don't do that much anymore."

"Kevin, it sounds like you're experiencing double shame right now—like you did that day at the movie theater after firing that nurse. Remember? You're thinking you shouldn't be allowed to react poorly now that you've learned so much," I point out.

Nodding, Kevin replies, "Yep. You're totally right. I got swept into that so fast." He takes a deep breath, clicking his teeth. "It's just so hard to accept something that I know is my fault!"

"Self-acceptance is a key aspect to moving away from the Monkey Mind. Let's say that right now, you completely let go of any shame you feel about your fight with Jamie. Instead, you fully accept that you communicated in a not-so-great way. How do you think this would feel?"

Cracking his neck sharply, Kevin replies, "It sounds great. And I feel like I'm making progress in doing that. But with Jamie, it just feels harder somehow. I feel like I *should* be able to let go of the shame, but, honestly, it still kind of feels like a cop-out."

I nod slowly. "I see. And in the past, Kevin, when you held on to that shame, you would end up beating yourself up over it, wouldn't you? You'd criticize and shame yourself for arguing with Jamie until, well, do you remember what would happen?"

Kevin sighs deeply. "I would end up at the bar."

"Would anything else happen?" I add lightly.

Clearing his throat, Kevin looks down at the floor. "I would question if I was a good husband, a good friend, a good person… and then it would get really dark," he quietly remembers.

"Remembering what happens when you don't honor your mistakes is perhaps the most powerful way to remind yourself why you *do* need to accept when you mess up," I affirm.

"It's just the Monkey Mind trying to use shame to motivate me to change again," he admits. "No matter how much I learn, it's still hard not to fall for its story sometimes."

"What if you had another way to help forgive yourself after you respond badly to Jamie?" I question.

"That'd be great. What is it?"

"Let's work up to it. First, can you tell me why you got upset with Jamie over her mom coming to stay?" I ask.

Kevin huffs, "Her mom and I don't get along that well, and I really don't want her staying with us for that long."

I clarify, "OK, that reason was about Jamie's mom. But what did *you* want that was being threatened?"

Kevin sits with this for a moment. "I mean, I've been really looking forward to spending time with Jamie and the baby... just our little family."

"Is there anything wrong with wanting that, Kevin?" I bring up.

"No..." Kevin responds, his eyes meeting mine.

"What if next time you fight with Jamie, instead of blaming yourself for arguing, you looked at the deeper reason why you fought—the desire you had that was being threatened?" I point out.

"Oh, so, like, in this instance, the desire that was being threatened was me wanting to spend time alone with Jamie and the baby?" Kevin clarifies.

"Exactly. There's nothing wrong with wanting to spend time alone with your family."

"Yeah, I can see that," he agrees, straightening the baby blue pillow behind his back.

"Now, you can see that becoming angry had a good intention behind it—you were fighting for your alone time with Jamie and the baby! You're not bad for wanting to defend that. Once you can see that, it's much easier to forgive yourself for what you said, while still acknowledging that arguing with your wife is not the way to achieve this desire," I illustrate.

"So if I can see my intentions are good, even if I do get mad, then I will be able to accept myself more when I do snap?" Kevin asks.

"That's it. You're not a bad person for arguing with Jamie—you had a good reason behind it."

"But does that really work for every argument? Sometimes I feel like I'm just in a bad mood and argue with her for no reason. That's when I feel the worst," Kevin replies, sliding his polka dot socks along the floor beneath his chair.

"Well, what's an example of when you think you're snapping just from being in a bad mood?"

Kevin leans his head back. "Hmm... let's see..." He darts his head back down to face me. "OK, so last week I got a haircut at this new barber. I wanted him to cut it a little shorter than normal, so he did. Then I came home, and Jamie asked, 'Whoa, why did he cut it so short?' And I snapped back, 'I asked him to. It is my hair!' I ended up apologizing a second later for being so short, but what was my desire that I was defending there, J.F.? What was my good intention?" Kevin asks.

"Well, why don't you take a guess," I counteroffer.

Kevin sighs and scratches his head. "Umm... well, I obviously assumed that Jamie didn't like my hair. And I want to be attractive to my wife... so, I guess my desire was that I wanted her to like how I looked, and I was trying to defend that?"

"That sounds right to me, Kevin," I reply.

"Huh. I guess you're right," he concedes.

"When it comes to accepting your mistakes, there are two things to keep in mind," I explain. "First, remember what happens when you don't accept your mistakes. Second, try to find the underlying desire that you're trying to protect, like wanting to have some intimate time with your family. When you combine these two ideas, you can learn to accept yourself after you have an outburst."

Kevin responds, "So I should identify what the deeper desires are behind my arguments...That's such an interesting idea. I'm really looking forward to trying this."

"Yeah, it's a very different concept than most of us are used to. But don't forget this is all still a learning process. When it comes to our behaviors, we often don't allow ourselves this learning phase because we're so busy judging our mistakes as a flaw in our character. When we stay in this shame-based way of thinking, we aren't able to look back and accurately see our growth," I add.

"Yeah, I can see what you mean. Here I am, obsessing over this little tiff I had with Jamie. But a few years ago, I wouldn't have given my response to our argument a second thought. I would have gotten pissed, gone to a bar, and drank until I blacked out. I have come a pretty long way," Kevin realizes, raising his head a bit higher.

Think of an example where you were upset with someone and you later regretted how you acted. Write down all the ways you shamed yourself. Then note what that judging led you to do—for Kevin, it led him to a bar. Next, think about what you were trying to protect by arguing, like Kevin wanting Jamie to think he's attractive.

Take a moment to recognize that you had a good intention. With this new understanding that shaming doesn't work and that you had a good intention, can you, in this moment, forgive yourself for your actions?

Chapter 35

WEAVE CONSCIOUS BREATH
INTO YOUR DAY

During our next meeting, Elizabeth proudly relays to me her regular Conscious Breath routine.

"I breathe every day. Right when I wake up and before I go to bed—for twenty minutes each," she announces with a smile.

"That's wonderful you have the practice down. Now, I want to teach you about the next level of Conscious Breath. Imagine if your breath wasn't something you focus on only twice a day — what if you were able to fully embody the concept of Conscious Breath throughout your entire day? The more you go to your breath, the less anxiety and negative responses you'll have. So, Elizabeth, when is the last time you reacted to something in a way you wish you hadn't?"

She ponders this for a moment, then quickly says, "Oh, I got one. A really bad one. Last week, I was at the store after a really long day. I was exhausted—I probably looked like a zombie. But Josh wasn't feeling well and wanted some ice cream, so I stopped on my way home.

When I got to the cashier, she looked me up and down and said, 'Wow. You look like you could use a drink.'" Elizabeth closes her eyes and shakes her head quickly.

"Oh man, that made my blood boil. Who does she think she is to say that to me? She doesn't know what I've been through…" Elizabeth starts ranting. Then she stops and takes a few deep breaths. She looks back up at me with a sheepish smile. "See? I'm getting roped into the Monkey Mind's voice even now."

I return her smile and nod for her to continue when she's ready.

"Her comment just totally caught me off-guard. So instead of cutting her some slack, I shot back, 'You really think it's OK to say that to a customer? Why don't you just keep your comments to yourself.' And she instantly turned bright red! She started stuttering an apology, but I was so mad I didn't hear any of it. As I was driving home, I started to realize how awful I had been. I mean, she was probably only nineteen or twenty. She didn't mean anything by it. I just snapped at her so hard. I'm sure it ruined her whole night," Elizabeth says, taking a deep breath.

"I started feeling so ashamed of how I'd acted. So I started asking myself some questions, and I realized how heavily my fear of drinking had gotten triggered."

I settle my breath to match Elizabeth's, allowing a moment of silence to pass between us. Then I point out softly, "You should pat yourself on the back for being able to recognize your shame so quickly and talk about that experience."

Elizabeth nods slightly, her eyes transfixed on her shoes.

"So, why do you think you responded to the cashier that way?" I prompt.

Elizabeth looks back over to me. "I don't think I even thought about how I was responding. It was just my knee-jerk reaction to what she said."

"Do you think you could have taken a breath before responding?" I ask curiously.

"Honestly... I don't know. It just happened so fast. I wasn't even aware of what I'd done until I was driving home," she says.

"This is exactly what happens to so many of us, Elizabeth. When we get triggered about such a deep-seated core belief, we just run with the first emotion that we feel. It seems so much harder to make a conscious, calm response when the topic is something that's very personal."

"That's completely true. When she brought up drinking, I went to a totally different headspace for that moment," Elizabeth concurs.

I nod in agreement. "The way to overcome these thoughtless reactions is to practice your Conscious Breath even more throughout your day. Say, for example, you had started your pattern of Conscious Breath while you browsed the store. There would be no particular reason you started breathing, other than the fact that you wanted to practice being mindful about your breath. So you breathe as you pick up the basket, choose the flavor of ice cream—you get what I mean. If you'd done this, when you reached the cashier and she said those things to you, how do you think you would have responded?"

Elizabeth considers this. "Maybe I would have been less harsh; it's hard to say. I've never done that before."

"Well, what happens to you in the morning and at night after you breathe?"

"I feel a lot calmer," Elizabeth responds quickly.

"Exactly. So, if you had been breathing in the store prior to being triggered, how do you think you would have responded?"

"I probably would have been more level-headed," Elizabeth confirms, her eyes softening.

"Conscious Breath is the doorway to accessing your Observing Mind, Elizabeth. While it is incredibly beneficial to consciously breathe twice a day, like you're doing now, it moves to a new level when you practice it throughout your day. The more often you do it, the more you're able to go to your breath when you get triggered," I explain.

I continue, "I'd like to recreate that moment with the cashier,

Elizabeth. I want you to fully experience the anger you felt when you heard her words. But this time, I want you to go to your breath before responding. Are you open to that?"

She says confidently, "Let's do this."

I sit down next to her, taking a deep breath myself. Then I say strongly, "Wow, you look like you could use a drink. You look awful— you could sure use a drink. You could really use a drink." I pause. "What are you feeling?"

Elizabeth doesn't respond and goes into her Conscious Breath to dissect this feeling. She breathes for several moments, taking the time to enter her body and notice what's coming up for her.

"Well, first I'm noticing my anger. Underneath that, I can feel my fear of relapsing coming up. But under that…" she pauses, closing her eyes. "I can hear my mind telling me I'm not going to succeed at staying sober because I'm not strong enough." She half smirks. "Gotta love that Monkey Mind."

"Can you see how you were able to access all that information from breathing?"

"Yeah, I can definitely see that."

"And the more you practice your Conscious Breath, the more you can eliminate these outbursts from your life."

Elizabeth opens her eyes and stretches her arms. She breathes deeply again and says, "I do see what you mean, J.F., I really do. But isn't it kind of inconvenient to practice Conscious Breath all the time? I feel like I just don't have the time to do that," Elizabeth openly admits, looking back over at me.

"It is something you have to commit to. But let me ask you a question: how long did you spend beating yourself up about your reaction to that cashier?"

Elizabeth laughs softly to herself. "That's a great point. I must have thought about it at least twenty times since."

"So which is actually more work? Criticizing yourself for responding poorly? Or training yourself to go to your breath instead?" I propose.

Elizabeth nods in understanding. "I get it. I'd say it's time for me to start practicing that breath more often then!"

Remember a moment when you overreacted, as Elizabeth overreacted with the cashier. Close your eyes and bring the scene back in your mind's eye. Begin to breathe. Remember your facial expressions, what was said, what the person was wearing, as many details as you can. Just keep breathing as you recount this situation.

Can you see the true cause of your reaction? What belief was present?

Ask yourself, as you're breathing right now, if you would have overreacted in that situation if you had taken the time to breathe?

Part 7

SHARING THE WISDOM OF THE OBSERVING MIND

Chapter 36

SPREADING THE LOVE

Of the many aspects of your life that change when you start listening to the Observing Mind, one of the most profound is how much your compassion for others tends to increase. Since you now understand that their behavior doesn't affect you, you're able to see the people around you more objectively. Coupled with this, you can see how their own Monkey Minds are influencing their lives. Once you can recognize this, you may naturally find yourself wanting to share the knowledge of the Observing Mind and help them start to address their own inner wounds. By starting these kinds of honest conversations, you can begin to build even deeper connections with the people in your life.

LIVING BY EXAMPLE

After working intensively with me, Elizabeth and Kevin have both learned to live differently. Even after overcoming their addictions, they continued to apply the Observing Mind to any obstacle that arose. They are now skilled enough to use the techniques they learned to help the people in their lives overcome their own Monkey Minds.

In the following chapters, you'll see how Elizabeth and Kevin are able to support people from all different walks of life. By embracing and living by the Observing Mind's guidance, it's easy to start living a life full of connection, support, and love.

Chapter 37

OVERCOMING PAST TRAUMA

"I'm not doin' so hot, Kev."

Kevin can hear the tension in his little sister Britney's voice on the other end of the phone.

"What's wrong?" he asks.

"So tonight, I went out with a few friends, and Megan's brother, Travis, came with us."

"That's the guy you've been hanging out with, right?" Kevin clarifies.

"Well, we've been hanging out, but not *officially* hanging out, you know?" Britney quickly rattles off.

Kevin takes a deep breath. Britney is almost ten years younger than him, and he sometimes forgets how big of an age difference that can be. "OK, so the two of you are just 'hanging out.' What happened tonight that has you so upset?"

"Well, we were dancing and then he leaned in and kissed me! And after like two seconds I pulled away and *ran* off, Kevin. Like some kind of crazy person! Who does that? I never used to be like this before that all happened..."

The last semester of her senior year of college, Britney was interning at a marketing firm. One fall night, after a long day at work, a handful of Britney's coworkers went to a bar to watch the game. After drinking three or four cocktails, her team scored. Britney threw her arms in the air, cheering loudly and spilling a little of her drink on the floor in the process.

Britney's much older manager, Keith, grabbed a napkin and knelt down to clean up the puddle on the floor. As he stood up, he subtly led his hand up the back of Britney's leg and cupped her behind. Britney stood frozen, unsure of what to do. She decided to not say anything and took the first opportunity to leave.

After this, things only got worse. Britney started finding anonymous, inappropriate notes on her desk at work. She still stayed quiet, hoping it was one of her work friends playing a joke on her. Finally, one night, Keith asked her to stay late to go over a project with him. As she entered his office, he cornered her, held her down, and forced himself upon her. The next day, Britney handed in her resignation and never saw anyone from the office again.

"Britney, it's OK. Just take a few deep breaths with me," Kevin instructs. He can hear his sister breathing quickly on the other end of the phone.

"How are you doing now?" he asks.

"A little better... God, I just can't believe I did that! Travis is a really nice guy, Kevin—you'd really like him. But here I am, hiding in the bathroom because I don't know how to handle a freaking kiss! I should just accept that I'm never going to be able to have a relationship ever again."

"Hey, it's OK, Brit. You've been through a lot. It's totally normal to respond in this way," Kevin reassures.

"But I don't *want* to respond this way! I don't care if it's normal or not—I just don't want this anymore. Maybe if I had a drink to loosen up that would help…"

"Britney. You don't need to go back down that road. You've been doing so well—if you drink now, you'd still be giving your old manager power over you. Is that what you want?"

"No," she firmly states. She takes a deep breath. "Thanks for that."

"Of course. What is it that you're afraid of, Sis? You've been going to therapy for a while now—has she helped you address this?"

Britney sighs. "Yeah… she and I have worked through a lot. I don't feel like it's my fault anymore, *finally*. But I feel like I'm damaged goods, Kev. Like no good guy is going to want me."

Kevin can hear Britney's voice break, followed by a sniffle. "Hey, you're not damaged goods, Brit. Look how far you've come."

Breathing in heavily, Britney relents. "Yeah, that's true. I just don't know what to do now. How do I go and face him?"

"What if you had an open conversation with him? You could say you went through a bad experience and then see what he says," Kevin suggests.

"Oh, I don't want to start talking about that kind of stuff! It's going to scare him away," she dismisses.

"I don't mean you have to go into the details, Brit. But if you put yourself out there, and then he shuts down or rejects you, is that really the kind of guy you want to be with? Or do you want to be with someone who knows what you went through and wants to support you as you work through it?" Kevin poses.

"Are there really guys like that out there?" Britney scoffs.

"Well, I mean, you're talking to a guy right now who would want to support a woman through that…"

"I know, I know. That's why I talk to you, Kev—to remind me that not all guys are scum," Britney says with a small laugh, sniffing again. "Ugh, I'm messing up all my makeup! I need to fix this before I go back out." She clears her throat. "Thanks for picking up the phone, Kev. I really needed that."

"I'm always here for ya, Sis."

"I know—you always have been, through all of this. Tell Jamie hi for me," Britney replies.

"Will do. Love you," Kevin says.

"Love you too."

Primping in the mirror for a few moments, Britney goes back out into the main room to find Travis. She spies him standing alone by a table.

"Hey," she sheepishly says, tucking a strand of hair behind her ear.

"Um, hey," he uncomfortably responds.

"I, uh," Britney stammers. Inhaling a deep breath, she pauses before continuing. "Sorry about freaking out back there. I've, uh, had some stuff happen to me. So it can be a little hard for me to open up." Britney is terrified to look up and see how this was received. But she knows she has to.

Travis' eyes are crinkled at the edges, a soft smile on his mouth. "You wanna get out of here? I know this diner a couple blocks away— we could get some coffee and just talk, if you want?"

She returns his smile. "I could really go for a waffle too," she giggles.

Travis strokes his chin, clearly exaggerating his thought process. "Waffles, waffles... I think I could arrange that," he says, revealing a bright grin.

The two leave the loud club for the intimacy of a diner in the twilight hours. After they've ordered, Britney starts opening up to Travis about her experience with her old manager.

"So I just, um, have a hard time trusting guys now," she concludes, playing with a packet of sugar.

"Wow... that's some serious stuff," Travis replies, his eyes wide. "I... uh... I'm sorry. That you went through that, I mean," he stumbles.

"Yeah, well, I'm doing a lot better than I was a few months ago," she says with an uncomfortable chuckle.

Leaning forward across the table, he asks quietly. "Have you... have you talked to someone about this?"

"Yeah. I have a therapist. She's helped me a lot," Britney replies, accidentally ripping the sugar packet and spilling its contents all over the table. "Oh, geez, sorry," she mumbles, grabbing a napkin to gather the mess with shaking hands.

"No worries," Travis replies. After helping her clean up, he leans back and takes a deep breath.

"Hey, thanks for telling me this, Brit. And you know, not all of us are like him," Travis says, giving her a small, reassuring smile.

"I know," she quietly says.

Travis' smile fades as he sighs, popping his knuckles unconsciously. "Actually, one of my best friends went through... a similar experience in college."

"Oh yeah?" Britney asks, surprised at this comment.

"Yeah. I think I was the only one she talked to about it. She was so scared of the guy that she wouldn't report it, you know? So I can imagine how scary that was for you."

Britney nods gratefully. "Yeah, it really was. I think that's why I freaked out when you kissed me. I don't want you to think that I didn't *want* to kiss you, it's just... hard."

"You know, I kissed you because I really like you, Brit," Travis says, looking up to meet her eyes. "But I remember how shut down my friend was after that happened to her, so I don't want you to think that I'm pressuring you. 'Cause I'm not. We can take this as slow as you need to," he reassures her.

"Thanks, Travis. You have no idea how much that means to hear you say that," Britney confides warmly.

The two end up talking for hours, diving into the difficult experiences each of them has been through in their lives. By the time they leave the diner, the two feel more connected than ever.

When Britney gets home, she can't seem to stop smiling. This night had gone so much better than she could have hoped! As she crawls into bed, the photo on her nightstand catches her eye. It's a picture of her on Kevin's shoulders at the Grand Canyon. Her smile grows even wider as she thinks about how lucky she is to have a loving brother like Kevin who supports her no matter what she's going through in her life. She makes a mental note to give him a call tomorrow to relay the happy events of the evening.

Chapter 38

QUESTIONING YOUR EXPECTATIONS

As he hears his son, Scott, park his car, Ravi takes out his frustration on the pan he's scrubbing. As soon as the door opens, Ravi starts hurling his accusations. "Really, Scott? You're failing world history? You love history!" Ravi screams, flicking water across the floor as he points to the notification letter.

"No, I don't," Scott spits back, leaning against the kitchen counter and looking at his phone.

"Put that down while I'm talking to you," Ravi snaps, snatching the phone out of his son's hand and slamming it on the table behind him.

"Hey! You're going to get it wet!"

Ravi ignores his son's comment. "What is going on with you? First English, now history? Are you doing this on purpose?" Ravi questions, throwing his hands in the air.

"I mean, why does it matter anyway? It's not like I'm going to need grades for anything after school. It's just a waste of my time," Scott sulks.

"You need good grades to get into college! To get jobs! If you don't have a good track record, no one is going to hire you. Then what are you going to do? Live here forever? I don't think so!" Ravi barks back.

"God, why can't you just leave me alone!" Scott yells, lunging behind his father to grab his phone. He quickly walks out of the kitchen and up the stairs to his room.

"Don't think this is over, young man!" Ravi shouts after him. He sighs and slinks into one of the kitchen chairs, feeling defeated. His Monkey Mind goes directly to the blame game.

Scott is ruining his life! He's going to end up like that good-for-nothing friend of his, Colton—working at some dead-end job and smoking weed all day. He's hopeless.

The next day, Ravi is still replaying the argument as he drops his daughter, Sophia, off at karate class. He decides to stay and watch after he spies Elizabeth in one of the chairs, watching Tiffany. Elizabeth flags her friend over to sit next to her.

"How are you, Ravi?" Elizabeth asks brightly.

He shakes his head. "Eh, not so great. Had a rough day."

"What happened?" Elizabeth asks.

"Scott is… well, he's really pushing my buttons. I just don't know how he can be so ungrateful sometimes! And now he's *purposely* failing classes, so he'll probably never get into college," he bemoans, placing his head in his hands. "This is one of those moments where I'd love to have a nice glass of bourbon."

"Hey, Ravi, we've gotten through a lot tougher situations than this before. You've been doing so great! And remember, you can call me anytime you feel like you're going to drink, OK?" Elizabeth offers wholeheartedly.

Ravi sighs. "I know, I know. You've been a godsend when it comes to all that. I'm not going to drink, but I'm at my wit's end with him. I don't know what else to do!"

"Why are you so attached to him going to college anyway?"

Ravi jolts slightly, surprised someone would even ask such a question. "Because I want him to do well in life."

"OK—but why does he need to go to college to do well in life?" Elizabeth reiterates.

"Well, what's the alternative? If he's going to make anything of himself, he needs to have a solid education."

"And there aren't other ways he can educate himself besides college?"

Ravi shakes his head in disbelief. "Elizabeth, you see how the world works! College is a necessity. It was so important to my career, and it will be for Scott's too!"

Elizabeth takes a deep breath, and Ravi unconsciously copies her. She replies, "Well, think about when you were Scott's age—were your parents pushing you as much as you're pushing him now?"

Ravi looks away, rubbing the back of his neck uncomfortably. "Um, Elizabeth, I don't think I've told you this, but, uh, my parents passed away in a car accident when I was nine. After they were gone, I moved in with my mom's sister. I think Aunt Natalie put a lot of pressure on herself to raise me in a way that my parents would have been proud of. So she sent me to one of those private schools where I had to wear a uniform and learn the school song and all that stuff. And she was always on my back about studying and getting my homework done on time. She's the reason I was such a good student, and that allowed me to get into a great school—I'm forever grateful for that."

Elizabeth gently touches Ravi's knee. "Oh, Ravi, I'm so sorry. I had no idea. You know you can always share that kind of stuff with me, right?"

"Yeah, I know. You and I have been through a lot," he acknowledges. "I just don't talk about it that much. It happened a long time ago."

"Well, Natalie sounds like a great woman," Elizabeth kindly says.

"She is. My kids think of her as their grandma," Ravi replies, a soft smile settled on his face.

"Do you think growing up with her might be part of why you're being so tough on Scott about going to college?" Elizabeth brings up.

Ravi sits up straighter and looks over to her. "I mean, that would make sense, wouldn't it? She was convinced that I had to go to college to make anything of myself. I never even questioned it—it wasn't an option to not go, you know? But I do remember being pretty stressed about choosing which college to go to."

Elizabeth adds, "What if that's how Scott's feeling right now? Not stressed about which college to go to, but stressed about going to college at all. Do you think he's feeling any pressure from you?"

"Probably some, but that's to be expected," Ravi dismisses. "If I didn't push him a little, I feel like he'd just give up completely and end up at some dead-end job. He's such a smart kid—he's just not applying himself."

Elizabeth suggests, "What if what he needs right now is a little time to decide for himself what he wants to do? You might be surprised with what he chooses."

"I don't know…" Ravi uncertainly replies.

"You know, I experienced this a little bit myself last semester with Tiffany. She was selected to be an applicant for the National Honor Society. She's only a junior, so this was a big deal. We practiced her interview over and over, and I helped her perfect her resume. Looking back, I was putting a ton of pressure on the poor kid's shoulders. And when the day came when they announced the inductees, Tiffany's name wasn't on the list."

Elizabeth pauses and inhales deeply. "And when she came home to tell me the news, she was so bummed. But I realized that it wasn't because she didn't get in; she was worried I'd be disappointed in her! When I saw that, I gave her a big hug and reminded her that she gave it a great shot, and she can always apply again next year. I could see the shift in her, like a weight had been lifted off her shoulders. Then I started thinking about why I had pushed her so much to get into NHS, and I realized that I felt like if she didn't get in, *I* was failing her somehow—like I should have practiced with her more or done something to help her achieve this. I had somehow decided that her getting into this group determined how good of a mom I am! It sounds ludicrous, but I really felt like if she didn't get in, I had done something wrong."

Ravi absorbs Elizabeth's anecdote, staying silent for a moment before responding, "I've never thought about it like that. So if Scott fails, I think *I* failed him... huh. I mean, now that I think about it, I do get this guilty feeling in my gut when I think about Scott's future."

"Yeah, and that's just going to snowball over time. And the funny thing is—it's not true at all! Of *course* we influence how our kids grow up. But at the same time, they each interpret us in ways we can't control. I mean, just look at Sophie. She thinks the world of you! Just because Scott doesn't want to go to college doesn't mean you did anything 'wrong' as a parent," Elizabeth assures.

"Thanks for saying that, Elizabeth," Ravi acknowledges softly.

"So, what if, instead of yelling at Scott, you opened up to him a little like you did with me? He's a smart kid, and you raised him well—maybe if he understood the pressure you were under when you were going into college, he won't push back as much."

"Yeah, you're right... I think it's about time I try something different."

That night, when Scott gets home from his job at the bowling alley, Ravi calmly calls him into the family room.

"What?" Scott snaps, ready for a fight.

"Scott, I want to say I'm sorry for how pushy I've been about you going to college," Ravi says sincerely.

Shocked at his father's words, Scott sits down in an armchair opposite him.

"Growing up with Aunt Natalie, she was always pushing me so hard to do well in school. I do appreciate it now, but I remember how stressed I was back then. I have a feeling I'm doing the same thing to you right now. I don't want you to feel that way. I want you to be able to enjoy your senior year," Ravi says, smiling faintly.

Scott doesn't back down so easily. "Well, right now I feel like you're putting a ton of pressure on me, Dad. College is all you talk about. Or, if you're not, you're yelling at me for not doing better in school. Do you think that's helping me *want* to do better? You just... you have to control every aspect of my life. I feel like I don't even have a say in what I do anymore! And it really sucks."

"I'm sorry, Scott. I really didn't realize I was doing that," Ravi quietly says, looking at his hands.

Scott leans back in his chair, taking this opportunity to state his mind. "And it's not even that I don't want to go to college, Dad. I'm just, like, freaked out that I'm going to pick a major, and you're not going to be happy with it, so you'll want me to change it. And then you'll want to check my grades constantly and make sure I'm doing well... I feel like college isn't even going to be fun because you're going to be breathing down my neck the whole time!"

Ravi's jaw clenches. "I... had no idea this was impacting you this much, Scott. What if I started to back off?"

"I can't even imagine that," Scott huffs.

"Seriously, Scott. What if I did back off? If I gave you some room, and didn't bring up college so much?"

Scott glares at his father, trying to read this new man. "So if you *actually* trusted me, you mean? Like Mom does?"

"Like Mom does?" Ravi asks.

"Well, yeah! Haven't you noticed how I always go and talk to *her* about everything? She hardly ever brings up college—she asks about how I'm doing now and my friends and stuff," Scott mutters.

"Oh...well, yeah. I could be more like Mom then," Ravi confirms.

"I mean, if you say so..."

"Scott, I... I'm sorry. Truly sorry. I know this last year has been tough on you. The reason I've been so hard on you isn't about you at all—it's about me. And about your grandpa."

Scott's ears perk up. His dad never talks about his father.

Ravi takes a breath and begins, "You know, Grandpa was really successful. He owned five restaurants around town—did I ever tell you that? And he was in the works to open another two restaurants before he passed. He was doing so well, and his employees all adored him. I would go to one of the restaurants after school, and they would take me back in the kitchen, wash me up, and let me knead the bread with my elbows." Ravi explains, a small smile crawling onto his face at this memory.

"Wow... I had no idea Grandpa ran restaurants. What was he like? Was he a chef too?" Scott asks with big eyes.

"Oh, he was the best. He made every single person who walked into the restaurant feel like family. He'd spend the time to get to know his regulars too—really learn about their families. So he was always invited to all of these weddings and baptisms and bar mitzvahs and anything else you can think of! Mom and him were gone most weekends to some event or another. And oh, was he a chef! He made the best lasagna in the world." Ravi leans in and whispers, "Even better than your mom's."

This comment gets Scott to snicker. "Wow, he sounds like he was really cool."

"He really was. I wish you could have met him. He would have loved you." Ravi pauses as his throat closes up. He takes off his glasses to pinch the bridge of his nose, pressing back the tears in his closed eyelids.

Scott is stunned. He's only seen his father cry a handful of times, and the emotional man before him doesn't seem so uptight anymore.

"You OK, Dad?" Scott gently asks.

His father clears his throat and takes a shaky breath. He opens his eyes and wipes away a few fallen teardrops. "Yeah, yeah I am. It's just hard to think about them."

Scott softly asks, "Is that why you don't talk about him? I feel like Sophie and I don't know anything about him or Grandma."

This initiates another tear. Ravi clears his throat again. "Yeah, bud. I've never really come to terms with their passing."

Scott nods solemnly.

Ravi takes a fuller breath and says, "And that's why I wanted to bring this up. When they did pass away, I felt like I had to live up to the expectation that Dad had set. I felt like if *I* was successful, it would have made him proud. So I worked my butt off, and I've done pretty well for myself. But, you know, I still feel like I should be better. I should be more successful or make more money... and I feel like I should be a better dad to you too. And if I don't set you up to have a great future, I feel like I've done something wrong."

Scott looks away, a tinge of guilt creeping over his features.

Ravi continues, "But I don't want to keep pressuring you, Scott. You're a smart kid. It would be really hard for me, but if you choose not to go to college, I'll be proud of you no matter what."

Scott perks up as he looks into his father's eyes. "Yeah? Thanks, Dad. That's really cool of you." He takes a deep breath, looks down to his hands, and mumbles, "I actually have been looking into some stuff that I haven't really told you about..."

"Oh yeah?" Ravi can feel his defenses come back on board, preparing for the worst, but he quickly catches himself and does his best to look supportive.

Scott scratches the side of his hand. "Well, there was this career fair at school a few weeks ago, and there was this guy who talked about a program that sounded pretty cool."

Releasing a relieved breath, Ravi asks, "Oh? What was it?"

"It's this program that's kind of like a gap year. You know what that is, right? Like they do over in Europe?"

"Yeah, I know what a gap year is, son," Ravi says, stifling a chuckle.

Scott continues on, "Well, the year is split into three sections—for the first part, I go and volunteer somewhere for four months. Like, it could even be out of the country. Which I think would be awesome! Um, and then you come back and do some classes around a few different areas you're interested in—like one of the courses that looked cool was a culinary course…"

"You have always liked to cook," Ravi chimes in.

"Yeah!" Scott excitedly agrees. "And then after that, you do a three-month internship in whatever field you liked best. And they help with the placement and stuff, so that's nice."

"Wow, that sounds like a great program, Scott!" Ravi beams, truly meaning it.

"Right? So I was thinking of looking into that a little more… then, after it's done, who knows what I'll do. Maybe then I'll decide I want to go to college. Or maybe culinary school. But at least I'll have an idea of what I want, instead of just going to college right away because that's what's expected of me," Scott states, sitting a little taller.

Ravi is impressed. "You've really thought about this, haven't you, Scott?"

"Yeah, I have," Scott says, full of confidence.

"Hey guys—dinner is ready!" Ravi's wife calls from the kitchen.

As they stand, Ravi fondly slaps his son on the shoulder. "Well, I think that sounds like a great option. Why don't you find out some more of the details, and your mom and I can sit down and look at it with you."

"Really?" Scott eagerly asks.

"Yeah! Scott, I really am going to try to start letting go. But it's going to take some getting used to. So if I do still seem like I'm trying to control you, just let me know," Ravi requests.

"Sounds good, Dad. Thanks. Do you think you could maybe tell us more about Grandpa over dinner? Like what else he cooked and more about his restaurant and stuff?" Scott asks as they walk into the dining room.

"Yeah, I think it's time you guys got to know a little more about him," Ravi agrees warmly.

After telling his family stories about his childhood, Ravi feels closer to his parents than he has for a long, long time.

As his kids clean up the dishes, Ravi sends off a message to Elizabeth, thanking her for the suggestion to connect authentically with Scott and letting her know how wonderful his evening ended up being.

Chapter 39

CONFUSING PEOPLE-PLEASING
WITH LOVE

Kevin is quietly enjoying his lunch in the hospital cafeteria when his coworker, Salma, sits down across from him with a thud. The two of them met through work, but over the last few years have developed a close friendship.

"Everything OK?" Kevin asks.

Struggling to get the lid off the container holding her lunch, Salma grunts loudly. "Oh, come on!" Finally, the lid pops off. As she's adding dressing to her salad, she answers. "Ugh. No. I just got off the phone with Andy and you're not going to believe what he said."

"What's that?"

"Well, I asked him if Mom was able to talk. And he said that she was busy making them lunch, so she couldn't talk with me right now. I mean, can you believe that? Like my mother cannot hold the phone in one hand while she stirs his damn soup with the other!" Salma rattles off, shuffling her salad leaves in annoyance.

Kevin shrugs. "Well, you know how he is, Salma."

"I know. I know." She takes a bite of a tomato. "I've talked to him, what, a total of three times since Christmas? I told you what he did then, didn't I?"

"Yeah, you did…" Kevin begins.

"About how he ordered my mom to go fetch him a beer, like she was his servant or something! Like, he was just sitting there, watching his stupid game, and she was in the middle of setting the table. And the worst part is, she was going to stop what *she* was doing to go get him one before I spoke up!" she huffs, stabbing another piece of lettuce.

"Yeah, I remember you telling me that," Kevin brings up lightly.

"And did I tell you about the fact that he has *never*, not once, done a load of laundry? I mean, if Marcus didn't do any laundry, I honestly would probably leave him."

"Maybe they just have an old-fashioned relationship," Kevin offers.

"Ugh, that's probably true. But still! She raised two strong women—why is she letting him treat her this way?" Salma argues.

Kevin gently puts his fork down and looks at his friend. "You know, Salma, I hate to bring this up, but… have you ever thought about how in some ways, you're pretty similar to your mom?"

"What do you mean?" Salma shoots back.

"Well, I mean last week you said that Marcus was dragging you to that new outer space movie, right?"

"Yeah. So?" she asks, an edge to her voice.

"Well, every time you've ever brought up going to the movies with Marcus, you're always going to something he wants to see," Kevin calmly says.

"Yeah, because I want to go see romantic comedies—he doesn't want to see those," Salma defends.

"But you don't want to see the movies he wants to see either, right?"

Salma shakes her head dismissively. "That's called being in a *relationship*, Kevin. Sometimes I do stuff with Marcus that isn't my favorite thing to do. You do it with Jamie, too. It's normal."

Kevin nods along. "Oh, definitely. Occasionally doing something just because your partner wants to is totally fine. But when you're *only* doing the things they want to do is when it starts to become a problem. Like when you're late for work over and over because Marcus wants to stop for coffee... are you doing that just because 'you're in a relationship'?"

"It's not really *that* often, is it?" Salma mumbles, looking down at her fork.

Kevin raises his eyebrows. "Well, it's usually a couple times a week. I've actually heard from a few nurses that they don't like to work mornings with you, because they know they'll be on their own until you 'decide to show up.'"

"Wow... I didn't realize it was happening that much. That's so embarrassing," she admits, tightening her pony tail.

Kevin questions lightly, "Why haven't you told Marcus that you don't want to stop for his coffee when you're already running late?"

Salma immediately shakes her head. "Oh, he'd throw a fit. If he doesn't get his coffee, he's *so* cranky..." she pauses, considering this. "But at the same time, him needing his coffee shouldn't mean that *I'm* late to work!" She swallows another bite then adds, "Geez, how many other times do you think I'm doing this?"

"I'm not sure..." Kevin begins with a shrug.

Salma interjects, "All these memories are just flooding in now! All those holidays! I even did this last weekend with Easter! I can't *believe* how much I do what he wants!"

"You're talking about how you went to Marcus's parents' for Easter this year, right?" Kevin clarifies.

"Yeah! Even though we went there last year too! And I've told you how my mom throws this big party for Easter for all my nieces and nephews and cousins... he knew how much I wanted to go, but he insisted that we go to his parents' instead," she says, nearly spitting in disgust.

"So why didn't you say anything to him?" Kevin brings up.

"Because we'd just end up bickering for days, and I'd probably end up giving in anyway to stop it… oh my God! Did you hear what I just said there? This is ridiculous!" Salma shrieks, looking at Kevin with wide eyes.

"How ya doing with this revelation?" Kevin jokes, trying to bring down the drama.

Salma lets out a hard laugh. "Honestly, I'm pretty pissed at myself for doing this!" she says, the volume of her voice returning to a normal level.

"And if you're doing this, it makes sense that your mom is doing the same thing with Andy," Kevin points out.

Taking a deep breath, Salma nods slowly. "Yeah, I'm sure that's where I learned it from. But it's probably even more engrained in her, you know? I'm sure she would feel absolutely terrible if Andy ever got mad at her, like she was the world's worst wife or something."

Salma lays her head on the table, and her voice is muffled by her cascade of hair. "This is a somber day, Kevin. The day I realized I turned into my mother."

Kevin laughs heartily. "Oh, it's not that bad, Salma! Look on the bright side—now you can consider changing what you're doing."

Salma perks her head up. "That's true." Then she changes her mind and sighs heavily. "But I've been doing this for years without knowing it, Kevin. I think it's going to be pretty hard to change. This does explain why I've been getting on Mom's case so much about Andy—I'm watching her do the same thing I do with Marcus."

"Well, you're both doing it because you don't want to fight with your husbands. There is a good intention behind it," Kevin mentions.

"I guess. And you know, even if I did bring this up to Mom, I doubt she would change what she's doing. I'm sure she thinks it's the loving thing to do—being at her husband's beck and call. She would never see it as unhealthy," Salma shrugs.

"Oh yeah?" Kevin asks.

"Oh, she'd feel so guilty if she stopped. And... I hate to admit it, but I can kind of understand that feeling." Salma says, taking a swig from her water. "Even now, when I'm imagining speaking up to Marcus about going to my family's for Easter, I feel *so* bad. I can see what I'm doing isn't good for me, but I'm really nervous to change it, you know?"

Salma looks to Kevin, hoping to get some empathy. Thankfully, he delivers. "I used to do this all the time with Jamie," he reassures. "I wouldn't speak up about my desires, but after a while, I noticed I had all this pent-up resentment toward her for not doing what I wanted to do. But then I realized how ridiculous that was. She didn't even *know* what I wanted to do! After that, I realized that sometimes the healthiest thing is to speak up and do what I want to do."

Salma can't help but try to poke holes in Kevin's idea. "But didn't she get mad?"

"Well, at first she did. But that's to be expected—for seven years I had always done things her way, so there was bound to be a bit of annoyance in the readjustment phase. But in any strong relationship, the person *will* readjust. I mean, do you honestly think Marcus would leave you if he stopped getting his way?"

"He better not!" Salma rebukes with a huff.

"I think it really comes down to how you talk to him about it. So, imagine that you had gone to your Mom's for Easter. And Marcus really didn't want to go, so you went without him," Kevin suggests.

"Oh, he'd never agree to that..." Salma inserts.

Kevin continues, "But just imagine he did. Now, instead of apologizing like crazy when you get back home, what if you had said something like, "Thank you so much for supporting me to go to Mom's for Easter, Marcus. It was amazing to see the kids' faces when they hunted for the Easter eggs. Baby Aubrey even took her first steps when she was out looking! It really meant the world to me.'"

"Dang, Kevin. That was really poetic…" Salma chuckles.

Kevin joins in her laughter. "I did do some slam poetry in college," he jokes. "But seriously, do you think Marcus would stay upset with you for long if you said that?"

Nodding, Salma replies, "It'd be pretty hard for him to stay mad, I'd guess. And even if he was mad, I'd probably be in such a great mood from seeing my family that I wouldn't care." She shakes her head, "And like you said, if I don't do what I want every once in a while, it's just going to keep building up resentment, like you had with Jamie."

She smiles and adds, "Thank you, Kevin, for talking me through this. It's so nice to be able to talk to you about this kind of stuff, and, you know, the stuff we see around here," she motions to the wall of the hospital. "Marcus and my other friends just don't understand what we go through."

Kevin nods. "I get what you mean. It's great to be able to talk to you about all this stuff too."

A broad grin forms on Salma's face. "You know, if someone had told me three years ago that *Kevin Smith* of all people would end up being my go-to person for advice, I would have said they were out of their mind!"

They both erupt in laughter. Kevin responds, "Yeah, I'd say I've changed a bit since then."

"Well, I'm glad you did. But now I think you're going to start to get sick of me… because I'm going to need a lot more of these encouraging chats as I go through Marcus's 'readjustment' phase!"

Chapter 40

MOVING PAST YOUR JUDGMENTS

While unbuckling her daughter out of her booster seat, Rebecca is simultaneously trying to keep her son from eating a week-old carrot he found in his car seat.

"Brandon! Put that down!" she hoarsely orders.

"Beckyyyyy! Good morning!"

A chill runs down Rebecca's spine. She honestly debates hopping in the car and pulling the door closed behind her—but, being a respectable member of the PTA, Rebecca instead decides to turn and to face the source of the voice.

"Morning, Jill," Rebecca curtly replies.

Next to Jill are her two perfectly manicured children. Her daughter even has ribbons tied around her perfect ringlet pigtails.

"Your hair looks so great this morning!" Jill compliments.

"Um, thanks. I didn't really do much…" Rebecca begins, twisting her limp ponytail around her finger.

Jill interjects, "I actually just got mine done yesterday! Have you ever been to Taylor over on 34ᵗʰ Street? She is amazing! Just look what a spectacular job she did!" She shows off her new hairdo with a flip of her hand.

"She did a great…" Rebecca begins, fighting the urge to roll her eyes.

Jill cuts in again, "Didn't she! I just *love* it!"

Rebecca's daughter pulls on the bottom of her t-shirt. "What is it, honey?" Rebecca says sweetly, trying to mimic Jill's 'perfect-mom' demeanor.

"Brandon has a carrot booger," her daughter says, pointing back to her brother, who now has the baby carrot sticking out of his right nostril.

"Brandon! Take that out!" Rebecca commands, lunging across the seat to reach him.

"Well, I gotta run, Becky. Have a wonderful day!" Jill sings with a delicate wave, quickly leading her kids into the school.

Rebecca's blood starts to boil, and her Monkey Mind starts running. *Jill has to be the most conceited person ever. She can twist any topic so she ends up talking about herself. Does she care at all what other people have to say?*

Rebecca's Monkey Mind is still running wild when she reaches her yoga class, where her cousin, Elizabeth, is awaiting her.

"I saved you a spot!" Elizabeth shouts from across the room, with a big, open-mouthed smile.

Hauling her yoga mat over, Rebecca throws it down with a thud. "Ugh, Elizabeth, I am so tired of self-centered people!"

"What's up?"

"There's this mom at school, Jill. She is *incredibly* conceited. I can't stand her," Rebecca complains.

"What does she do that you find so annoying?" Elizabeth asks calmly, sitting down on her mat.

"She never lets me get a word in edgewise. All she talks about is her amazing life and her amazing kids and blah blah blah," Rebecca exasperates, plopping down next to Elizabeth. "And she calls me Becky. I *hate* when people call me Becky! Where did she get the idea that's OK?!"

"Have you told her you don't like to be called Becky?"

"Well... no..." Rebecca stumbles.

"Mm-hmm... anyway, a lot of people like to talk, Rebecca. Why is she bugging you so much?" Elizabeth asks.

"It just makes me feel like she doesn't care what I have to say. This morning it was all about *her* and *her* hair and *her* stylist." Rebecca responds, mimicking Jill's hair flip.

"You know, you say that a lot—'I feel like they don't care what I have to say.' Whenever I hear you say that, it always reminds me of Grandpa. You used to say that all the time when we'd be over there as kids," Elizabeth remembers.

"Ugh, right? I forgot about that. He always used to shut me down. And you remember how much I was over there—practically seven nights a week. And every night, I'd help Grandma make dinner and set the table. Man, could she cook," Rebecca reminisces fondly.

Elizabeth nods her head in agreement. "Oh, yeah. I sure miss her."

"Yeah, me too." Rebecca takes a deep breath. "I just remember how every night, after we had dinner all set up, she'd call for the boys and Grandpa to come eat. The whole meal, they'd talk about the boys' football or baseball games. And if I ever tried to talk about my cheerleading competitions or any of the clubs I was in, Grandpa would just change the subject back to their sports. And that happened *every day*. I'm surprised I even try after so many years of that," Rebecca finishes with a sneer.

"It's impressive we turned out as well as we did," Elizabeth says with a laugh. "And, you know, it's not bad to stand up for yourself. Like right now, you feel threatened when Jill talks a lot. There's nothing wrong with that." Elizabeth leans in closer to her cousin and adds,

"But it's important to remember that not everyone who likes to talk is like Grandpa. Who knows—maybe Jill's childhood was even worse than ours. There could be a lot of reasons why she feels like she has to control a conversation."

Rebecca sighs and lies down on the mat. "I know… everyone has a reason for what they do. I just have to remember not to take it personally next time she cuts me off," Rebecca notes.

"Yeah! I mean, it's so *tiring* judging people. It's so much easier to just accept them," Elizabeth says with a half-smile.

"You're right. I don't even know anything about Jill. Maybe next time I see her, I could try to get to know her a little," Rebecca suggests.

"Well, look at you, being so mature, Miss Rebecca!" Elizabeth says with an exaggerated smile.

"Me? Look at *you*, Elizabeth! Who is this wise woman standing in front of me!"

The yoga teacher walks out, asking everyone to rise for the beginning of class. Rebecca looks over to Elizabeth, sending her a grateful smile. Elizabeth winks back in reply.

A few days after her talk with her cousin, Rebecca is flipping through a magazine in her dentist's waiting room when in walks Jill.

"Becky! How funny to see you here!" Jill shouts from across the room.

Rebecca feels her face start to heat up. She feels her gut clench, but she decides to push that discomfort aside.

"Jill, it's lovely to see you. How are you?" Rebecca calmly and kindly asks.

"Oh, I'm OK. I've had quite the day," Jill says with a small, nervous laugh. Rebecca notices the hard swallow Jill takes after her comment.

"What happened?" Rebecca asks.

"I… actually just got back from the hospital." Jill sighs. "My sister is going through chemo for breast cancer, so I sat with her for a little while," she explains with a hunch of her shoulders.

Rebecca puts her magazine down as Jill sits next to her.

"Oh my goodness. I'm so sorry," Rebecca says.

Jill's eyes start to become misty. "Thank you. It doesn't look too good, and it's hitting all of us really hard," she says, her voice catching.

Rebecca feels like the air has been suddenly squeezed from her lungs. Her stomach drops, in an oh-so-familiar way. "Jill, if you need anything, please don't hesitate to ask," Rebecca offers, trying to blink back tears.

"Oh no, I don't want to trouble you," Jill begins, wiping a stray tear away quickly.

Rebecca takes a moment to breathe and collect herself. "I… actually lost my grandmother to breast cancer last year," Rebecca stops, grasping for words. Her eyes well up.

Jill looks over to Rebecca, their eyes reflecting each other's pain.

Rebecca explains, "My grandma was always there for me. My parents weren't super present in my childhood, so my brothers and I were always at our grandparents. I swear, I was like my grandma's shadow. Wherever she was, I was. Whatever she was doing, I had to be doing. She's the one who taught me how to sew all those years ago," Rebecca pauses, thinking back to the fond memory.

Jill quietly asks, "Aren't you a designer now?"

Rebecca bites her lip for a moment. "I sure am. Worked my way through fashion school, then up the corporate ladder. But it all started with Grandma Elsie. She showed me how to use a sewing machine, inside and out. And she was just so darn kind. Anything you could ask of her, she'd do it. I mean, here she was, practically raising four kids after her children were grown. But she never complained, and she was rarely upset with us. She just loved us unconditionally."

"She sounded lovely," Jill comments tenderly.

"She was. A real gem of a woman," Rebecca says, wiping away more tears.

"That's how I feel about my sister, Liz—a gem of a woman. I mean,

I've always been the overly loud, boisterous sister, and she was the sweet, kind sister. Everyone loved her in school and at work... she's one of those that would never hurt a fly, you know? And now, for *her* of all people for this to happen to... it's just not fair. She's the good one. This wasn't supposed to happen to her," Jill weeps.

"It's hard, Jill. It's so, so hard," Rebecca takes Jill's hand in her own. "But having the right people to support you can make all the difference. After Grandma died, I wanted to crawl into a hole. I couldn't motivate myself to do anything for weeks. My friend came over one night when I was in a really dark place, and she happened to be there at the exact moment I needed her to be. I know we don't know each other very well, but... it would mean a lot to me to help you through this," Rebecca softly affirms, squeezing Jill's hand.

Jill leans over and hugs Rebecca tightly. "Thank you," Jill whispers back, the tears refilling her eyes.

"Jill Prescott!" the secretary announces.

"Well, aren't I in the perfect state to get a root canal?" Jill asks, quickly wiping under her eyes and trying to salvage what eye makeup she has left. They both laugh and hug once more.

"Go get your root canal, and we can talk more later," Rebecca says.

Gathering her things, Jill walks to the hallway, glancing back at Rebecca and sending her one more appreciative smile.

Later that month, Elizabeth is at her yoga class when Rebecca rushes in and throws her mat down, minutes before the class is to begin.

"Where have you been? You've missed the last two classes," Elizabeth questions.

"Yeah, I've been really busy. Remember last class, how I was telling you about Jill? You were so right! She really is great. She's just... going through a lot right now."

"Oh?" Elizabeth asks in a worried tone.

Rebecca sighs. "Her sister has breast cancer. After I found out, I told her I'd go to one of those support group meetings with her, the ones that are for the loved ones of breast cancer patients. That first meeting was really tough—all I could think of was Grandma, and what she went through…"

Her own eyes filling with tears, Elizabeth nods along to her cousin's words.

"But the more I listened to these people share, the more connected I felt. To them, to Jill, even to Grandma… so now, I've been to three meetings with Jill. And last weekend I met her sister, and we all went shopping to get her sister some new hats. I thought it was going to be a pretty somber occasion, but we ended up laughing all day and having a great time! Her sister really is amazing."

"That's so wonderful, Rebecca. It warms my heart to hear how you were able to turn your nemesis into a friend," Elizabeth says with a laugh, dabbing at the fallen tears.

"Seriously though—thank you. If it weren't for you, I would have been robbing myself of a wonderful friendship," Rebecca sincerely acknowledges, lightly grasping Elizabeth's arm.

Touched by Rebecca's authenticity, Elizabeth nods her head slightly. "Don't mention it." She adds, "And I hope Jill knows how lucky she is to have found a friend as wonderful as you."

Chapter 41

CONQUERING A HEALTH CRISIS

Heather sits outside Kevin's office, nervously twisting her hospital bracelet. She's been coming to the hospital for regular checkups with her OBGYN, and today was a bit more stressful than the others.

Soon, Kevin turns down the hall and spots Heather.

"Hey! How did today go?" He leans down and gives her a side hug as she stays seated.

"Eh. Not the best," she replies, deflated.

Not long ago, Kevin was making his rounds when he recognized a patient as being the wife of one of his golf partners. They'd only met once or twice, but she looked really upset, so he went over and chatted with her.

Since then, the two have met up every time she's come into the hospital for another round of tests or procedures. Heather has opened up to Kevin about many of her painful experiences, and he has become an important emotional support for her.

"I'm just so fed up with all this. Now, they're talking about putting me on *more* pain meds! It started with oxycodone after the hysterectomy. Then that wasn't working, so they upped it. I didn't like that, so I tried to reduce how much I was taking. But then the pain was just debilitating. So, they upped it again. All I want is to get off all this crap, but I still have this deep-set soreness. It just never seems to go away. I don't know what to do," Heather explains solemnly.

"Sorry to hear that, Heather. Opioids are a tricky one. It's good you're keeping an eye on how much you're taking though," Kevin softly assures her.

"Yeah, I know. But I feel like I'm going to be stuck on them for the rest of my life! Ever since the surgery, it's just been issue after issue. And every day, I have to look at this hideous thing." She motions to her stomach. "This scar is healing in the most unattractive way possible," she details, laughing sarcastically.

"I'm sure once it's further along it will start to fade," Kevin reassures.

"Hmph. Maybe. We'll see. You know, I haven't even let Tony see my stomach since the surgery. Isn't that pathetic?" she scoffs.

"I don't think that's pathetic at all, Heather. This surgery was a big thing. Don't blame yourself for needing time to process it," Kevin affirms.

"I guess. I'm just so sick of it. I'm sick of the pain. I'm sick of the drugs. And I'm sick of myself—even now, here I am complaining to you about all of this. I'm so tired of being a victim, but I just feel like there's no way out," Heather softly says, fighting back tears.

"Heather, have you ever thought about how much your mindset plays into your pain?" Kevin asks gently.

"Like mind over matter stuff?" Heather asks.

"Something along those lines. I'd love to show you what I mean, if you'd be open to it."

"Sure, I'm willing to try anything that can help."

"Give me one second," Kevin states, before jogging out the door. He soon returns with four balloons from the nurse's station. "We keep these for when people have birthdays around here. Would you mind blowing one up?"

She nods and, soon, the balloons are all full.

Kevin explains, "This is something I learned from a mentor of mine. The goal of this game is to toss the balloons up in the air and do everything we can to prevent them from hitting the floor. Really let go when you're doing this, Heather—it's a lot of fun!"

"I'll try, but I don't think I'll be very good at it," she replies, slowly pushing herself up off the armrests of the chair.

At first, Heather stands hunched over as Kevin throws the balloons in the air. She moves slightly to hit a close balloon.

"Come on, Heather! Don't let that one fall!" Kevin shouts, hitting up a balloon himself.

Heather starts to giggle and bops the balloon. Then she moves a little more to hit another. Soon, the two of them are laughing away and completely focused on keeping the balloons in the air. Five minutes later, without any warning, Kevin grabs a balloon and asks, "What happened to your pain?"

Heather stops dead in her tracks. Slowly, she backs into a chair, with a puzzled look on her face.

Kevin asks again, "What happened to the soreness?"

"I'm not sure," Heather replies, putting a palm to her lower stomach. "It seemed to disappear for a while."

"Why do you think that is?" Kevin asks with a raised eyebrow.

"Because... because I wasn't thinking about it?" Heather ventures uncertainly.

"Can you see how much power your mind has over your pain?"

A stunned look is still sprawled across Heather's face. "I guess so..."

"We don't really realize how much our mind—our anxiety—can affect our health. I mean, think about it this way. Which do you think about more: your pain? Or the idea that you could live with this pain for the rest of your life?" Kevin poses.

"I... I don't know. Both, I guess?" she uncertainly replies.

"Well, let's look at what just happened with the balloons. In that moment, were you thinking about how you may have to live with this pain for the rest of your life? Were you feeling any of that anxiety?" Kevin asks.

"No..."

"And your pain—how was it when we were playing with the balloons?" Kevin brings up.

"I was so focused on playing that I didn't even feel it," Heather admits.

"What I'm trying to show you is that your mind has a lot of power to lessen or worsen your pain. Just now, you gave your anxiety a rest when we were having fun. This means the anxiety isn't always present, Heather—it can pass. And when the anxiety runs its course, your pain can lessen. Did you feel that?" Kevin asks.

"Yeah, I did," Heather confirms.

He continues, "Now, think about when you've tried to stop taking your pills. Was it the pain that was unbearable? Or was it the *anxiety* about the pain that made it unbearable?"

"I... there was a lot of anxiety I was feeling. Maybe that was part of it," she says.

"Remember how you mentioned that they had to up your medicine recently?" Kevin brings up.

"Yeah."

"How anxious do you think you were feeling before they agreed to up your dosage?"

"Oh, man. It was right around my daughter's graduation from high school. I was getting ready for the party for weeks. God, I was so anxious! I didn't even think about that at the time," Heather recognizes.

"So can you see how that anxiety might have played into how much pain you were feeling?" Kevin asks.

"Yeah, it really might have." Heather pauses. "So how do I do this?

You know, actually start to lessen my pain?" Heather asks, a glimmer of hope arising in her voice.

"You could look more at the anxiety you have around your pain with a therapist. Then once you're aware when your anxiety is triggered, you can start to control your response to it. For example, for a lot of people with chronic pain, they can start to feel the tingles of the pain before it fully kicks in. Do you know what I mean?" Kevin asks.

Heather nods firmly.

"When most people feel those first stages, they tense up. They're *preparing* themselves for the discomfort. This can actually make it a whole lot worse. Not only are you now more anxious about the pain coming on, but your muscles are physically tighter, which could lead to more extreme pain," Kevin points out.

"So I should just relax when I feel the pain coming on? That's going to be so hard to do," Heather trails off, her eyes wide as she processes the idea.

"It takes practice, Heather," he confirms. "This may not be an easy feat. To work up to it, you could start by doing some kind of activity that relaxes you. Is there something you've done before where you felt completely at ease?"

"I used to *love* going to this dance class downtown, but since the surgery, I haven't been able to go because it hurts so much to move like that. Do you think I could do that?" she excitedly asks.

"Eventually, you might be able to! Remember what you experienced with the balloons? You can do a lot more when you're not feeling anxious about the pain. But let's take some baby steps first. Is there a less vigorous activity you could do in the meantime as you work up to dance class?"

"Actually, my neighbor hosts this qigong class in the park every morning and was telling me about how healing it can be. I went once; it was great, but I just got busy with other stuff. Maybe I could try that again," Heather suggests. "Thanks for showing me this, Kevin. You're one of the only people I know who hasn't gotten sucked into my 'woe is me' tale. It's really refreshing to see that by managing this anxiety, I might actually have more control over my pain than I thought. I mean, who knows? Maybe I can even get to the point where the pain is manageable enough to get off these pills completely," Heather says, giving a laugh filled with disbelief at this idea.

"Well, I've had a lot of practice avoiding getting wrapped into stories, Heather. And I'm sure once you start working at it, you'll be stronger than you ever thought."

Chapter 42

FEELING CONFIDENT IN YOUR OWN SKIN

Carrying a pie in one hand, Michelle scopes out the park. There must be close to fifty relatives at this reunion. To the left, the little ones are playing tag. The aunties are all fumbling with the food table, making sure each dish has its serving spoon. Finally, in the sea of bodies, Michelle spots Elizabeth.

"Lizzie!" Michelle announces, walking up behind her.

Elizabeth spins around, holding a plate piled with chips and salsa. "Michelle! So glad you could make it!"

Michelle continues scanning the faces. "Is Nathan here yet? I haven't seen him for a few weeks and need to ask him about alimony." With her free hand, Michelle nonchalantly plays with the skirt of her dress, hoping Elizabeth will comment on it.

Looking around, Elizabeth doesn't catch Michelle's hint. She shakes her head. "I'm sure he'll be late. My brother is not known for his timeliness. I mean, you know that better than anyone."

"Don't I!" Michelle huffs, dropping her skirt a little disappointedly.

"So how's the new place? You settled in OK?" Elizabeth asks.

"Oh yeah! Still have a few boxes left to unpack, but it's coming along well. I know I've said it a million times, but thank you again for letting me stay with you while I was… going through all this," Michelle says, her gaze falling to the ground.

"Don't mention it. You're stuck being family with us forever, Michelle—whether you have the last name or not," Elizabeth promises.

Michelle giggles. "I know. Thank you."

Elizabeth lowers her voice and leans in, "And how is that… other thing going?"

Whispering into Elizabeth's ear, Michelle says, "I dumped everything I had down the toilet. Haven't gotten any more since."

Straightening her back, Elizabeth cheers, "Yay! Oh, good for you, honey! I'm so proud of you."

Michelle's cheeks grow red. "Thank you. Again," she quickly states. "I'm going to go put the pie on the dessert table. I'll be back in a sec."

As Michelle makes her way to the covered area, she passes by her teenage niece, Anna, who's sitting at a picnic table with some of her cousins.

"Hi, Anna," Michelle warmly says, giving her shoulder a squeeze.

Anna puts down her fork and glances behind her. "Hi, Aunt Michelle!" She jumps up and gives her a hug. After looking her aunt up and down, she exclaims, "Man, your dress looks like it's from the sixties!"

"Oh, yeah," Michelle sputters, not finding any words to respond. "I'm, I'm just going to go put the pie down," she stammers, pointing behind her.

Michelle's Monkey Mind has a field day. *Why did you wear this dress? Why did you think big polka dots was a good idea? No wonder Elizabeth didn't compliment you—it's horrible.* She becomes so self-conscious that she can't focus on any of the conversations she's having with her other relatives. After a few minutes, she makes up an excuse of having an upset stomach and slips away.

On her way home, Michelle's Monkey Mind continues chipping away at her self-esteem. She decides to pull over into a parking lot and give Elizabeth a call.

Elizabeth answers, the noise of the reunion in the background. "Hiya, Michelle! Where'd you go?"

"I had to leave..." Michelle struggles to get out.

"Michelle, why don't we take a deep breath together, OK?" Elizabeth firmly and lovingly instructs. Michelle follows Elizabeth's directions, copying her pattern. Soon, she's present enough to have a conversation.

"Sorry, it's so hard to remember to breathe when I get so worked up," Michelle embarrassingly admits.

"Don't apologize, Michelle. I used to be the same way. Now, tell me what happened," Elizabeth requests.

"Anna said my dress looks like it's from the sixties! I just couldn't stay there knowing I look like a big idiot!" Michelle cries, her breaths becoming shallower already.

"Oh, I see. And you took that as an insult, it sounds like?" Elizabeth asks.

"Well, yeah," Michelle replies defensively.

"Couldn't she have meant it as a compliment?" Elizabeth suggests.

"I... I guess. Are the sixties in fashion again? What did you think of it? Did you like it?" Michelle asks, an excitement rising in her voice.

"It doesn't matter what I think, or Anna thinks—what matters is that you don't let one comment ruin your whole day. I mean, what she said got under your skin so much that you *left!* Do you think this could maybe be about more than just the dress?"

"Probably... I don't know. I just haven't been complimented in such a long time. I was kind of looking forward to today because I hoped at least *one* person would say that I looked nice! But when

Anna said that, I started thinking that I looked like a fool in front of everyone… I just couldn't do it," Michelle quietly responds.

"Whether she meant it as a compliment or not, you're strong enough to hear the statement and take it in stride. What she says doesn't determine how you feel, Michelle," Elizabeth encourages over the phone.

"You're right, Lizzie…. You know, I actually really liked how I looked this morning! And I let that one little remark wash away all those positive feelings… If I like how I look, who cares if anyone else does!" Michelle strongly states.

"That's it, Michelle! Why don't you just sit and breathe for a few minutes, then decide if you want to come back. I'm sure everyone would be thrilled if you did," Elizabeth points out.

Soon after they end their conversation, Michelle feels confident enough to return to the reunion. One of the first people she runs into is Anna.

"Aunt Michelle, I thought you'd left!" Anna says with a wide smile.

"I did, but I'm feeling better, so I came back! So, I never got to hear more of what you thought about my dress," Michelle asks, doing a small turn.

"Your dress? It's… kind of weird." Anna says bluntly, with the iciness only a teenager's voice can deliver. "No offense," she adds quickly.

Michelle's Monkey Mind fires off, *See! You do look absolutely horrible! Everyone thinks you look ridiculous. Elizabeth doesn't know what she's talking about.*

Michelle takes a deep breath, calming herself before her skin becomes the color of a tomato. She remembers what she discussed with Elizabeth just moments ago and stands her ground.

"Anna, I appreciate your opinion, but I think the sixties will always be in fashion."

Feeling more confident, Michelle walks away and over to Aunt Margie, whom she hasn't connected with yet today.

"Aunt Margie! How are you?" Michelle asks with a hug.

"Oh! Michelle, my dear. I'm doing very well. How about you?" Margie asks in a hoarse voice.

"Can't complain! I actually just got a pretty big promotion at work a few weeks ago..." Michelle begins.

"Did you bring anyone with you?" Margie cuts in, adjusting her glasses and scanning the close perimeter.

"Excuse me?" Michelle asks, a bit startled.

"Aren't you dating anyone, my dear? It's been a while since you and Nathan split up. It's about time you found yourself a new husband!"

Michelle is completely blindsided and struggles to remain polite.

"I... I mean, no, I didn't bring anyone..."

Margie cuts her off again. "My, my, Michelle. You're not getting any younger. If you don't hurry up, all the good ones are going to be gone!" she says with a harsh chuckle.

"I... um, would you excuse me for a moment, Aunt Margie?" Michelle says, completely flustered.

Michelle quickly walks away from her aunt with tears in her eyes. Her Monkey Mind is running wild. *You are such a loser! What's wrong with you? You'll probably never find another husband. What man would want you?*

Michelle doesn't stop until she's on the other end of the park, far away from the party. She slumps down against a tree, and the crying commences. Fortunately, Elizabeth had been keeping an eye on her since she came back to the party.

"Mind if I join you?" Elizabeth asks, approaching her friend.

Michelle nods, wiping away a few tears. "I can't do this, Lizzie. I'm not as strong as you!"

"What happened?" Elizabeth questions compassionately, rubbing Michelle's arm.

"Aunt Margie just asked when I'm going to get *remarried!* I can't handle this anymore. It was stupid to come back. I'm not ready to do this," Michelle anxiously cites.

"Good lord, Aunt Margie," Elizabeth says, rolling her eyes. "She would be the one to add to an already rough day."

"And she's right! I feel like such a *complete loser*," Michelle wails, wiping her nose with a wadded-up tissue from her purse.

"Why are you buying into her story, Michelle?" Elizabeth asks.

"Because I agree with it! I might never find another husband!" Michelle cries, quickly looking behind her back to make sure no one is near her.

"Michelle, look at me for a second, honey." Michelle looks up at Elizabeth, heaving a shaky breath. Elizabeth continues, "What if you were to meet the man of your dreams today at the party? Do you think he would be more attracted to a warm, confident woman who is rocking her polka-dot dress? Or a woman who is distracted by what others think of her?"

"Yeah, I know what you mean," Michelle answers, looking back down and picking a blade of grass out of the ground.

"Can you see the change that would happen if you stop seeking approval from other people?" Elizabeth asks.

"Of course, I can see that! But I don't know if I can *do* it," Michelle replies honestly.

"Well, I don't know... did you see Anna again when you came back? She was right over there by the entrance, wasn't she? How did that go?" Elizabeth asks hopefully.

"You know, pretty well actually. It does turn out that she hates my dress, but somehow I didn't let it get to me," Michelle says flatly, shrugging.

"What! That's amazing, Michelle! You literally just left the party because of a comment Anna made, and now you were able to brush it off! Do you see how huge that is?" Elizabeth points out.

"Yeah, I guess so," Michelle acknowledges, lifting her head a bit higher.

"Let's go back there and show them how confident you can be!" Elizabeth suggests, extending her hand to help Michelle up.

As Michelle grasps Elizabeth's hand, she struggles getting up.

"Geez, if I could just lose twenty pounds, I'm sure it'd be even easier to be confident," she says, releasing a hard breath once she's standing.

"Oh, Michelle, stop that! Why do you always have to be so self-deprecating?" Elizabeth points out.

Michelle shrugs as they walk back toward the reunion. "It just comes so naturally. I grew up in the South. Need I say more?"

"Was it really that bad?" Elizabeth inquires softly.

"I know your dad was hard on you guys, but I think my mom was even worse. I remember this one time when I was in some school play. I can't remember what it was… Peter Pan? No, that can't be it…" Michelle disputes as they walk through the grass.

She shakes her head and continues, "Anyway, I was a fairy in this play with two other girls. We all had the same costume, and they did our hair up the same way. Mom had gotten me contacts to wear so my glasses wouldn't make me stick out. I'd never used contacts before, so on the day of the play, I was trying to put them in and dropped one down the sink. It was like twenty minutes to curtain, so I had to wear my glasses. We did the play, and everything went perfectly—I remembered all my lines. But after the play… man, I swore my mom was going to whoop me right there in the gym. She grabbed me by my arm and pulled me off to the side. She started asking what kind of fairy has glasses and why did she waste perfectly good money on those contacts if I wasn't going to wear them."

Michelle stops walking for a moment, closing her eyes, trying to get away from the memory. She looks over at Elizabeth. "And the saddest part is—I really liked those little pink glasses. I thought I had looked great." Michelle defeatedly drops her shoulders.

"Geez, Michelle. That's intense."

"Yeah, well, it is what it is," she shrugs it off. She continues her pace back toward the crowd.

"Michelle, do you think how your mom treated you growing up could somehow be related to how you're reacting to Aunt Margie's comment? Or Anna's?"

"Oh, I don't know about that..." Michelle quickly dismisses.

"Well, right now, do you have that same feeling that you had as a little girl when your mom made fun of your glasses?"

Michelle blinks her eyes several times. "Now that you say it, yeah. I do. I feel like an out-of-place loser."

Walking straighter, Elizabeth says, "Well, Michelle, you are one of my best friends in the world. If my best friend is a loser, what does that say about me?"

Michelle laughs, unable to hold back at the ludicrousness of the statement. "Obviously you're not a loser, Lizzie."

"We are two beautiful women, with plenty of flaws. So let's go back there and own it!"

As they approach their family members, they spot Anna speaking to Aunt Margie with a flustered look on her face.

"And you know what else," Elizabeth says in a conspiratorial tone, "you're not the only one who's talking to Aunt Margie today. Every person here is feeling self-conscious, so let's embrace who we are and enjoy ourselves!"

Part 8

MAKING PEACE WITH
THE MONKEY MIND

Chapter 43

THE WAR IS OVER

After years of listening to our programming (which is decades for some people) we've been trained to have a tendency to make something "bad" or "wrong" if we want to make a change. For example, if we want out of a relationship, we start to villainize our partners, to give us a reason to break up with them. Or if we want to change jobs, we find new things to complain about at our current position.

This same thing often happens when we first become aware of the Monkey Mind — we're upset that it's there. We try to convince ourselves that it shouldn't be there.

When we get to the point where we no longer insist on making the Monkey Mind bad or wrong, we graduate to a new level of consciousness. This is where we can clearly comprehend the importance of the Monkey Mind's role in facilitating our awareness, and we no longer strive to get rid of it.

Reaching a peaceful relationship with our Monkey Minds is one of the most freeing experiences we can have. Look at Elizabeth and Kevin. They've each reached a place where they're no longer at war with their own inner critics. They can hear the Monkey Mind's commentary and release the negative thought in the same breath. They have embodied what it means to live from the Observing Mind's perspective.

Let's see how Elizabeth and Kevin respond when they encounter the primary sources of their programming: their fathers.

Chapter 44

ELIZABETH

As Elizabeth pulls into the familiar driveway, she can feel her heart racing. While going through her healing journey, she made a conscious decision to give herself some space from her father. She knew he was going to be her biggest trigger, and she wanted to be sure she was strong and skilled enough to face him.

Last week, Elizabeth's mother told her that her father was having hip surgery and was going to be laid up for a few weeks during recovery. After the call, Elizabeth thought long and hard about if she was ready to see her father. After breathing through it, she decided she was.

Now, she notices her hand shaking as she knocks on the door.

"Lizzie! Oh, honey, it's so good to see you!" Elizabeth's mom exclaims, bringing her in close for a hug.

"Aww, you too, Mom," Elizabeth says, squeezing her mother's small frame. The two catch up a bit, but Elizabeth notices her mom glancing towards the steps.

"So... how is he?" Elizabeth quietly inquires.

"Oh, you know how he is. It's driving him crazy to have to sit still for so long."

"Well, I suppose I should go say hello…" Elizabeth says, the saliva running dry from her mouth.

"Would you mind bringing him up some soup? I was just about to before you got here," her mother begins, shuffling off into the kitchen. She returns with a tray holding a bowl of chicken noodle soup and a glass of water. "Thanks, dear," she finishes, handing off the food to Elizabeth.

"No problem," Elizabeth whispers. Carefully balancing the tray, she tiptoes up the steps. The hallway to her parent's room seems longer than she remembers. Finally, she takes a deep breath and gently knocks on the door.

"Come in!" a harsh voice orders from the interior.

Balancing the tray against her body, Elizabeth turns the doorknob and enters.

"Oh, it's you," her father sneers. His pale body is propped up by two pillows behind his back.

"How are you doing, Dad?" Elizabeth greets as warmly as she can.

"Well, I did just have metal put into my body, so not the best," he scoffs, coughing loudly.

"Mom asked me to bring up some soup," Elizabeth replies, placing the tray on her father's nightstand.

"Yeah, I've been waiting an hour for it." As he lifts the bowl to suck up a spoonful of broth, he mumbles his thanks. Then he groans and drops the dish back onto the tray. "It's cold! Jesus, I can't even get a hot bowl of soup…"

"Want me to go warm it up?" Elizabeth quickly offers.

"No, no. It's fine. I wouldn't want to be a bother to anyone," he sarcastically replies.

"So, how have you been, Dad?" Elizabeth asks, wringing her hands behind her back.

"Fine."

"What's been going on around here?"

"What's been going on for the last year and a half? Quite a bit," he huffs.

Elizabeth breathes, allowing several moments of silence to pass between them. Her father grunts and picks up the bowl to take another bite.

"The kids are doing well, by the way," she brightly reports.

This gets her father's eyes to flash up to meet hers. "Oh? Still doing well in school?"

"Oh yeah! A's and B's for both of them!"

"How many B's?" he questions.

"Each of them had one or two last semester is all. I think Josh's was in his calculus class, which was so hard anyway…"

"All A's would be better."

"Well, regardless, they're both doing very well. And they're both in a lot of activities this year. Tiffany is actually about to get her red belt in karate…"

"Karate! She's still doing that?" He slurps another spoonful with a scowl. "I'll never understand why you let her do that. Girls shouldn't be fighting each other, if you ask me."

Inhaling deeply, Elizabeth focuses on her internal responses. She can feel her anger starting to rise within her, but she breathes through it. "A lot of girls do it now, Dad. And it's great for her to know how to defend herself." She breathes again, squeezing her thumb tightly. As she releases her breath, she adds, "But I love that you're trying to look out for her."

"Mmm," he mumbles, sucking up a noodle from the corner of his mouth.

"I have a picture of them from the other day…" she begins, quickly swiping through the photos on her phone. "Ah! Here it is."

She approaches her father and shows him the screen. This results in the first smile on his face since she entered the room.

"Josh is getting so tall!" her father remarks with a wide smile.

"Isn't he! He passed me a long time ago, and even Tiffany a few months ago. Pretty soon he's going to be taller than his dad!"

Elizabeth can feel her father's warm attitude shift into a cold disapproval.

"How is Ted? Do you still talk to him at all?" he questions coldly.

"Yeah, of course. We talk at least a couple times a week. We're actually getting along better than when we were married," Elizabeth jokes, adding an uncomfortable laugh.

"I'd imagine it was pretty hard to get along with a drunk," her father spits back, wiping his mouth with the back of his hand.

Now, Elizabeth can feel the full force of her anxiety. Her Monkey Mind is already playing its tune. *You did ruin your marriage! It's your fault!* "There were a lot of reasons our marriage didn't work, Dad. We're both much happier now…" she begins, keeping her voice as calm as possible.

"It doesn't matter what the *reasons* are, Elizabeth! It's a marriage! You don't just quit when it gets hard!" he hisses, throwing his now-empty bowl down on the nightstand.

Elizabeth's Monkey Mind wants nothing more than to throw that comment back in her father's face. *Doesn't matter what the reasons are? What about having affairs with numerous women, Dad? That's a pretty good reason to end a marriage!*

Fighting hard to stay away from this negative voice, Elizabeth looks down at the floor and focuses on her gratitude around her father. She murmurs, "I appreciate your dedication to marriage, Dad, but…"

"If that were true you wouldn't have gotten divorced!" Elizabeth's father yells, throwing up his hands. His quick movement strains his incision, and he yelps out of pain.

This snaps Elizabeth's focus back to caring for her father. "Dad? You OK?"

He nods strongly. "Can you get my pain meds off the bathroom counter?" he asks in a strained voice, his eyes tightly closed.

"Of course." She runs into the en suite bathroom and quickly spots the prescription bottle. Glancing up in the mirror, Elizabeth can see her father wincing in pain in the reflection. He coughs violently, covering his mouth with a handkerchief. From here, her father is the spitting image of her grandfather.

Elizabeth's mind transports her to a memory from her childhood. She was with her father and grandfather at a department store, and Elizabeth spotted a doll that she really wanted.

"Daddy, can I have it?" she begged, her pigtails bouncing up and down.

"No, honey, you don't need another toy," her father had replied, stroking her hair gently.

Her grandfather glared at her father, then said, "Lizzie, sweetie, I'll get you the doll." As he grabbed it off the shelf, he pulled out his monogrammed handkerchief to wipe a smudge off the doll's face. Bending down to her eye level, Elizabeth's grandfather continued, "And if there's ever anything that you want but your Daddy can't buy for you, just let me know."

As Elizabeth spun her new doll around, she heard her grandfather tell her dad, "If you had a decent job, you'd be able to afford dolls for your little girl."

Elizabeth, now back in the present, takes another deep breath. Her Observing Mind takes this break from her Monkey Mind to pose a question to her. *Look at your father objectively right now. What do you see?*

Instead of the strong man that raised her, Elizabeth sees an elderly, weak man sitting before her. This frail stranger is nearing the final stage in his life, and Elizabeth realizes that fighting with him isn't going to do anything to stop that clock. He has his own Monkey Mind that was programmed just the way hers was, but he never had the opportunity to stop listening to it. She can feel her emotions shift immensely away from anger into love.

"Here, Dad," she says, handing him the pills.

"Thanks," he mumbles, dry swallowing the large caplets.

"No problem at all," Elizabeth compassionately replies.

Just then, Elizabeth's cell phone starts ringing. She sees that Sarah is calling and silences the phone.

"Need to talk to someone more important than me?" her dad harshly comments.

"No, no. It's fine. I'll call her back later." She adds, "That was actually Sarah. Have you talked to her lately?"

Her dad shakes his head slightly, though she can tell he has perked up at the mention of this. "No, I haven't. Your mother has, I think. She's doing well?"

"Yeah, she is. She's doing really well." Elizabeth takes a deep breath and decides to go for it. "You know, I never really found out why you brought Sarah to live with us, Dad. One day, you just came home with this girl none of us had met and said she was going to be staying with us. I mean, Mom used to talk about how she brought in those foster kids before we were born, but you had never done anything like that. Why did you? With Sarah?"

Her dad huffs. "Your mother wanted me to pick her up was all…"

Elizabeth cuts in, "None of the bull, Dad. Mom told me she didn't know anything about Sarah before you brought her home that day. It would mean a lot to me if you'd just give me a straight answer."

Her father clears his throat. "Well, if you're going to get all touchy about it… fine." He sighs. "I actually met Sarah's father in Vietnam."

Elizabeth feels her mouth start to gape open. She makes the effort to shut it and continue listening.

"Over there… we saw stuff. You form a bond with those guys that none of you can ever understand." He breathes in deeply. "Joe and I made a pact that if anything happened to either of us, we'd look after each other's families. He had Sarah. I had you and your brother. Anyway... after we came home, Joe didn't cope with civilian life so well. One day, I got a call that he had overdosed. Just like that." Her father stares blankly in front of him, sitting silent for a few moments.

He continues, "Once I heard, I called his wife to give my condolences and found out she wasn't in the picture anymore. So I stepped in, and Sarah moved in with us. And that's that."

"Dad... that's..." Elizabeth begins slowly.

"Yeah, yeah. It is what it is. No need to dwell on it," he quickly dismisses.

But Elizabeth has come here to say something, and she is determined to get it out. "You know, Dad, since I stopped drinking, I've done a lot of work on myself. A *lot*. And I realized that I have a lot of unresolved issues with you. Particularly, the, um, cheating..."

"Oh, not this again..." he cuts in.

"Please." Elizabeth strongly declares, locking eyes with her father. "I know you're not a perfect person. But none of us are. Now that I can take a step back, I can see, regardless of your mistakes, that you are a good man, Dad. You were always very kind to people, and I ignored that because I was so fixated on your critiques of me. But even now, as you're criticizing my failed marriage, I can see that you care for me. You've always cared for me, and Nathan, and Mom, and Sarah. And for the first time, I can really see that."

"Well, umm..." Her father clears his throat. "Your mother told me about you stopping drinking and all. How long has it been now?" he asks, trying to be nonchalant about it.

"Over a year. Closer to a year and a half, actually."

Her dad glances up at her, making eye contact with her. "Well, good for you." Then he coughs and looks down. "That stuff'll kill you if you're not careful."

She takes a deep breath. "Dad, in the past, I would have taken that really personally. But I'm not going to right now. Because I've realized that one of the main reasons why I did drink was because I felt like I wasn't good enough. I was constantly seeking your approval. You'd say things to me, and I'd feel like I was just a waste of space…" Elizabeth father's eyes meet hers as she talks, and she's surprised to spy a look of sadness has settled on his face. She continues, "I'm sorry about that, Dad. Because I realized that's not true. I *am* good enough, and I don't think you ever thought I wasn't. It took me… a lot to figure that out. I know you love me, and I love you," Elizabeth responds with a small, grateful smile.

Her father swallows deeply. "Well… um, I'm glad you're not drinking anymore."

"Thanks, Dad," Elizabeth says warmly.

"Yeah… well… I think I'm going to lay down for a while. That medicine makes me pretty tired," he gruffly responds.

"Sounds good, Dad. I'll go talk to Mom for a bit then."

Elizabeth's father slowly sinks down into the sheets. Picking up the tray with his bowl, Elizabeth sneaks out of the room and flicks off the light. She feels an immense sense of pride. Her anxiety is nowhere to be found as she refocuses her mind on love. As she's walking down the staircase, she looks over some photos from her childhood.

There's one of Elizabeth and her brother on their first day of school, many of the family trips to the lake, Sarah playing in the snow one winter. Near the bottom of the steps, there's a photo of a four-year-old Elizabeth on her father's shoulders. Her wide grin is dwarfed in comparison to the open-mouthed smile sprawled across her father's face.

Staring at this picture, Elizabeth can feel the enormous love her father has for his children. While he may not have been the perfect parent, he tried, and he passed on what he thought would help them.

For the first time, Elizabeth is able to look past the narration of the Monkey Mind when it comes to her father and see the real man that he is. Now, Elizabeth has the power to decide if she wants to take on the lessons he taught her or exchange them for something else. Elizabeth is no longer a victim to her father's voice, the Monkey Mind, or anyone else.

Elizabeth is the person in charge of her life.

Chapter 45

KEVIN

Kevin is pacing outside the hospital room. Everything had gone so well with the birth, but after the delivery of his beautiful baby boy, the doctors whisked the newborn away, saying his breathing was irregular. Jamie had ordered Kevin to go after him, but the doctors wouldn't let him in the room.

So now, Kevin waits. After nearly a half an hour of silence, a voice behind him asks, "How you doin', son?" Kevin turns to see his father behind him, his hands dug into the pockets of his jeans.

"Honestly... I'm pretty scared, Dad," Kevin replies, his voice cracking.

His dad walks forward and grips his shoulder tightly. "I know." He clears his throat. "But no matter what happens, you have to be strong through this."

Kevin nods, his eyes tearing up. He inhales a broken breath, closing his eyes. "How did you get through this with us, Dad? When Mom was in labor—were you scared?" Kevin asks, opening his eyes to look at his father.

Coughing abruptly, Kevin's father doesn't reply for a moment. "Yes,

I was. You can never plan for childbirth, but you'll get through it."

"If something were to happen to him... I just don't know what I'd do," Kevin confides, his voice breaking.

"It's not something any parent ever wants to experience," his father replies. Sighing, Kevin's father continues, "You know, the first time your mother got pregnant, everything was going great until about the eighth month. Then she started having these sharp pains..."

Kevin cuts in, "I didn't know Mom had complications with Patrick?"

"She didn't. This was... with our first little girl," his father says quietly. He takes a deep breath, then sits down on one of the gray, well-used chairs. Kevin sits next to him in shock, wiping away a tear.

"It was an ice-cold December morning, and I remember trying to scrape the windshield as fast as I could so we could get to the hospital. But when we got there, it was too late. They said it was some heart abnormality that no one could have known about. Anyway, after they, um... got her out, your mother and I got to spend a moment with her. She was beautiful." His father pauses. This time, it's his voice that is cracking. Kevin even sees a tear glistening in his father's eye—something he can't recall ever seeing before.

Kevin witnesses his Monkey Mind coming on board. *Why didn't they ever tell you about this? What else have they kept from you?*

Kevin can feel that his Monkey Mind is starting to separate him from this beautiful connection from his father, something he's craved his entire life. So, just as quickly as the judgmental thoughts came, Kevin chooses to let them go.

His father quickly clears his throat, patting his chest with the knuckles of his fist before resuming his story. "After they took her away, your mother and I never spoke of her again. We just didn't know how to tell you kids about her. But I remember when we found out she was pregnant with Patrick. I was terrified, absolutely terrified. Probably like you are now, son."

His father takes another breath and sits up straighter. "But I sucked it up and put on a tough face for your mother. And that's what you need to do with Jamie—you need to be a rock for your wife."

"I… I had no idea," Kevin says, his mouth still hanging open in shock. "I'm so sorry, Dad."

Kevin's father tenses up for a moment. Relaxing his shoulders, he responds, "Well, we ended up with three great kids, so I can't complain too much." He smiles at Kevin. "You know, I have a feeling your little boy is going to be just fine. If he's anything like his father, he's a tough one."

"Thanks, Dad," Kevin whispers, bowing his head slightly.

Within moments, they are joined by Jamie's mother, June.

"Kevin! Have you heard anything yet? We've been staying with Jamie and are just *beside ourselves* with worry! Won't they let you in there? Have you asked them for an update? Oh God, what if they have to do surgery! Maybe we should give blood, so he has blood if he needs it…" Jamie's mother babbles on, waving her hands wildly around her.

Patting his dad on the back as he stands up, Kevin walks over to his mother-in-law and takes her hands in his. "June, why don't we take a deep breath?" Kevin inhales deeply, and June copies him. "And out," Kevin instructs.

They do this several more times until Jamie's mother is able to keep an even breath.

"How are you doing, June?" Kevin asks calmly.

"A little better," she replies, still clearly shaken.

"June, is being worked up helping anything right now?" Kevin asks gently.

She scoffs. "Well, I'm sure not, but how could I *not* be!"

"We're strong enough to get through this, June," Kevin calmly states, continuing to take deep breaths and trying to get her to do the same.

"But what if something bad happens? I mean, heaven forbid, but he could *not make it*, Kevin! Have you prepared yourself for this option? God, has *Jamie?* She could never handle that... why aren't they telling us anything?" she yells harshly at the closed door.

"We've both prepared ourselves for all possibilities. But I have this feeling that he's going to be OK. He's a tough one. He's a Smith," Kevin says, giving his dad a grateful look.

June sighs and sits down next to Kevin's father. "I'm sorry, Kevin. Here you are, so calm and collected, and I'm a batty mess over here. I should be the one comforting you, not the other way around."

Showing a small smile, Kevin takes the seat next to her. "I can tell how much you care, June. No need to apologize. How about we breathe together some more?"

She looks over at Kevin. "Yeah, that sounds good." Then, she adds, "I'm glad Jamie has someone like you to go through this with."

Giving an appreciative nod, Kevin starts breathing in and out slowly. June follows his rhythm, her fingers massaging the rosary beads in her hand. Soon, even Kevin's father joins in on the breathing pattern, his inhales and exhales matching up to his son's. The three continue sharing this moment until a doctor finally emerges from the room.

"Kevin, your son is going to be fine, he just had some fluid in the lungs. We can bring him back out to Jamie in a few minutes," the doctor says.

Kevin hops up and shakes the doctor's hand, thanking him for everything he had done. Then he turns back to his father and mother-in-law as tears of happiness rain down his cheeks. His mother-in-law soon joins him in crying happily, while his father pats Kevin on the back enthusiastically.

Within minutes, Kevin is sitting with Jamie on her bed, their beautiful son wrapped in her arms. "Look at how *little* he is!" Jamie expresses, bouncing him up and down gently.

"He's perfect," Kevin says, playing with one of the baby's fingers.

Jamie looks over to Kevin. "Thanks for waiting for him outside that room, hon. I couldn't bear the thought of neither of us being near him."

"Of course," Kevin says, kissing his wife on the forehead.

"And sorry for sending my mom out on you... I just couldn't handle her anymore," Jamie says with a shake of her head.

Kevin laughs. "I had a feeling that's what it was. No problem, honey." He looks up at the clock, then caresses his son's head gently. "We've been in here for a while... I think we better let them in now."

"Do we have to?" Jamie pleads. She smiles broadly and kisses Kevin. "Go get them before they knock down the door."

As Kevin ushers in his family, he stands back a moment and watches the pure elation on each of their faces. Kevin can't help but take in this moment—here they are, all together sharing this joyous event, while not long ago, Kevin barely spoke to half of these people.

Before, Kevin's mother-in-law wouldn't speak his name. Now she gushes to her friends about her daughter's composed, supportive husband.

Before, Kevin would have taken his father's presence as a sign that he had done something wrong—that his dad didn't trust him enough to be a father. Kevin would have been anxious simply standing in the same room as him.

Most importantly, Jamie probably wouldn't have even been here. Kevin and she would have broken up long ago, and she might be in a delivery room with another man. But now, she tells everyone that she feels like the luckiest wife in the world.

Looking around, Kevin can feel the overwhelming amount of love in the room. He loves each of these people in their own way. And he's finally learned to turn that love inward. Kevin knows he's a good man, a good husband, and will be a good father.

As he soaks all this in, Kevin can't help but think, in this moment, there is absolutely nothing bad in the world—there is only family, friends, and this one, perfect being.

Kevin's heart has never felt fuller.

Chapter 46

THE LIFELONG BENEFITS OF THE OBSERVING MIND

When teaching the concept of the Observing Mind, people often express surprise and doubt at first, saying, "Wow, it can't be that easy!" The Monkey Mind has trained them to think that change must be hard. Yet, when they shift into observing and learning from the Monkey Mind's stories, things become easier.

As people embark on this journey, they start to feel a sense of peace as they reinterpret the source of their addiction and their anxiety. They feel appreciation and unconditional love in the same situations that used to leave them seething with frustration. They stop arguing with the world and what's in it by shifting their focus inward. They become present, witnessing the events of their lives with clarity and acceptance. They're compassionate with others because they can identify how they're battling their own Monkey Minds. Instead of reacting to stories, they accept who they are in the moment and move with joy toward who they want to become. They learn that they have the power to direct their own lives.

I have found that living our lives without the Monkey Mind running the show is the most freeing feeling in the world. Once you learn the skills to overcome your sabotaging programming, your life is forever changed.

I feel immense gratitude to have witnessed so many people overcome their addictions and transform their lives. The successes of people like Kevin and Elizabeth are completely within your reach if you incorporate the tools of this book into your daily life.

I have enjoyed sharing my work with you and hope that this book has been helpful. Now that you've stepped into a new experience, may your Observing Mind keep growing and enriching your life.

ABOUT THE AUTHOR

Jean-Francois (J.F.) Benoist has been counseling people struggling with addiction, mental health, and relationship issues for over twenty years. He co-founded The Exclusive Hawaii, a non-12-step residential addiction treatment center, with his wife, Joyce, in 2011. He is the creator of the therapeutic methodology Experiential Engagement Therapy™ (EET), which focuses on addressing a person's underlying core beliefs. He is well-known for his authentic, experiential techniques, which maximize long-term change.

Benoist is a Certified Option Process Mentor/Counselor. He is an internationally certified leader in The Mankind Project, a nonprofit organization dedicated to promoting men's personal growth. He began his studies in human development and empowerment with Robert Hargrove and Relationships Inc. in 1980 and has been deeply involved in facilitating change in others ever since.

Benoist offers in-depth workshops, professional trainings, and speaking engagements to help individuals further learn how to change their self-sabotaging programming.

To find more information about the author, J.F. Benoist, and the residential addiction treatment program he created, please visit the following websites:

www.TheExclusiveHawaii.com

www.JFBenoist.com

ACKNOWLEDGMENTS

To my family, Joyce, Aaron, Seraphim, Lucca and my mother Micheline; thank you from the bottom of my heart for loving me unconditionally.

To my dear friends Mark and Desiree who have loved me and supported my work.

To my clients and students over many years, all of whom have been an inspiration and a testament to the strength and heroism of human beings.

To David Cates, the editor of the first edition of this work.

To Danielle Anderson, for her editorial assistance.

A special thank you to Emily Mast, who was instrumental in assisting with the organization and rewrites of the content.